Jonson's Moral Comedy

Alan C. Dessen

Jonson's

NORTHWESTERN

Moral Comedy

UNIVERSITY PRESS · 1971

Open access edition funded by the National Endowment for the Humanities/Andrew W. Mellon Foundation Humanities Open Book Program.

Alan C. Dessen. Jonson's Moral Comedy.
Evanston, Ill.: Northwestern University Press, 1971.

ISBN 978-0-8101-0318-4 (cloth)
ISBN 978-0-8101-3830-8 (paper)
ISBN 978-0-8101-3831-5 (ebook)

Printed in the United States of America

Original edition LCCN 76-126900

To Cynthia

Contents

Acknowledgments ix

Prologue 1

CHAPTER 1
The Dramatic Legacy of the Elizabethan Morality 8

CHAPTER 2
Jonson and the Morality Tradition: The Early Plays 37

CHAPTER 3
The Movement toward Moral Comedy: *Volpone* 70

CHAPTER 4
Comic Synthesis: *The Alchemist* 105

CHAPTER 5
The World in Panoramo: *Bartholomew Fair* 138

CHAPTER 6
The Decline of Moral Comedy: *The Devil is an Ass* and *The Staple of News* 221

CHAPTER 7
Jonson's Moral Comedy 243

Index 251

Acknowledgments

DURING the journey to Publication, this book has benefited from the Good Counsel of many people. In particular, I wish to thank Jackson Cope, Madeleine Doran, Walter Rideout, Samuel Schoenbaum, and, at Northwestern University Press, Richard Barnes and Janice Feldstein. Vestiges of Idleness or Ignorance are solely the responsibility of the author.

Portions of Chapters 1, 3, and 4 appeared in *Studies in Philology*, *Modern Language Quarterly*, and *Renaissance Drama*. I am grateful to the editors of those journals for their permission to incorporate that material here.

My deepest obligations are to Lawrence Ross, to whom I owe my enthusiasm for Elizabethan drama, and my wife, who held off the slings and arrows of outrageous children.

Alan C. Dessen

Prologue

ALTHOUGH Shakespeare was "not of an age, but for all time," Ben Jonson, the author of that tribute, has appealed to the select few, particularly the academic few. Bardolatry may spring up everywhere, but it is usually the scholar surveying the Elizabethan terrain who is attracted to Jonson's literary and dramatic corpus. Among the reasons for this academic appeal is the fascinating combination of theory and practice evident in Jonson's work, for this formidable figure has bequeathed not only a wealth of plays, poems, and masques but also a great deal of explanation and justification. Given the scholarly rage for order, the modern critic has needed no Mosca or Face to tempt him to relate Jonson's statements about drama and poetry to the literature itself. Such efforts have produced many valuable studies of Jonson's sources, his prose, his conception of dramatic satire, and his literary credo. Not all readers, to be sure, have been equally enthusiastic, for some have looked at the same material and seen "one of the most marvelous instances in all literature of the way the wings of genius may be clipped by the shears of doctrine and clogged by the cobwebs of conventional prescription."[1]

Neither friend nor foe would deny that Jonson allied himself and his work with literary antecedents and authorities; even when absorbed in the present a significant part of his artistic consciousness was involved with the past. But any fair evaluation of Jonson's art must go one step farther and consider how and to what effect this learned poet, dramatist, and critic made use of his sources and prescriptions. Jonson's own statements, as usual, are to the point. His editors, after observing in the introduction to his critical writings that Jonson turned to classical antiquity "in a spirit not of blind adoration, but of keen and critical inquiry," quote a telling passage from lines 129–40 of *Discoveries:*

> I know *Nothing* can conduce more to letters, then to examine the writings of the *Ancients,* and not to rest in their sole Authority, or take all upon trust from them; provided the plagues of *Iudging,* and *Pronouncing* against them, be away. . . . For to all the observations of the *Ancients,* wee have our own experience: which, if wee will use, and apply, wee have better meanes to pronounce. It is true they open'd the gates, and made the way that went before us; but as Guides, not Commanders: *Non Domini nostri, sed Duces fuêre.* Truth lyes open to all; it is no mans *severall.*

Herford concludes: "To study the ancients critically, with a view to extracting from them anything that threw light on the life or art of his own day, was the guiding principle of Jonson's reading."[2]

1. Unsigned review of A. C. Swinburne, *A Study of Ben Jonson,* in *Athenaeum* (March 8, 1890), p. 317. Quoted by Freda L. Townsend, *Apologie for Bartholmew Fayre* (New York, 1947), p. 14.

2. *Ben Jonson,* ed. C. H. Herford and Percy and Evelyn Simpson,

This guiding principle is present throughout Jonson's career. In the Induction to *Every Man Out of His Humour*, for example, Cordatus observes that the contemporary poet or dramatist "should enjoy the same license, or free power, to illustrate and heighten [his] inuention" as had the ancients, "and not bee tyed to those strict and regular formes, which the nicenesse of a few (who are nothing but forme) would thrust vpon vs" (ll. 266–70). In his *Discoveries*, Jonson argues that "nothing is more ridiculous, then to make an Author a *Dictator*, as the schooles have done *Aristotle*. The dammage is infinite, knowledge receives by it. For to many things a man should owe but a temporary beliefe, and a suspension of his owne Judgement, not an absolute resignation of himselfe, or a perpetuall captivity" (ll. 2095–2100). The subsequent lengthy and quite orthodox discussion of *imitatio* maintains that the true poet should be able "to convert the substance, or Riches of an other *Poet*, to his owne use."

> Not, as a Creature, that swallowes, what it takes in, crude, raw, or indigested; but, that feedes with an Appetite, and hath a Stomacke to concoct, divide, and turne all into nourishment. Not, to imitate servilely, as *Horace* saith, and catch at vices, for vertue: but, to draw forth out of the best, and choisest flowers, with the Bee, and turne all into Honey, worke it into one relish, and savour:
> (ll. 2472–78)

The other extreme must also be avoided, for the poet "must beware, that his Studie bee not only to learne of himself; for,

---

11 vols. (Oxford, 1925–52), II, 444–45. All quotations from Jonson are from this edition, which will hereafter be cited as H & S.

hee that shall affect to doe that, confesseth his ever having a Foole to his master" (ll. 2505–7).

Jonson's attitude towards earlier writers is neatly summed up by the title affixed to his gleanings (*Explorata: or, Discoveries*) and by his motto (*tanquam explorator*) cited by Aubrey and found in many of his books and inscriptions. Both uses of this image allude to a passage in which Seneca announces he is about to discuss an idea borrowed from Epicurus, adding: "soleo enim et in aliena castra transire, non tamquam transfuga, sed tamquam explorator." [3] Like Seneca, Jonson saw himself as an *explorator* or scout, venturing into the various *aliena castra* represented by his wide reading and returning with material relevant to the battles he was continually waging. His motto provides another revealing insight into his flexible attitude towards the past as a guide to the present.

To appreciate fully Jonson's role as *explorator,* however, one cannot limit the *aliena castra* to the works of the ancients. Many of the passages found in *Explorata,* for example, have been culled from sixteenth- and even seventeenth-century writers (Vives, Heinsius, the Scaligers, Bacon). As Richard Altick has pointed out, moreover, the reader interested in sources should maintain "a ceaseless awareness of the amount of verbal and conceptual material that in every age belongs to the common domain. Every writer's total debt as an artist is, on the whole, less to a handful of authors by whom he was especially influenced than to the mingled currents of art and ideas, traditional and new, in the midst of which he cannot

3. Seneca, *Ad Lucilium Epistulae Morales,* ed. and trans. Richard M. Gummere, Loeb Classical Library (London and New York, 1917), I, 8–9. Gummere translates the entire passage as follows: "The thought for to-day is one which I discovered in Epicurus; for I am wont to cross over even into the enemy's camp,—not as a deserter, but as a scout."

help living."[4] Such a common domain for any dramatist, especially one who started as an actor and patcher of plays, can be found in the fund of material in the native dramatic tradition. Thus *Cynthia's Revels,* with its elaborate use of mythology and witty pages, provides evidence for Jonson's awareness of the type of play associated with John Lyly, while *The Devil is an Ass* has interesting (although often ironic) connections with the "devil plays" which were apparently quite popular during the early seventeenth century. Jonson's *aliena castra* for dramatic purposes include more than Plautus, Terence, and Seneca.

Such an observation is not meant to impugn Jonson's credentials as a student of the ancients or his independence and originality as an artist. No casual observer of the quarto of *Sejanus* can question the former, nor can any sympathetic reader of plays as disparate as *Every Man Out of His Humour* and *The Alchemist* question the latter. Rather, I am seeking to establish Jonson's flexible attitude towards sources and antecedents without adopting an overrigid view of his classicism and learning which might prevent consideration of his contact with the English popular dramatic tradition. In particular, we should not overlook the major area yet unexplored as a potential influence upon Jonson's comedies—the native morality play tradition, especially the Elizabethan morality.

Although a connection between Jonson's comedies and the morality tradition has often been suggested, there are several reasons why no detailed study of the subject has yet been made. First, to connect the crude and often banal moral abstractions of the moralities with the fully realized characters of *Volpone* and *The Alchemist* has seemed to many

4. *The Art of Literary Research* (New York, 1963), p. 87.

scholars a degradation of Jonsonian comedy. Equally important is the fact that many of the Elizabethan moralities have received scant attention from both editors and historians of the drama; as a consequence, scholars are often unaware of the potential raw material available in that common domain. To correct such a situation, the first chapter of this study will be devoted to the dramatic legacy of one sizeable group of Elizabethan moralities, a group which in purpose and technique might have appealed to a dramatist of Jonson's inclinations. Obviously, such a limited study cannot encompass the entire legacy of the late moralities. But by establishing such dramatic possibilities and then considering Jonson's comedies in their light, I hope to provide additional insight into his best plays.

The need for reassessment of the distinctive qualities of Jonsonian comedy has been noted by several of his most careful readers. Four decades ago, T. S. Eliot observed that Jonson had achieved "his own style, his own instrument" in comedy.[5] More recently, Edward Partridge has asked whether in *Volpone* Jonson "either failed to create anything aesthetically pleasing or created a drama too complex in nature and unique in effect to be encompassed by the traditional categories." [6] Is *Volpone,* in other words, a failure, or is it a type of play for which we have no definition? In the dedicatory epistle to the play Jonson himself raises the same issue, for there he admits that according to "*the strict rigour of* comick *law*" parts of his play might meet with censure, but still asks "*the learned, and charitable critick to haue so much faith in me, to thinke it was done off industrie,*" not inadvertently (ll. 110–12). Elsewhere Jonson argues:

5. *The Sacred Wood* (London, 1928), p. 107.
6. *The Broken Compass* (London, 1958), pp. 70–71.

> Nor, is the moving of laughter alwaies the end of *Comedy*, that is rather a fowling for the peoples delight, or their fooling. For, as *Aristotle* saies rightly, the moving of laughter is a fault in Comedie, a kind of turpitude, that depraves some part of a mans nature without a disease.
>
> (*Discoveries*, ll. 2629–33)

If one admits the possibility of a more complex view of comedy in which its "end" is more than merely "the moving of laughter," consideration of morality or pseudo-morality elements in Jonson's mature plays may prove useful. To eliminate such a possibility may be more in keeping with "*the strict rigour of* comick *law*" but may also prevent the reader from being that "*learned, and charitable critick*" to whom Jonson addressed himself.

CHAPTER 1

The Dramatic Legacy of the Elizabethan Morality

In recent years the English morality play has been subjected to intensive scholarly investigation. Studies made early in this century by Thompson and Mackenzie,[1] to be sure, had sketched in the general history and development of the morality, but not until the pioneering work of Willard Farnham's *The Medieval Heritage of Elizabethan Tragedy*[2] was the importance of this native English form for Shakespeare and his contemporaries firmly established. Subsequent studies by Spivack, Ribner, and Bevington[3] (to name only a few) have provided further insights by viewing Elizabethan-Jacobean drama in the light

1. E. N. S. Thompson, "The English Moral Plays," *Transactions of the Connecticut Academy of Arts and Sciences,* XIV (1910), 291–414; W. Roy Mackenzie, *The English Moralities from the Point of View of Allegory* (Boston and London, 1914).

2. Willard Farnham, *The Medieval Heritage of Elizabethan Tragedy* (Berkeley, Calif., 1936).

3. Bernard Spivack, *Shakespeare and the Allegory of Evil* (New York, 1958); Irving Ribner, *The English History Play in the Age of Shakespeare* (Princeton, N.J., 1957); David Bevington, *From "Mankind" to Marlowe: Growth of Structure in the Popular Drama of Tudor England* (Cambridge, Mass., 1962).

of its simpler and cruder ancestor. The morality play, as a result, has been used successfully as a critical scalpel to lay bare the essential structure of such significant and highly developed plays as *Doctor Faustus,* 1 and 2 *Henry IV,* and *Othello.*

In spite of the admitted morality legacy bequeathed to Elizabethan drama, however, relatively little attention has been paid to the morality play after 1560. The reasons for this neglect are clear. The fifteenth-century moralities, as Farnham points out, were "mainly intent upon grasping human nature in some form of abstraction standing for mankind as a whole," but in the sixteenth century "the protagonist tends to lose the abstract quality of *Humanum Genus.*" [4] Finding only "a heterogeneous collection of incidents," "mere conglomeration," and little "dramatic cohesion" in a representative group of moralities from the 1560s and 1570s, Farnham concludes that "the morality in Elizabeth's reign is obviously drawing near the end of its service as a literary form. With few exceptions it shows distinct loss of ability to attain unification in a central character, and it shows a related tendency to rambling diffuseness." [5]

Similar conclusions are reached by Ribner and Spivack. The former argues that the morality of Elizabeth's reign substitutes "extraneous horseplay" for that "underlying regularity of structure" found earlier.[6] Spivack, in his more extensive investigation, points out how the morality's "human hero was subject to a constant process of limitation," becoming "divided and specialized into man religious, man political, man juvenile, man intellectual, and so on," eventually "producing contrasted types of good and bad humanity in respect to a limited moral thesis." The effect of this process, he argues,

4. Farnham, *Medieval Heritage,* p. 209.
5. *Ibid.*, pp. 244, 247, 245, 242.
6. Ribner, *English History Play,* pp. 42–43.

"is to disorganize the original metaphor and to dispossess the personifications of vice and virtue from their original function." He therefore concludes: "It is now the Vice whose role bounds the scope of the play, as Mankind degenerates, in a dramatic sense, into a series of incidental figures upon whom he repeats his performance and multiplies the display of his cunning." [7] Thus, according to most scholars,[8] the late sixteenth-century moralities, which do not attain the requisite "unification in a central character," represent a degeneration of "the original metaphor" and "underlying regularity of structure" of the pristine fifteenth-century form.

Certainly, if the structure of *The Castle of Perseverance* or *Mankind* is used as a standard, such a judgment is valid. The decline and fall of the morality play is therefore considered to be worth only a sentence, at best a paragraph, in most treatments of Renaissance dramatic history. Other types of available evidence, however, suggest the dangers of such easy dismissal of the serviceability of this dramatic form. On the basis of the total number of both extant and lost plays, for example, one *could* argue that the period between 1558 and 1590 represents the golden age of the morality play; thus a recent study lists about fifty moralities during this thirty-year period compared with forty to forty-five for the preceding

7. Spivack, *Shakespeare and the Allegory of Evil*, pp. 305–7.

8. Some exceptions should be noted. Bevington, for example, does deal with the structure evolved by the intermediate moralities owing to the demands of the small troupe (e.g., the need for doubling of parts). He does not, however, consider the equally interesting problem of what happened to the morality structure when such limitations ceased to exist—when moralities were performed in the public theaters during the 1580s (*The Three Ladies of London*, for example). For comments on the continuing importance of the morality, see Madeleine Doran, *Endeavors of Art* (Madison, Wis., 1954), pp. 110–11; and A. P. Rossiter, *English Drama from Early Times to the Elizabethans* (London, 1950), pp. 101, 152–53.

one hundred and fifty years.[9] Such a numerical criterion is admittedly arbitrary and perhaps misleading, but the resulting total does make it difficult to envisage the morality withering away during Elizabeth's reign.

Investigation of what is known about these fifty plays, moreover, reveals that, rather than becoming moribund, the Elizabethan morality remained a supple form which could be used for a variety of purposes and under a variety of auspices. During this period, several moralities which have not survived were performed before Queen Elizabeth,[10] while an extant play, *Liberality and Prodigality*, was performed before her as late as 1601–2.[11] In addition to entertaining such an august audience, the moral dramatists were able to use their medium to dramatize the many controversies of the age. Plays like *King Darius* and *New Custom*, for example, expressed the polemical anti-Catholic sentiment of the early Elizabethan period. In a lost play, Martin Marprelate appeared "dressed like a monstrous ape on stage, and wormed and lanced to let the blood and evil humours out of him," while "Divinity appeared with a scratched face, complaining of the assaults received in the hideous creature's attacks upon her honour." [12] In answer to Puritan attacks upon the stage, the players themselves responded with *The Play of Plays and*

9. Samuel Schoenbaum's revision of Alfred Harbage's *Annals of English Drama, 975–1700* (London, 1964) lists forty-two "morals" between 1558 and 1590; a note on p. 40, in addition, lists another group of plays which can be roughly dated within this period, of which about eight are probably "morals."

10. E.g., *The Marriage of Mind and Measure*; *Beauty and Huswifery*; *Loyalty and Beauty*; *Error*; *Truth, Faithfulness, and Mercy*. For a full list of moralities performed at court see E. K. Chambers, *The Elizabethan Stage* (Oxford, 1923), III, 178, n. 2.

11. Rossiter, *English Drama*, points to this performance "as an example of quite unambiguous Morality in the highest of high places in Shakespeare's mature manhood" (p. 101).

12. Chambers, *Elizabethan Stage*, I, 294–95.

Pastimes, which argued through dramatic allegory that Life, when led away from Delight and Recreation by Zeal, only becomes subject to Glut and Tediousness.[13] But the largest single group of Elizabethan moralities, as Louis B. Wright has demonstrated,[14] attempts to come to grips with current social and economic problems; plays like *Enough is as Good as a Feast*, *The Tide Tarrieth No Man*, *All for Money*, and *The Three Ladies of London* offer a telling indictment against greed and materialism by providing a disturbing picture of a society corrupted by the worship of money.

Such diversity of purposes is another indication that the modern reader should hesitate before agreeing with Farnham that the Elizabethan morality was "near the end of its service as a literary form." Still, these plays with few exceptions do fail to attain that "unification in a central character" which he found to be typical of the earlier tradition. But is such unification a requisite feature of a morality play? With how much justification has this restrictive definition of "morality" been established? Need a morality play, by definition, have a central figure named Everyman or Youth or Wit? After all, many of the monuments of dramatic and nondramatic literature of the period (e.g., Sidney's *Arcadia*, Spenser's *Faerie Queene*, Jonson's *Bartholomew Fair*) provide a "multiple unity" which arises from diverse elements rather than the simple structural unity found in the early morality play.[15]

13. For a plot summary of this play, see Stephen Gosson, "Plays Confuted in Five Actions," *The English Drama and Stage Under the Tudor and Stuart Princes 1543–1664*, ed. W. C. Hazlitt (1869), pp. 201–3.

14. "Social Aspects of Some Belated Moralities," *Anglia*, LIV (1930), 107–48.

15. See, for example, such diverse studies as Walter R. Davis, "Thematic Unity in the *New Arcadia*," *SP*, LVII (1960), 123–43; Freda L. Townsend, *Apologie for Bartholmew Fayre* (New York, 1947), pp. 71–76 and *passim*; and particularly Doran, *Endeavors of Art*, pp. 370–76 and *passim*.

Can we safely ignore what may be an Elizabethan development of an established form rather than an Elizabethan degeneration of an established form? Spivack himself has pointed, albeit briefly, to a group of plays, such as *The Three Ladies of London* or *The Cobbler's Prophecy*, which display: (1) a common concern ("the jeopardy of the state"); (2) common issues (e.g., usury, decay of hospitality); and most important (3) a common technique (the use of social types or "estates" to represent "the trades and stations of life").[16] These late moralities from the 1580s and early 1590s, one might add, are quite close chronologically to those mature Elizabethan plays in which Farnham, Spivack, and other such scholars are ultimately interested. Without disputing the significance of the structural pattern built around a *Humanum Genus* figure, both for the early morality and for such plays as *Doctor Faustus* and *Macbeth*, one can still admit the possibility raised by this often ignored evidence that the later morality tradition may have developed other methods of unification and presentation which, in turn, may have made their own contribution to the "literal" or nonallegorical drama that followed or grew up alongside.

A complete revaluation of the dramatic legacy of the morality play is far beyond the scope of this study. Rather, in the remainder of this chapter I propose to examine the techniques and structure of one group of late moralities, a group that has some bearing upon subsequent drama. Instead of judging such plays on the basis of a standard established by their predecessors, my focus will be upon the distinctive methods they use to dramatize the problems facing society. The essential question remains: does the morality play have heirs other than *Doctor Faustus* and *Othello?* Could a dramatist like Jonson, whose plays lack any *Humanum Genus*

16. *Shakespeare and the Allegory of Evil,* pp. 235, 209–11.

figure at their center, have found in the late morality any dramatic possibilities appropriate to his purpose?

Emergence of the Public Vice

The largest single group of Elizabethan moralities consists of plays concerned with social and economic issues or, to expand the category even further, plays concerned with the general condition of the kingdom. Pre-Elizabethan dramatists had also been interested in such public issues. To express them in dramatic form, however, they had retained, for the most part, the traditional dramatic structure built around a protagonist besieged by conflicting forces of good and evil, only substituting for Everyman or Mankind a central figure, such as Respublica or Albion Knight, who represented England as a whole. The forces of evil in such plays were embodied in Vices such as Avarice and Injury whose machinations closely resembled the activities of earlier Vices which beset Youth or Wit or Magnificence.

After mid-century, on the other hand, many of the moralities display what Spivack has termed the "fission" of the *Humanum Genus* hero.[17] Thus a Marian play, *Wealth and Health* (1554),[18] enacts the recent history of England through the fortunes of Wealth, Health, and Liberty, who are corrupted by Ill-Will and Shrewd-Wit (Protestant private judgment) but are finally restored to health by Remedy (proper authority). Instead of using a figure such as Respublica or Albion Knight to stand for the kingdom as a whole, the anonymous author has used three "heroes" to

17. *Ibid.*, p. 229.

18. Ed. W. W. Greg for the Malone Society (1907). Dates cited for this and subsequent plays are approximate and in accordance with those given in *Annals of English Drama.*

demonstrate how England's assets can be and have been lost or undermined. With no single figure on stage to represent England, moreover, the role of the Vices has been somewhat altered. Ill-Will and Shrewd-Wit, who have brought England into this deplorable situation, do not represent psychological forces within the three heroes but rather allegorize forces active among the general public or the kingdom as a whole which have led to the decline of wealth, health, and liberty.

Several of the early Elizabethan moralities provide interesting examples of such departures from the *Humanum Genus* structure. In *King Darius* (1565),[19] the audience is presented with two biblical scenes, which display the two notable virtuous acts of the titular hero (the entertaining of the four kings and the demonstration of the impartiality of a true prince), and three allegorcial scenes, which set forth the triumph of the Reformation over Catholicism by means of a conflict between virtues and vices. Although the Vice (Iniquity), his subordinates (Importunity and Partiality), and the virtues (Constancy, Equity, and Charity) have no explicit connection with King Darius, their presence is still quite relevant to the purpose of the play; as David Bevington has demonstrated, "in both plots the virtues of constancy, equity, and charity receive their reward." [20] Foregoing a central Everyman or Respublica figure as a focal point for contention, the dramatist instead has his vices and virtues either argue with each other (Charity vs. Iniquity, Equity vs. all three vices) or directly address the audience. So Charity, having been unable to convert Iniquity, concludes:

19. *Anonymous Plays*, ed. John S. Farmer, 3d ser. (London, 1906), pp. 41–92.

20. "*Mankind*" *to Marlowe*, p. 176. See also Spivack, *Shakespeare and the Allegory of Evil*, pp. 260–61.

O dissembling and flattering generation,
God will you destroy (O wicked nation)!
In mouth you profess God's holy name,
But in your thoughts you sure abuse the same.

(p. 48)

Similarly, Equity resumes where Charity left off:

A brother of mine was here, as I heard say,
But with your folly you did drive him away;
So I thought it good hither for to come
To turn you from your error, O ye people dumb,
Without knowledge and understanding
And yet so deceitful in wicked working.

(p. 53)

The general tendency of the virtues to address the vices and the audience at the same time, best seen in the deliberate confusion of "you," "your," and "ye people" in Equity's speech, shows how the author's desire to deal with the condition of the kingdom has altered the traditional role of the Vice and his henchmen. According to Charity and Equity, Iniquity and his subordinates gain their power through the acquiescence and permissiveness of the audience before them who represent the general public. The Vice emerges not as the tempter of Mankind or King Darius but rather as a dramatic symbol for that attitude or force within the kingdom which the dramatist wishes to single out as a basic cause of contemporary evils.

Such a public role for the Vice takes various forms. In a play like *Horestes* (1567),[21] as Douglas Cole points out,

21. Ed. Daniel Seltzer and Arthur Brown for the Malone Society (Oxford, 1962).

the Vice becomes "symbolic of a particular kind of evil, an evil which is demonstrated not only in the main line of action, but also in subordinate scenes of broad comedy which echo the play's major theme." [22] After Revenge has persuaded Horestes to kill the murderers of his father, the audience is treated to an entertaining brawl between two soldiers who end up swearing their "revenge" upon one another, thereby "demonstrating by implication the base and destructive nature of the revenge principle." Earlier in the play, the two country bumpkins, Rusticus and Hodge, had been a match for the Vice until he had turned them against each other, whereupon they became victims of a beating at his hands. The actions of Horestes, which nearly bring chaos to the kingdom, are thereby the central but not the sole examples of the power of Revenge and social division. By the end of the play, the marriage of Horestes and Hermione demonstrates the triumph of Amity over Revenge, so that Truth can draw the moral:

A kyngdome kept in Amyte, and voyde of dissention,
Ne deuydyd in him selfe, by aney kynde of waye,
Neather prouoked by wordes, of reprehention,
Must nedes long contynew, as Truth doth saye.
For desention and stryfe, is the path to decaye.
And continuinge therein, must of nesecitie,
Be quight ruinate, and brought vnto myserye.

(ll. 1371–77)

The "desention and stryfe" which can lead to decay and ruin have here been demonstrated by the effect upon both Horestes and several subordinate figures of a Vice who em-

22. *Suffering and Evil in the Plays of Christopher Marlowe* (Princeton, N.J., 1962), p. 34.

bodies that attitude singled out as most detrimental to the health of the state.

Another example of such a public Vice is provided by R.B.'s *Apius and Virginia* (1564).[23] In order to extend the scope of the moral, the author has added to the familiar story from Livy an allegorical structure centered around the Vice Haphazard. Before the appearance of the judge himself, the audience sees the Vice in action with Apius' servants, Mansipulus, Mansipula, and Subservus. Even though all three realize that they should be attending their master and mistress, Haphazard can still persuade them to tarry with him, for: "It is but in hazard and yf you be mist, / And so it may happen you feele not his fist" (ll. 323–24); or, in the terms of their song, "The worst that can hap lo, in end is but beating" (l. 344). Haphazard, who by nature is opposed to such absolutes as duty or true service, embodies that attitude which causes men to chance future punishment or loss for the sake of present satisfaction. To emphasize the widespread range of his power, Haphazard provides a lengthy soliloquy which catalogues his influence over various parts of society. For example:

> A Plowman perhaps or ere that he die,
> May hap be a Gentleman, a Courtier or Captaine,
> And hap may so hazard, he may goe a begging:
> Perhap that a Gentleman, heyre to great land,
> Which selleth his liuing, for mony in hand,
> In hazard it is the bying of more,
> Perhaps he may ride when spent is the store.
>
> (ll. 393–99)

23. Ed. Ronald B. McKerrow and W. W. Greg for the Malone Society (1911).

When Apius subsequently reveals (ll. 393–99) his desire to possess Virginia, the audience has been prepared for the plan offered by the Vice, who suggests that "if you will hazard, to venter what falles, / Perhaps, that *Haphazard*, will end al your thralles" (ll. 476–77). Although the following scene involving Apius, Haphazard, Conscience, and Justice does suggest the *psychomachia* conflict, the Vice here and throughout the play represents not merely a weakness or evil to which Apius alone is susceptible but rather an attitude, prevalent in society, of which Apius is one famous example. Thus, on the different levels set up by the play, Apius is willing to ignore Conscience and Justice for the sake of his private lust; the servants (who, unlike their master, manage to escape punishment) are willing to neglect their duty and chance a beating for the sake of present pleasure; and the social types catalogued by the Vice are willing to chance the future for possible gain in the present. Haphazard is a dramatic representation of the amoral attitude, "Take a chance—perhaps you may get what you want," which pervades the play, as contrasted to the chastity of Virginia and the honor of Virginius, which alone are worthy of Comfort, Fame, and Reward. The author is using his Vice and allegorical apparatus not merely to make explicit the motivations of his central figure but to isolate and indict an attitude felt to be responsible for unworthy actions on various levels of society.[24]

The Marian and early Elizabethan moralities discussed so far, although differing in many ways, have several interesting

24. According to Jackson I. Cope, Haphazard "motivates the action so thoroughly as to rise above it as symbol rather than cause" (" 'The Best for Comedy': Richard Edwardes' Canon," *Texas Studies in Literature and Language*, II [1961], 511). For a discussion of how the Vice is used for "isolating the tragic implications" of these plays, see P. Happé, "Tragic Themes in Three Tudor Moralities," *SEL*, V (1965), 207–27.

features in common. First, the traditional morality pattern of conflict over a central *Humanum Genus* figure was no longer a universal choice for dramatists interested either in bringing social issues on stage or in adapting a famous story for didactic purposes. Some contemporary plays, to be sure, still made structural use of a figure resembling Everyman (*The Longer Thou Livest, The Marriage of Wit and Wisdom, Impatient Poverty*); others retained a similar structure but focused on a historical hero (*Cambises, Horestes*). The various changes —sometimes slight, sometimes major—in the dramatic representation of Mankind or Respublica inevitably produced concomitant changes in the role of the antagonist, the Vice. In differing ways the altered roles of Ill-Will, Shrewd-Wit, Iniquity, Revenge, and Haphazard show how different dramatists were attempting to isolate for dramatic investigation those forces or attitudes within society felt to be responsible for the evils depicted in the play as a whole. Emphasis upon public issues and wider scope has, in a sense, pushed some of the Vices out of the *psychomachia* conflict and into a new arena as yet only partially defined.

The "Estates" Morality

To see the new direction in store for both the public Vice and the morality of social criticism, one can turn to Wapull's *The Tide Tarrieth No Man* (1576).[25] Although Farnham characterized this play as "a heterogeneous collection of incidents," Bevington has argued for some measure of dramatic unity through the central position of Courage the Vice, who "conducts a series of cleverly interwoven intrigues with secu-

25. Ed. Ernst Ruhl, *SJ*, XLIII (1907), 1–52.

lar social types who represent the sinful excesses of man."[26] After Courage has opened the play by inviting the audience to join him on the Barge of Sin (an Elizabethan Ship of Fools containing representative types of corruption and folly), the Vice proceeds to practice his wiles upon a series of figures who form a cross section of society. Even though Wapull has provided allegorical names for Courage's victims (Greediness, Wastefulness, No Good Neighborhood), they nonetheless represent such social types as the landlord, the courtier, the usurer or merchant, and the young married couple. The story of Wastefulness and Wantonness, here only one strand of a larger action, shows the adaptation of subject matter (the effects of "corage" upon Youth) which formerly might have served for an entire play (*Lusty Juventus*). In Wapull's play, however, the fall of youth functions not as the center of a *Humanum Genus* structural pattern but rather as one example of the various segments of society corrupted by the Vice and all he represents. In place of Mankind or Respublica and a *psychomachia* conflict, Wapull has used Courage, who advocates the "misdirection of human energy toward acquisition, ambition, and sensual fulfillment,"[27] and his henchmen (Hurtful Help, Painted Profit, Feigned Furtherance) to isolate those attitudes felt to be responsible for the ills of society. To provide specific demonstration of the effects of such attitudes, he has then used his social types or "estates" along with a few virtuous figures (Faithful Few, Christianity). The resulting thesis-and-demonstration structure shows how at least one dramatist in the 1570s has combined extensive examples from contemporary society with the allegorical structure made possible by the public Vice to provide an analysis of the condition of the kingdom.

26. *"Mankind" to Marlowe*, p. 150.
27. Spivack, *Shakespeare and the Allegory of Evil*, p. 231.

A similar technique is employed by Thomas Lupton in one of the major scenes of *All for Money* (1577).[28] Here a series of petitioners parades before All for Money, the magistrate, who has instructions to grant only those suits approved by Money. The audience is presented with Gregory Graceless, a ruffian and thief, who is excused of his crimes; a woman who has murdered her child, who is let off; William-with-the-two-wives, who is relieved of the legal one in favor of the younger one; Nichol-never-out-of-the-law, who is granted a piece of land that rightfully belongs to his poor neighbor; Sir Lawrence Livingless, the foolish priest, who becomes All for Money's chaplain; and Old Mother Croote, who buys false witnesses in order to catch a young husband. Only poor Moneyless-and-Friendless is refused. In accordance with his promise on the title page of "plainly representing the maners of men and fashion of the world noweadayes" (p. 145), Lupton has offered his audience a specific demonstration of how the venality in various parts of society contributes to the corruption of justice. Through a combination of allegorical personae, who embody the thesis (All for Money, Sin), and social types or "estates," who provide the demonstration, the moral dramatist has made his point about the materialism of society.

Such use by Wapull and Lupton of a cross section of social types to illustrate the effects of the public Vice can be contrasted with the prevailing technique in earlier, and even in many contemporary, plays. In *Respublica* (1553), for example, the effects of the ascendancy of Avarice, Adulation, Insolence, and Oppression had been set forth by the complaints of People and the bragging of the vices about their respective achievements. Many moralities contain such sum-

28. Ed. Ernst Vogel, *SJ*, XL (1904), 129–86.

mary exposition of abuses through set speeches by either the vices (as in the vaunts of Ignorance, Perverse Doctrine, Avarice, and Cruelty in *New Custom*) or figures such as People (*Respublica, The Longer Thou Livest*), Vulgus (Phillips' *Patient Grissill*), or Commons' Cry and Commons' Complaint (*Cambises*). Wapull and Lupton, on the other hand, manage to achieve the same end, the demonstration of the power of vice over "people," by maintaining the allegorical framework embodied in the Vice while adding specific figures and events that enact rather than describe what the kingdom has become. Instead of castigating such dramatists for their debilitation of the figure of Mankind, perhaps we should give them credit for their innovations in providing representative victims for the public Vice.

The first extant play to take full advantage of such new dramatic possibilities is Robert Wilson's *The Three Ladies of London* (1581).[29] This play, as Madeleine Doran has pointed out, is concerned with "public ethics, and gives a lesson in the characteristic evils that beset the body politic and the saving ideals that should govern it." [30] London, the focus of the play, is represented not by a central figure in the tradition of Everyman or Respublica but rather by three female figures (Love, Conscience, and Lucre) who embody the city's assets or essential features. The central allegory of *The Three Ladies* presents the degradation of Love and Conscience in a world in which Lucre "rules the rout," for, as the opening scene makes clear, "They forsake mother, prince, country, religion, kiff and kin; / Nay, men care not what they forsake, so Lady Lucre they win" (pp. 249–50). The subjection of

29. *A Select Collection of Old English Plays Originally Published by Robert Dodsley in the Year 1744*, ed. W. Carew Hazlitt, 4th ed. (London, 1874), VI, 245–370. (Hereafter cited as Dodsley.)
30. *Endeavors of Art*, p. 110.

Love and Conscience and the ascendancy of the four knaves or vices (Dissimulation, Fraud, Simony, and Usury), who by gaining important positions in the service of Lady Lucre become active forces let loose in London, effectively embody the author's vision of his society.

Wilson, moreover, like Wapull and Lupton, is also concerned with demonstrating the specific effects of such conditions upon the general populace or "the man in the street," for, as the title page tells us, this play is meant to be "*A Perfect Patterne for All Estates to looke into*" (p. 246). Once the evils of contemporary London have been established in allegorical terms, a series of social types appears to demonstrate the effects of such corruption upon the various "estates" or segments of London society. The poor Artifex, who seeks help from Lucre, is told to be deceitful in his trade; the Lawyer, who in the past had pleaded for Conscience and Love, is told to keep his clients in the law for years and to twist the truth if he wishes Lucre's favors; and Sincerity, a poor scholar from Oxford seeking a benefice, is given the parsonage of St. Nihil and empty promises from Sir Nicholas Nemo. In contrast, Peter Pleaseman, who promises that his religion will offend no one and agrees to give up half his income to Simony, is granted a benefice; and Mercatore, who is willing to give up anything (including his religion) for Lucre, thrives, at least temporarily. By means of such recognizable types, the specific effects of the allegorical ascendancy of Lucre in the overplot are demonstrated to the audience.

Another related structural feature of this play is the role played by Simplicity, the country bumpkin, who provides a low comedy equivalent for the degradation of Love and Conscience. He, like Conscience, is reduced to beggary and, like all three ladies, is punished for his crimes, although innocent of the robbery and murder for which he is stripped and beaten. In Simplicity we can see the only reflection in this play of the traditional morality pattern based upon a *Humanum Genus* figure. Although the true subject of *The Three Ladies* is London, Simplicity represents hapless and unprotected humanity in a Lucre-dominated society. Wilson, like Wapull in his Wastefulness-Wantonness plot, is here adapting an earlier dramatic convention as one part of his desired effect.

Wilson's allegorical superstructure or overplot, although more elaborate, thus functions in much the same way as did the Vices and other allegorical personae of the earlier plays discussed above, for his use of the three ladies and the four knaves effectively isolates for the audience's edification those forces or attitudes in society responsible for the evils of the kingdom. The real step forward in the play lies in the various ways in which the announced subject, London society as a whole, is specifically anatomized. The abundance of such devices here (one could also point to the disappearance of Hospitality who is haled off the stage by Usury, never to return again to England) can be attributed to the new centering of theatrical operations in London. In contrast to *All for Money*, which Bevington has shown to be a tour de force with thirty-two parts for four actors,[31] *The Three Ladies* has more personnel at its disposal; the dramatist, released from the severe limitations of a small troupe, can thereby attempt effects on a larger scale. The central personification of *Humanum Genus*, so effective as an organizing principle for plays facing the performance requirements of the earlier popular tradition, could now give way, even more than in the

31. *"Mankind" to Marlowe*, p. 165.

moralities of the previous decade, to new experiments, a process which enabled Wilson to present the same type of allegorical thesis without sacrificing such specific *exempla* as the "estates," Simplicity, and Hospitality. New theatrical conditions have made possible a new dramatic formula specifically designed to diagnose the health of Respublica.

Little of the popular drama of the 1580s has survived, making it difficult to determine to what extent such trends were characteristic of the London moralities. One reference does point to a lost play which certainly belongs to this group. Sir John Harington, answering the charges of "lightnes & wantonnes" made against the drama in the late 1580s, provides the following examples:

> Then, for Comedies, how full of harmeles myrth is our Cambridge *Pedantius*? and the Oxford *Bellum Grammaticale*? or, to speake of a London Comedie, how much good matter, yea and matter of state, is there in that Comedie cald the play of the Cards, in which it is showed how foure Parasiticall knaues robbe the foure principall vocations of the Realme, *videl.* the vocation of Souldiers, Schollers, Marchants, and Husbandmen?[32]

The Play of the Cards as described by Harington appears to have been a morality along the lines of *The Three Ladies* in which the four knaves of the deck, like Dissimulation and his group, plot against characters who represent various "estates" or "vocations." Again, as in the earlier moralities, the particular evils to be emphasized can be isolated in the knaves or vices, while, as in Wapull, Lupton, and Wilson, the effect upon Respublica is acted out by social types.

32. "A Preface, or rather a Briefe Apologie of Poetrie," *Elizabethan Critical Essays*, ed. G. Gregory Smith (Oxford, 1904), II, 210.

Although *The Play of the Cards* has not survived, the same general principle of dramatic organization can be seen in Robert Wilson's *The Cobbler's Prophecy* (1590).[33] Although the scene is ostensibly Boeotia, Wilson presents his social thesis by having the Vice, Contempt (who stands for "envy and dissension among the several estates and for the resultant turmoil and injustice in the realm"),[34] practice his wiles upon selected types from sixteenth-century English society. Sateros, the noble soldier, whose main concern is for the health of the state, is contrasted with Emnius, the treacherous and lecherous courtier, and the cowardly country gentleman, who tries to bribe his way out of military service. The duke, his daughter, the priest, and the scholar, all of whom are endowed with representative failings, undergo a reformation in character by the end of the play, so that once they have made their pledges and burned the cabin of Contempt, peace and prosperity return to the kingdom. When the soldier and the scholar embrace in the finale, the health of Boeotia-England has been symbolically restored, for arms and art have regained their true roles as supports of the state. In the midst of the mythological machinery and comic buffoonery of this play, the health of the kingdom is dramatically explored by means of representative "estates" who act out their parts within a larger allegorical framework centered around a Vice which epitomizes those attitudes responsible for the evils in the kingdom.

Although the plays discussed so far use "estates" or "vocations" along with vices or knaves, there are other possible combinations. Lodge and Greene's *A Looking Glass for Lon-*

33. Ed. A. C. Wood and W. W. Greg for the Malone Society (Oxford, 1914).

34. Spivack, *Shakespeare and the Allegory of Evil*, p. 210.

don and England (1590),[35] for example, dispenses with the allegorical apparatus entirely. This best seller (four editions by 1617) uses wicked Nineveh rather than Boeotia to "set a looking Glasse before [the] eyes" (l. 2400) of the London audience. The vices of Nineveh (elaborately called to the attention of the audience by the prophets Oseas and Jonas who act as chorus) are set forth on three levels: Rasni and his corrupt court, who are presented as the source of the diseases of the kingdom; Thrasibulus and Alcon, the citizen and the peasant, who are degraded and eventually destroyed by usury and corruption in the city; and the servant-clown, who beats his master and takes his wife. The allegorical superstructure of *The Three Ladies* or *The Cobbler's Prophecy* has here been replaced by the historical overplot involving Rasni and his court, but the authors of *A Looking Glass* are using Thrasibulus, Alcon, and the clown in much the same way as Wilson had used his "estates" and Simplicity. Once more the source of corruption has been defined, so to speak, by the overplot, while the specific effects of that corruption are acted out by representative figures. Two Elizabethan dramatists, maintaining a realistic or "literal" mode of presentation, have here combined a historical *exemplum* with an "estates" structure in order to deal with the health of Respublica.

Such a movement away from allegorical elements in drama, however, is by no means all-inclusive. Perhaps the best example of the use of "estates" within an allegorical framework in the 1590s is *A Knack to Know a Knave* (1592).[36] Ribner has pointed to this play, which apparently was popular enough or well-known enough to call for a "sequel" (*A Knack to Know an Honest Man* [1594]), as "of peculiar

35. Ed. W. W. Greg for the Malone Society (Oxford, 1932).
36. Ed. G. R. Proudfoot for the Malone Society (Oxford, 1963).

interest for the evidence it furnishes of the strong survival of morality play forms at the very end of the sixteenth century."[37] The author of *A Knack* has used an overplot based upon legendary English history to frame his satirical titular plot which depicts the evils of contemporary English society. In the opening scene Honesty, the central figure of the play, is granted a commission by King Edgar and Bishop Dunstan to seek out knaves in the state and bring them to justice; much of the remainder of *A Knack* is devoted to the devices used by this allegorical undercover agent to expose the four knaves (Perin the courtier, Cuthbert the coneycatcher, Walter-Would-Have-More the farmer, and John-the-Precise the priest) before the King. In the denouement Honesty can therefore conclude:

> You that wil damne your selues for lucres sake
> And make no conscience to deceiue the poore:
> You that be enemies of the common wealth:
> To send corne ouer to inrich the enemie:
> And you that doe abuse the word of God,
> And send ouer woolle and Tin, broad cloath and lead,
> And you that counterfeyt Kings priuie seales,
> And thereby rob the willing minded Communaltie,
> I warne you all that vse such subtill villanie,
> Beware least you lyke these be found by Honestie.
> (ll. 1877–86)

In addition to the exposure of these knaves and their representative evils, *A Knack* also provides, by way of contrast, several characters who function in a manner befitting their place in society. Juxtaposed with Walter the farmer, whose selfish ends leave no room for charity, are the Knight and the

37. *English History Play*, p. 227.

Squire, who argue for the old hospitality and obligations. To demonstrate to the King the effects of the present export policies, Honesty brings in Piers Plowman, who was once a valuable member of the kingdom but is now in deplorable condition owing to the export of corn. Finally, Bishop Dunstan, who gives good advice to the King whether it is welcome or not, is contrasted to Perin, the archetypal false courtier. Such ideal characters, however, are in the minority in this play which, as the title makes clear, is primarily concerned with the exposure of knavery.

A Knack, in several respects, provides a convenient middle ground from which to view the earlier moralities and the literal drama that is to grow out of them. As in *A Looking Glass*, the author has replaced the allegorical superstructure of the various Wilson plays with a historical overplot which deals with the uncovering of a different kind of deception (King Edgar's wooer by proxy who secretly marries the girl) and thereby sets up interesting analogies in the manner of many Elizabethan double plots. The dramatist's use of allegorical figures is sparing; rather, the social thesis is developed primarily through the four knaves who represent four major "estates" or areas of society (the court, the priesthood, the farms, and the city). Despite such increased literal emphasis, however, the role of Honesty still firmly connects the play with the morality tradition. This allegorical prime mover functions not as a vice nor as an abstraction acting in behalf of a divine order (God's Merciful Promises) but rather as an ideal principle within this particular kingdom, a potential force by which the people can cure themselves. The author of *A Knack*, although seeking the scope and breadth of the earlier moral dramatists, was unwilling to sacrifice specificity and recognizable details of contemporary life. His solution was to deal, for the most part, with representative or typical, rather than allegorical, figures and to have his central allegorical figure perform his tasks within a dramatic world primarily literal in nature. This combination of what a modern audience might regard as contradictory modes of presentation produces a valuable document of dramatic history, for we can see how a popular dramatist of the 1590s with a social thesis could modify the traditional allegorical drama in order to have it coexist with the nascent literal drama growing up alongside.

Nor does *A Knack* represent the end of the use of "estates" within an allegorical structure. Certainly the best known example in the 1590s is *Histriomastix* (1599)[38] which, unlike most of the plays discussed so far, has received considerable scholarly attention. Anthony Caputi has described this play as a "crude allegorical dramatization of two Renaissance commonplaces": that the fortunes of society are governed by a continuous cycle; and that the way out of the cyclical trap is through learning and Christian Stoicism.[39] Each of the six acts deals with one phase of the cycle, presenting "the appropriate allegorical figure and his or her attendants," who "preside over the action and influence in characteristic ways" representative elements of society. Act I, for example, displays the effects of Peace: the four nobles adopt the arts, the

38. *The Plays of John Marston*, ed. H. Harvey Wood (Edinburgh and London, 1939), III, 243–302.

39. *John Marston, Satirist* (Ithaca, N.Y., 1961), pp. 82–84. More recently, Philip J. Finkelpearl has pointed out that "in each act the author exemplifies the state of the kingdom under its particular presiding allegorical deity, first by means of general statements and then by the introduction of a succession of characters—nobles, lawyers, merchants, actors, and so forth—who depict a cross section of the commonwealth" (*John Marston of the Middle Temple* [Cambridge, Mass., 1969], p. 122). Finkelpearl argues convincingly that *Histriomastix* is not merely a revision of an old morality play but rather represents an original piece which Marston specifically designed for the Inns of Court.

merchants and lawyers decide to improve themselves through study, and the commoners, here represented by harvest folk, sing a song of plenty and rejoice in their contentment. As Plenty, Pride, Envy, War, and Poverty successively take over as presiding deity, the same pattern is repeated with minor variations until Peace finally returns in Act VI. Within this symmetrical scheme, Chrisoganus, with his theses about learning and Stoic fortitude, and the players, with their buffoonery and satire, are the mobile elements. Regardless of the conflicting theories about the proto-*Histriomastix* and the revisions, the 1599 version imparts its message by means of an "estates" technique within an elaborate allegorical framework. Although the emphasis upon learning and the obvious appeal to an elite audience are rather far in spirit from the popular tradition, Marston's adaptation of the popular drama's thesis-and-demonstration structure with its use of a cross section of society as data for an allegorical purpose provides an example of a full-scale "estates" morality at the very end of the sixteenth century.

An even later example of a play in the same tradition is *Nobody and Somebody* (1605).[40] This strange play (acted, as the undated edition tells us, by a Jacobean company) is a late "hybrid" which attempts to deal with social injustice and the evils of the kingdom on two different yet related levels. The vicissitudes of King Elidure, who is trying to act justly and charitably despite the machinations of a tyrannical elder brother, two ambitious princes, and a corrupt court, are juxtaposed with the ill fortunes of Nobody, a symbol of the old virtues and hospitality, who is discredited and eventually arrested as a criminal by his sworn enemy Somebody. The parallel is enforced when both Elidure and Nobody, at the

40. Ed. John S. Farmer for the Tudor Facsimile Texts (1911).

nadir of their respective fortunes, are imprisoned in successive scenes. Justice finally triumphs in the denouement, however, for Elidure becomes king for the third time and Nobody is vindicated at the expense of Somebody and Lord Sycophant. Although a large part of the titular plot is given over to "nobody" jokes, the various social questions and the condition of the kingdom still represent the dominant concern of the play, a concern dramatized by means of a fanciful variation upon the techniques of the late morality tradition. As in *The Three Ladies* or *A Looking Glass,* the author has used his overplot to define the condition of the kingdom and then used the Nobody and Somebody plot to act out the effects of such evils upon the general populace. As in *A Knack,* the allegorical figures used to set forth the social criticism of the play are contained within an over-all historical or literal structure provided by legendary English history. The substitution of Nobody and Somebody for Honesty and the "estates" shows how a later dramatist turned to a traditional literary and pictorial *topos* in order to find a suitable vehicle for his social message.[41] The resulting juxtaposition of literal and nonliteral modes of presentation may jar the modern sensibility, but such a dramatic formula was, apparently, still a viable means of bringing social questions to the attention of the audience of *Hamlet* or *Volpone.*

This survey of selected plays from five decades of Elizabethan drama is one answer to the scholarly indictment of the late morality for its "rambling diffuseness" and "extraneous horseplay." Although these moralities may not please our dramatic palates, many of them exhibit techniques and an over-all rationale which are of definite interest both in their

41. See Gerta Calmann, "The Picture of Nobody: An Iconographical Study," *JWCI,* XXIII (1960), 60–104.

own right and in their potential relationship to the more sophisticated drama that follows. Even though the evidence may not be as exhaustive as one might wish,[42] certain conclusions about this group of Elizabethan moralities now appear justified. The mid-sixteenth-century popular dramatist about to put his social thesis into dramatic form would probably have been thinking in terms of a *Humanum Genus* structure with Respublica or England as the central figure. Between 1560 and 1580 other dramatic forms came into use, particularly a new thesis-and-demonstration structure (suggestive, at times, of the preacher's text and *exempla*) in which the thesis, usually supplied by the proverbial title, is embodied in the Vice and other allegorical personae while the demonstration is provided by the victims of the Vice who, upon occasion, form a cross section of social types. Vices like Haphazard and Courage (and Contempt some years later) embody forces within society as a whole, not within individual man, and can thereby be used to isolate for dramatic purposes those attitudes or evils responsible for the diseases of the kingdom.

With the centering of theatrical operations in London around 1580, better facilities and increased personnel enabled dramatists with the same interest in social reform, such as Robert Wilson, to employ a wider range of techniques and effects. Thus, in *The Three Ladies of London,* the allegorical superstructure effectively defines the causes of contemporary evils in a manner much more elaborate than would have been

42. Chambers, for example, has pointed out that although there are 307 plays extant for the period between 1586 and 1616, there is reason to suppose that this total "only represents a comparatively small fraction of the complete crop" of those years (*Elizabethan Stage,* III, 182). The plays that have survived, it is safe to assume, represent the cream of the dramatic crop, but those that, for whatever reason, did not find their way into print probably included among their number much of the ephemeral or journeyman work in which one would expect to find examples of the less sophisticated popular drama.

possible for Wapull or Lupton, while Wilson's use of the "estates," Simplicity, and Hospitality spells out the effect of such conditions upon the public at large. Similarly, in *The Cobbler's Prophecy* Wilson is able to provide a more specific account of the pernicious influence of his Vice upon society than had been found in the earlier dramatists.

By the 1590s, moreover, several revealing changes have taken place. The elaborate allegorical superstructure of *The Three Ladies,* for example, has given way in several instances to a historical overplot coupled with a comparatively sparing use of nonliteral personae. The authors of *A Looking Glass* use Rasni's corrupt court rather than the three ladies and four knaves to define the true nature of their city and employ Thrasibulus, Alcon, and the clown rather than the "estates" and Simplicity to display the effects of such evil conditions. *A Knack,* on the other hand, has no such close equivalent for Wilson's allegorical overplot but rather uses as its framework a historical story which functions in the manner of a standard Elizabethan overplot. The host of allegorical personae characteristic of the earlier tradition has here given way to a historical kingdom in which an allegorical figure, who embodies a standard of conduct available to all, brings representative types to literal justice.

Such emphasis, moreover, upon representative types, which often provide a cross-sectional or panoramic view of society as a whole, emerges as a distinctive feature of many late moralities. This device, used by Wilson as part of his total effect in *The Three Ladies,* becomes in *A Looking Glass, The Cobbler's Prophecy,* and *A Knack* (and, in a slightly altered fashion, in *Histriomastix* and *Nobody and Somebody*) the dramatist's primary means of setting forth his social thesis. So Alcon, Thrasibulus, and the clown demonstrate the effects of a corrupt Nineveh; the duke, his daughter, the priest, the scholar, the soldier, the courtier, and the country gentleman act out the effects of the ascendancy of Contempt and Venus in Boeotia; and the courtier, the coneycatcher, the farmer, and the priest display the faults inherent in four major areas of English society. Such a dependence upon social types rather than allegorical qualities provides valuable evidence that the "estates" play around 1590 was moving away from the morality as we usually conceive of it.

The concern for the health of Respublica found in the earlier morality tradition has thus persisted, even though new theatrical conditions and new trends in drama have brought about significant changes in the means used to provide a dramatic representation of the kingdom. Besides filling in a somewhat neglected chapter in English dramatic history, study of a major group of Elizabethan moralities has uncovered dramatic forms and techniques, particularly the use of "estates" and the public Vice, available to later Elizabethan and Jacobean dramatists concerned in their own ways with the condition of the kingdom. Such findings, moreover, raise several interesting questions. To what extent does the growing emphasis upon literal effects seen in *A Knack* lead into the sophisticated Elizabethan-Jacobean drama which, in general, lacks overt allegory? Is there any significant connection between the goals and techniques of the Elizabethan morality and those of the various literal dramatists who follow? And, of major interest to this study, does analysis of the dramatic possibilities provided by such late moralities offer any insight into the techniques and structure employed by the master of Jacobean satirical comedy, Ben Jonson?

CHAPTER 2

Jonson and the Morality Tradition: The Early Plays

THE association of Ben Jonson with the morality play and the allegorical tradition is a long and hallowed one. C. R. Baskervill was the first to emphasize Jonson's borrowings from the moralities, especially in *Every Man In His Humour* and *Cynthia's Revels*.[1] L. C. Knights, among others, has pointed to "the obvious 'morality' influence in such plays as *The Devil is an Ass* and *The Magnetic Lady*" and has described *The Staple of News* as "a morality play on the power of money." [2] Harry Levin has seen English morality conventions "in Jonson's casts and plots, in the *redende Namen* of his characters, in the beast-fable of *Volpone* or the gaping Hell-mouth of *The Devil is an Ass*." [3] Madeleine Doran, in her discussion of the mature

1. *English Elements in Jonson's Early Comedy* (Austin, Tex., (1911).
2. *Drama and Society in the Age of Jonson* (London, 1937), pp. 188, 220.
3. Ben Jonson, *Selected Works*, ed. Harry Levin (New York, 1938), p. 11.

comedies, has conceded their outward resemblance to Latin and Italian models but has still concluded: "In their moral-psychological combination of motives they seem to me to have closer affinity with the morality play tradition." [4] And recently Robert E. Knoll has argued that Jonson's plays like the moralities are "both realistic and allegorical," offering "eternal truth wrapped in contemporary garb just as they did." [5]

In spite of the abundance of such observations (of which the above are but a representative sampling), there have been few critical studies which have argued for a definite relationship between any of Jonson's major comedies and the morality tradition. Perhaps the main reason for such silence is the widely held conception of "morality play." Thus Maurice Hussey, who views Jonson's moral values as being, "in dramatic terms, closely related to the Morality Play," can describe *The Alchemist* as "a morality play on the lusts of covetousness and licentiousness" with Epicure Mammon as the central character.[6] Even though Mammon may be the most memorable figure in the play, he can scarcely be viewed as a *Humanum Genus* prototype around whom the entire plot is organized. At least one scholar seeking to establish a connection has therefore been forced to wrench the structure of a major Jonsonian comedy in order to fit it into the standard scholarly definition of "morality play."

Certainly there is no reason to question Jonson's familiarity with the *Humanum Genus* morality pattern, but, as a spectator in Westminster in the 1570s and 1580s and as a journeyman player in the 1590s,[7] he was just as likely to be aware

4. *Endeavors of Art* (Madison, Wis., 1954), p. 169.

5. *Ben Jonson's Plays: An Introduction* (Lincoln, Nebr., 1964), p. 165.

6. "Ananias the Deacon: A Study of Religion in Jonson's *The Alchemist*," *English*, IX (1953), 299.

7. For a discussion of Jonson as a member of a "strolling company,"

of later developments in morality structure and technique. If in the course of his dramatic career he had wished to draw upon this native tradition, one might well expect him to turn to more recent plays with which he would have had firsthand contact. Given such conjectural possibilities, the following chapters will ignore the *Humanum Genus* will-o'-the-wisp and will instead investigate Jonson's comedies, particularly *Volpone*, *The Alchemist*, and *Bartholomew Fair*, in the light of the findings about vices, virtues, and "estates" presented above.

Jonson's most obvious use of morality elements comes late in his career, particularly in *The Devil is an Ass* (1616) and *The Staple of News* (1626). By the time of the latter, moreover, Jonson evidently felt it necessary to reeducate his audience during the course of the play so that they would fully understand how he was transforming the now defunct allegorical tradition. The choric comments of the foolish gossips can thereby provide the modern reader with revealing statements about the dramatist's aims and techniques. The

---

see H & S, I, 13–14; and Fredson Thayer Bowers, "Ben Jonson the Actor," *SP*, XXXIV (1937), 392–406. There is as yet no authoritative treatment of what such troupes had in their repertoires or of the more general problem of what earlier plays were known in the 1590s. For conflicting interpretations of the evidence offered by the player in *Sir Thomas More*, see Bevington, *From "Mankind" to Marlowe: Growth of Structure in the Popular Drama of Tudor England* (Cambridge, Mass., 1962), p. 68; and Arthur Brown, "The Play Within a Play: An Elizabethan Dramatic Device," *E & S*, XIII (1960), 37. A touring company, the Earl of Pembroke's Men, apparently performed a morality, *Like Will to Like*, at the Rose as late as October 28, 1600. See *Henslowe's Diary*, ed. R. A. Foakes and R. T. Rickert (Cambridge, Eng., 1961), p. 164. Although there is insufficient evidence for establishing just how Jonson's notion of "morality play" would correspond to ours, there is certainly every reason to assume that he would have been aware of developments during the 1570s and 1580s in morality structure and technique.

second intermean, for example, contains the following dialogue:

> MIRTH. *How like you the* Vice *i' the Play?*
> EXPECTATION. *Which is he?*
> MIR. *Three or foure:* old Couetousnesse, *the sordid* Peny-boy, *the* Money-bawd, *who is a flesh-bawd too, they say.*
> TATLE. *But here is neuer a* Fiend *to carry him away. Besides, he has neuer a wooden dagger! I'ld not giue a rush for a* Vice, *that has not a wooden dagger to snap at euery body he meetes.*
> MIRTH. *That was the old way, Gossip, when* Iniquity *came in like* Hokos Pokos, *in a Iuglers ierkin, with false skirts, like the* Knaue *of* Clubs! *but now they are attir'd like men and women o' the time, the* Vices, *male and female!* Prodigality *like a young heyre, and his* Mistresse Money (*whose fauours he scatters like counters*) *prank't vp like a prime* Lady, *the* Infanta *of the* Mines.
>
> (ll. 5–20)

Here Jonson is glossing his own play to explain how morality personae are being clothed in "modern" (1626) dress. "*The* Vices, *male and female,*" who had formerly strutted around the stage with their wooden daggers before being carried off by the Devil, have now been "*attir'd like men and women o' the time.*" "*The old way*" of using figures such as Covetousness, Iniquity, and Prodigality has been replaced by a "new way" which metamorphoses the traditional allegorical figure into a recognizable contemporary figure (a young heir, a usurer) whose function in society is in some way analogous. By means of such choric exegesis, Jonson is hoping to establish both connections and distinctions between his comedy and the morality tradition. Of greatest interest for this study, he is suggesting that the Vice of 1626 may have retained his traditional function and identity, while being adapted in some manner to fit the realities of contemporary society.[8]

Few scholars would quarrel about the presence of morality elements in *The Staple of News*. A more controversial point, however, is the importance of the moralities for many of the previous plays, particularly for *Volpone*, *The Alchemist*, and *Bartholomew Fair*. Does the theory of adaptation set forth by Mirth, in which allegorical personae are to appear somehow in modern dress, apply only to the plays of Jonson's so-called "dotage," or can this process of dramatic metamorphosis also be found in earlier plays which maintain a consistent literal surface? Is the method described in *The Staple of News*, in other words, a new innovation, or is Jonson spelling out for us a hitherto unrecognized process by which he has been creating dramatis personae throughout a long career?

The difficulties in answering such questions are manifold. Certainly there is little profit in combing through Jonson's plays in the hope of reducing his successful comic creations to moral abstractions in order to prove a point. Jonson's greedy merchant, Corvino, to take one example, acts out within the comic framework of *Volpone* the same concept of covetousness which many a moral dramatist had introduced by means of an allegorical Vice (e.g., Covetouse in *Enough is as Good as a Feast*) or an "estates" figure (e.g., Mercatore of *The Three Ladies*). But for several reasons such a relationship cannot in itself provide any firm evidence for indebtedness to the morality tradition. First of all, the morality was scarcely the only available source for examples of greedy merchants, especially for an author with Jonson's command of Renaissance and classical literature. Equally important is the fact

8. The point is essential to *The Devil is an Ass* in which the ludicrous and outdated attempts of Pug, the inept devil, to corrupt mankind are contrasted with the skillful "modern" operations of Meercraft, the projector, who clearly represents a Vice "*attir'd*" as a man "*o' the time*." See Chapter 6 below for a full discussion.

that the use of a "character" to embody an abstraction or universal concept in some concrete form is basic to Renaissance literary theory, as any reader of Sidney or Spenser will testify.[9] Corvino's avarice, especially when one takes into account the entertaining comic spectacle which it provides, cannot in itself substantiate any firm connection. To establish Jonson's indebtedness to the morality tradition or his use of morality personae in modern dress, then, the investigation must be broader and deeper, with an emphasis upon features of his plays that cannot be explained with reference to hitherto explored sources or influences. Perhaps the question to be entertained in the following chapters can best be summed up as follows: does knowledge of the structure and techniques of the late morality, as set forth in the previous chapter, coupled with the theory of adaptation derived from *The Staple of News,* help us to understand Jonsonian comedy more fully? In brief, does such an approach allow the modern reader to be that "*learned, and charitable critick*" at whom *Volpone* was directed?

The Case is Altered and *Every Man In His Humour*

With the exception of *Cynthia's Revels,* the Jonsonian comedies that precede *Volpone* offer little evidence for the influence of the late morality structure discussed above. Nevertheless, a brief consideration of these plays is necessary to set forth various problems in structure and technique that provide a valuable background to the mature comedies.

9. See, for example, Edward W. Robbins, *Dramatic Characterization in Printed Commentaries on Terence* (Urbana, Ill., 1951), p. 66 and *passim;* Baxter Hathaway, *The Age of Criticism: The Late Renaissance in Italy* (Ithaca, N.Y., 1962), pp. 129–202; and Doran, *Endeavors of Art,* p. 256 and *passim.*

The first plays to be noted are Jonson's starting point in comedy, *The Case is Altered* (a play he apparently wished to disown), and *Every Man In His Humour* (his first success).[10] In both plays Jonson was seeking to adapt the plot, characters, and conventions of Roman intrigue comedy to his own purposes. In *The Case is Altered*, he intertwines plots borrowed from two Plautine plays, adding Juniper with his big words, Onion with his buffoonery, and various satiric thrusts at French manners, courtly dialogue, and Antonio Balladino. Romance conventions are much in evidence throughout the play, particularly in the double *cognitio* of the denouement (Gasper is found to be Camillo, and Rachel, Isabel), but equally apparent is the author's unsure hand. The reader, accustomed to Jonson's skill in dramatic exposition in the mature plays, cannot help being struck by the clumsiness and heavy-handedness here, as in the filling in of Jacques's past (II.i) or the rather obvious announcements about Gasper-Camillo (I.ix.63–85; IV.iv.20–31). Even more revealing is the treatment of comic providence (described by Herford as the "convention of easy forgiveness"),[11] for in spite of the dilemmas often raised by the action, the audience is aware of an underlying assumption that matters will somehow work out satisfactorily. Perhaps most typical of the manner in which this early play raises and resolves moral issues is the handling of Angelo's attempted rape of Rachel. Paulo has entrusted her to the care of his supposedly trustworthy friend, but Angelo, with little hesitation, pursues Rachel for himself. His first two attempts to seize her are interrupted

10. *Tale of a Tub* is omitted from this discussion owing to its anomalous position in the Jonsonian canon. For a recent argument placing this play in Jonson's mature period, see J. A. Bryant, Jr., "*A Tale of a Tub:* Jonson's Comedy of the Human Condition," *Renaissance Papers, 1963*, pp. 95–105.

11. H & S, I, 316.

fortuitously (IV.vi.29–30), but finally, in Act V, Angelo seems to have achieved control over his intended victim. Foreshadowing Celia some years later, Rachel then comments upon the baseness of human motives when governed by appetites, not obligations:

> ô heauen, can it be,
> That men should liue with such vnfeeling soules,
> Without or touch of conscience or religion,
> Or that their warping appetites should spoile
> Those honor'd formes, that the true seale of friendship
> Had set vpon their faces?
>
> (V.viii.14–19)

As opposed to *Volpone,* however, such moral questioning is not in keeping with the assumptions and tone of this play. Rather than posing any real threat to a helpless victim, this sequence of events is building towards the discomfiture of Angelo, the false friend, for during Rachel's speech the audience has been visually aware of Paulo standing in the background, ready to intercede at the most opportune moment. Here, as elsewhere in the play, the "heauen" that Count Ferneze had earlier observed as throwing "iust affliction" upon man "most deseruedly" (III.iv.22,40–41) is in clear control, even at the expense of the sometimes interesting issues raised by the action.

The same general assumptions about comedy and comic providence are to be found in *Every Man In His Humour,* although here they are handled in a less arbitrary and far more skillful fashion. Once again Jonson makes heavy use of elements derived from Roman intrigue comedy (the conflict between generations, the wily servant, the parasites and pretenders, the ordering through a disinterested party), but his adaptation of such materials here is certainly more worthy of the definition of *imitatio* in the quotation from *Discoveries* cited earlier (p. 3): "to convert the substance, or Riches of an other *Poet,* to his owne use . . . to draw forth out of the best, and choisest flowers, with the Bee, and turne all into Honey, worke it into one relish, and savour." Both the Italian and the English versions provide that characteristically Jonsonian mixture of the old (here the conventions of Roman comedy) and the contemporary (the gulls and "humours" of the 1590s); the result is an entertaining yet revealing comic spectacle of the various types of folly found in the world of young Lorenzo and Prospero. The limited definition of "humour" supplied by Piso ("a monster bred in a man by selfe loue, and affectation, and fed by folly" III.i.157–58) helps to categorize and explain the various "monsters" or offenders against Nature (Stephano, Mattheo, Bobadilla, Thorello, and, to some extent, Lorenzo Senior). The many fine moments in the play arise out of such comic monstrosity or absurdity. So in Bobadilla's big scene (IV.ii), the braggart warrior blows himself up to Mammon-like proportions with his vaunts about his prowess and his heroic plans, only to have his comic inflation punctured by the downright Giuliano who beats and disarms him. The audience's reaction surely echoes that of Lorenzo Junior: "Oh God that this age should bring foorth such creatures?" (ll. 130–31)

As Jonson tells us in his famous Prologue to the revised version, *Every Man In* is concerned "with humane follies, not with crimes" (l. 24), with affectations and misjudgments rather than threats to the health of society. The most successful scene in the play, the confrontation of various characters with each other and with themselves at Cob's house (V.i), acts out the comic absurdity of such misjudgments. Here a series of characters (Lorenzo Senior, Bianca and Piso, Thorello, and finally Cob himself) arrive with false expectations and assumptions about what they are to find. The accusations and counteraccusations of Bianca and Thorello both demonstrate the absurdity of such unfounded jealousy and, equally important, degrade the dignified Lorenzo Senior into "this hoary headed letcher, this olde goate" (l. 47). Lorenzo's realization of how far he has been led astray by his unfounded suspicions of his son ("how haue I wrongd my selfe in comming here" ll.77–78) can thereby cure his own manifestation of folly, the mistrust of the younger generation. To climax the scene, Jonson introduces Cob who, like Thorello with his wife or Lorenzo with his son, jumps to conclusions about Tib's behavior. The beating which Cob administers to his wife (obviously to be played in as broad a fashion as possible) can function as a *reductio ad absurdum* of the misjudgments of the other two men on stage.[12] Now Lorenzo Senior can accept the advice of Doctor Clement, who had observed:

> your cares are nothing; they are like my cap, soone put on, and as soone put off. What? your sonne is old inough, to gouerne himselfe; let him runne his course, it's the onely way to make him a stay'd man: if he were an vnthrift, a ruffian, a drunkard, or a licentious liuer, then you had rea-

12. The superiority of the revised version can be seen in the various ways in which Jonson has clarified the essential point of this scene. Lorenzo's reaction ("how haue I wrongd my selfe in comming here") is expanded into the Elder Knowell's: "Though I doe tast this as a trick, put on me, / To punish my impertinent search; and iustly: / And halfe forgiue my sonne, for the deuice" (IV.x.61–63). Similarly, Lorenzo's advice to Cob ("Friend haue patience . . .") is transformed into Knowell's "Friend, know some cause, before thou beat'st thy wife, / This's madnesse, in thee" (ll. 75–76). Both changes, when noted, call attention to the way this scene serves as a microcosm for the madness and impertinence in the play as a whole. For a discussion of such changes, see J. A. Bryant, Jr., "Jonson's Revision of ***Every Man In His Humor***," *SP*, LIX (1962), 641–50.

son: you had reason to take care: but being none of these, Gods passion, and I had twise so many cares, as you haue, I'ld drowne them all in a cup of sacke:

(III.iii.132–39)

This speech and the denouement brought about by Clement clarify the assumptions underlying the play. The youths, who have been using the gulls for their (and for our) entertainment, are not dissolute or dangerous but rather are misunderstood by the older generation (Lorenzo Senior). Once the father has been educated by the examples set by Thorello and Cob, the good-natured laughter of Doctor Clement can emerge as the dominant tone of the play.

The highly entertaining comic spectacle of *Every Man In* is certainly not devoid of insights into the eccentricities and aberrations of late sixteenth-century society, but the tone of the laughter evoked and the role of the young men rule out any extensive moral emphasis or investigation. The role of Musco, the clever slave of Roman comedy, *could* have been fused with the function of the morality Vice in order to introduce some specific thesis into the play while still keeping Musco a man *"o' the times."* But far from being a Vice in modern dress, this particular wily servant (as opposed to Mosca or Face) lacks any specific rationale but rather serves as an important but thematically neutral prime mover in the unfolding of the plot. In tone and structure, *Every Man In* has little in common with the "estates" morality and the public Vice, for Jonson's *explorata* here have clearly been in other *aliena castra.*

Every Man Out of His Humour

Every Man In demonstrates how eccentric or aberrant elements can be reclaimed by a healthy society, for those characters who seek to be something other than their true selves or mistake the true identity of others receive appropriate discomfiture and correction. But in spite of the Prologue's claim that the revised version embodies "an Image of the times" (l. 23), the individual eccentrics are not really typical of all of society but rather represent curable extremes befitting the somewhat limited definition of "humours" being used. *Every Man Out of His Humour*, Jonson's next play and the first of the so-called comical satires, obviously has more ambitious and panoramic concerns, for Asper promises in the Induction:

> Well I will scourge those apes;
> And to these courteous eyes oppose a mirrour,
> As large as is the stage, whereon we act:
> Where they shall see the times deformitie
> Anatomiz'd in euery nerue, and sinnew,
> With constant courage, and contempt of feare.
>
> (ll. 117–22)

The subsequent action of the play substantiates Asper's claims, for the audience is offered representative examples of "the times deformitie" from many different walks of life. Included among these representative figures, moreover, are social types and professions quite similar to the "estates" of many late moralities; the play's panoramic survey includes a courtier (Fastidius Brisk), a merchant (Deliro), a farmer (Sordido), a youth (Fungoso), and a knight (Puntarvolo). But even though Jonson's goals are in some respects analogous to those of Wapull or Wilson, there is only the most general resemblance between *Every Man Out* and such plays as *The Tide Tarrieth No Man* and *The Cobbler's Prophecy*. Rather, Jonson is strenuously and ingeniously seeking to transfer the methods and materials of an established literary form, nondramatic verse satire, to a new medium, the stage.

To see the essential difference between Jonson's comical satire and the late morality, one need only look closely at his chosen prime movers. Instead of a public Vice like Courage or Contempt whose machinations could prey upon and thereby exhibit the weakness of each "estate," *Every Man Out* brings about its various exposures of vice and folly through the activities of Asper-Macilente and Carlo Buffone who function as dramatic equivalents for the figure of the satirist found in the nondramatic tradition. As Alvin Kernan has demonstrated, the Elizabethans were highly conscious of the distinction between the public and private personality of the satirist, between the mask or persona and the author himself. The public face of the satirist, moreover, was often envisaged as the satyr figure, a figure of many contradictions:

> although he is the inveterate foe of vice, he himself has dark twists in his character: he is sadistic and enjoys his rough work; he is filled with envy of those same fools he despises and castigates; he has a taste for the sensational and delights in exposing those sins of which he is himself guilty; he is a sick man, his nature unbalanced by melancholy, whose perspective of the world is distorted by his malady.[13]

In the figure of Asper-Macilente, Jonson "went to some trouble to make clear that the character of the satirist is a mask which an author assumes for the purpose of making some lasting impression on the world he is attacking." So the Induction introduces Asper, who is morally indignant at the

13. Alvin Kernan, *The Cankered Muse: Satire of the English Renaissance* (New Haven, Conn., 1959), pp. 116–17.

abuses of the age (ll. 4–20) but "is not morally culpable like the satyr," while in the play proper Asper takes on the role of Macilente, a much more unsavory character, obsessed with envy, who betrays various trusts and even poisons Puntarvolo's dog. After Macilente's distasteful actions (combined with the jeers of Carlo) have revealed the truth about the various fools, the satyr figure (his job done) can then revert to the identity of Asper. Kernan concludes:

> The more unsalutary aspects of the character of the satirist are thus treated as merely the tools which the writer of satire uses to accomplish his end. What Jonson did in *Every Man Out* was to develop in dramatic terms the relationship between author and satirist which is axiomatic in both Elizabethan formal verse satire and critical discussions of the genre.[14]

The highly original combination of the fools and knaves, the Grex, and Asper-Macilente offers an excellent example of Jonson's role as *explorator*, in this instance of the *aliena castra* of formal verse satire.

Such analysis of the satyr-satirist in *Every Man Out* can offer valuable insights into Jonson's adaptation of available techniques into his own distinctive synthesis, but as Kernan goes on to point out, the presence of such a highly original device does not in itself make the play a success. In nondramatic satire, "the satirist appears to stand on the edge of a turbulent and silent mass of humanity and characterize the fools as they pass," a pose that emphasizes "his rocklike moral stance before a world of giddy change," but such immobility produces a quite different effect on stage because "the essence of drama is movement, and the audience no longer stands still with the satirist but sits outside observing both him and the

14. *Ibid.*, pp. 137–38.

moving crowd of fools."[15] As Oscar J. Campbell has demonstrated, Jonson strenuously sought to prevent this play from being merely a "procession of fools who follow one another over the pages of a formal satire,"[16] but most readers have agreed with Herford that Asper's satiric mirror reflects "not breathing nature, the very age and body of the time, his form and pressure, but a collection of pathological specimens, labelled and classified."[17] As a *play* (as opposed to an extension of formal verse satire), *Every Man Out* represents "a heroic failure, a brilliant and original failure," largely because its author has "rejected even the minimal suspense needed to hold an audience in the theater."[18] A tension clearly exists between Jonson's literary aims and the basic demands of the theater, a tension which results in elaborate and often confused scenes. A striking example is the formal, dancelike pattern which takes place in Paul's aisle (III.i–vi), where an enormous array of characters meet, exchange remarks, and then change partners; the effect is summed up in the revealing stage direction: "*Here they shift. Fastidius mixes with Puntaruolo, Carlo and Sogliardo, Deliro and Macilente, Cloue and Orange, four couple*" (III.iv.82.s.d.).

Although *Every Man Out* may well be a "heroic failure" as a play, it still can tell us a good deal about Jonson's goals in comedy, goals which he later achieved with greater success. The best scenes in the play offer more than just a display of pathological specimens, for at times Jonson is able to provide both examples of what is wrong with his society and analysis of the causes of such evils. Thus Fungoso's obsession with the latest style in clothing (epitomized for him in Fastidius

15. *Ibid.*, pp. 160–61.

16. *Comicall Satyre and Shakespeare's "Troilus and Cressida"* (San Marino, Calif., 1938), p. 70.

17. H & S, I, 378.

18. Jonas A. Barish, *Ben Jonson and the Language of Prose Comedy* (Cambridge, Mass., 1960), p. 104.

Brisk) is given wider significance through the comments of Macilente, who at one point gains access to new clothes and to the court:

> I was admiring mine owne out-side here,
> To thinke what priuiledge, and palme it beares
> Here, in the court! Be a man ne're so vile
> In wit, in judgement, manners, or what else;
> If he can purchase but a silken couer,
> He shall not only passe, but passe regarded:
> (III.ix.8–13)

Further experience at court teaches Macilente that such concern for surfaces arises from an absence of any absolute standards:

> Why, all their *Graces* are not to doe grace
> To vertue, or desert: but to ride both
> With their guilt spurres quite breathlesse, from themselues.
> 'Tis now esteem'd *Precisianisme* in wit;
> And a disease in nature, to be kind
> Toward desert, to loue, or seeke good names:
> (IV.iv.84–89)

The world of the play is characterized by such lack of concern for absolute qualities ("vertue, or desert"); instead, most of the characters exhibit some type of obsession with surfaces (Fungoso with style, Sogliardo with Shift's qualities, Fallace with Brisk's manners, Brisk with Saviolina's wit, Deliro with Fallace's beauty, Puntarvolo with romantic conventions, and so on). Perhaps the most telling single incident is the inability of the supposedly witty Saviolina, who should embody the superior wisdom and insight of the court, to perceive the difference between a true lout (Sogliardo) and a gentleman posing as a lout for her benefit. In a world in which surfaces are so significant, loyalties and standards lose all validity. So Carlo can comment upon friendship: "Pish, the title of a friend, it's a vaine idle thing, only venerable among fooles: you shall not haue one that has any opinion of wit affect it" (IV.iii.111–13). Similarly, any sense of the responsibilities that accompany rank and wealth has disappeared, so that Sordido, to be sure of making his profit, is willing to hoard grain and live miserably himself: "What though a world of wretches starue the while? / 'He that will thriue, must thinke no courses vile' " (I.iii.144–45). In Macilente's terms, the various characters display "a deale of outside," but once "their inward merit" is examined the observer (echoing Lorenzo Junior) can only conclude: "Lord, lord, what things they are!" (II.v.42,46–48)

Even such a general summary of the themes of *Every Man Out* can suggest how much Jonson had to say about the faults of his society. The momentary similarity between the reactions of Macilente and Lorenzo Junior to the folly around them, moreover, cannot disguise the basic differences between the two nominally similar plays. Not only the satiric conventions but also the sardonic, even savage tone and the emphatic social and moral concerns of verse satire have transformed Jonson's comic world from the good-natured sunshine mood of Doctor Clement and Lorenzo Junior to this darker picture of the vicious and irresponsible side of human behavior. Certainly *Every Man In,* with its emphasis upon follies rather than crimes, fits in well with accepted notions about comedy, especially the stipulation that its province should be the ridiculous (which by definition embodies that which cannot injure others) rather than the horrible.[19] Many of the

19. For a general discussion of accepted notions about comedy and Jonson's comical satires, see Campbell, *Comicall Satyre,* pp. 1–14.

characters of *Every Man Out* also fall within the province of the ridiculous (Fungoso is perhaps the best example), but parts of the play, as Jonson was himself aware, do not fit as well with inherited notions about comedy. Thus the Induction, in several famous passages, argues for a strong measure of independence from rigid application of the laws of comedy, while the choric commentary of the Grex continually defends and explains Jonson's practice. A good example is the treatment of Sordido's attempted suicide, the event in the play farthest from the spirit of the ridiculous. Mitis objects that even though "his purpos'd violence lost th' effect, and extended not to death, yet the intent and horror of the obiect, was more then the nature of a *Comoedie* will in any sort admit" (III.viii.82–85). As Herford points out, Cordatus' justification (in which he cites as a precedent the attempted suicide of Alcesimarchus in Plautus' *Cistellaria*) is not really satisfactory.[20] Here as elsewhere in this highly original play (Cordatus describes it as "strange, and of a particular kind by it selfe" Induction, ll. 231–32), "the intent and horror" of many of the events and issues is "more then the nature of a *Comoedie*" in the traditional sense will "admit." Having left behind the tidy traditional structure of *Every Man In*, Jonson as yet lacks a suitable dramatic container in which to package his new tone and scope, one which would allow him to combine conventional comedy with analysis of social evils and demonstration of their effects.

Cynthia's Revels

The panoramic scope of *Every Man Out* suggests a very general correspondence to some Elizabethan moralities, a

20. H & S, I, 385 n.

resemblance that is probably fortuitous. *Cynthia's Revels,* on the other hand, the second of the comical satires, provides firmer evidence for indebtedness to the "estates" morality. C. R. Baskervill (who finds an "allegorical tendency" latent in all of Jonson's early comedies) points out that "the plot of *Cynthia's Revels* as given in the Induction is a pure allegory, the characters bearing allegorical names and the relations existing among them having an allegorical significance, so that the reversion of the humour types to the older abstractions is here almost complete." [21] Baskervill then argues for a specific connection between Jonson's comedy and Wilson's *The Cobbler's Prophecy*. In addition to some similar details (the presence, for example, in both plays of Echo and Mercury), he finds the supremacy of Contempt over the various representative figures "similar in spirit to the prevalence of self-love in the evil court group of *Cynthia's Revels* as a result of drinking of the Fountain of Self-Love." [22] In Wilson's play, the causes of the disease in Boeotia had been embodied in Contempt and Venus while the effects had been enacted by such "estates" as the soldier, the scholar, the courtier, and the country gentleman. In Jonson's play, the Narcissus story, the Fountain, and Echo's speech set forth that quality, Self-Love, which lies at the heart of the perversions acted out by the eight pretenders to courtly virtue. Thus, after the already corrupted false courtiers have drunk the water of the Fountain at the end of Act IV, their perversity (in terms of the mythological imagery of the play) grows "into a presumptuousness equal to that of Niobe's and Actaeon's" [23] so that without compunction they can intrude into the presence of

21. *English Elements,* p. 214.

22. *Ibid.,* p. 244.

23. Ernest Talbert, "The Classical Mythology and the Structure of *Cynthia's Revels,*" *PQ,* XXII (1943), 208.

Cynthia herself. To Baskervill, Jonson's plot and general procedures show a firm structural connection with the late morality play.

But in several important respects, the differences between *The Cobbler's Prophecy* and *Cynthia's Revels* are more revealing than the similarities. Contempt, although not the most memorable of the Elizabethan Vices, is still an active figure with some stage presence whose arguments and intrigues supply much of the action of his play. His successful machinations can thereby convey the power over contemporary society of the attitude he embodies. Jonson's Fountain of Self-Love, on the other hand, although perhaps not quite as inappropriate as Herford suggests,[24] has distinct limitations as a dramatic center. Clearly Jonson is seeking to offset the tendency towards lack of focus and proliferation of events found in *Every Man Out,* but as Jonas Barish has pointed out, "the greater cohesiveness" and increased "structural coherence" of *Cynthia's Revels* have been achieved only at "a terrible price," what amounts to boredom and the stifling of theatrical movement.[25] Indicative of the problem is the role of the Fountain and its waters. Instead of providing a Vice-like figure to initiate an intrigue which might convey a thesis, Jonson relies upon an inert, static, central symbol which the false courtiers send for in Act II and then dutifully await throughout Act IV. Meanwhile, the failings of these pretenders to courtly virtue are seldom demonstrated by any

24. Herford complains that although Jonson introduces the fountain in the opening scenes "with striking wealth of mythic apparatus and the emphasis of italics," it subsequently "disappears with the rest of the mythic scenery, and the references to its transforming water, which from time to time recall it, are felt as incongruous and irrelevant interruptions to dramatic business which goes on, such as it is, not merely in another place but on another plane of reality" (H & S, I, 399).

25. *Jonson and the Language of Prose Comedy*, p. 113.

significant action or interaction but rather are commented upon for our benefit by Jonson's spokesmen (Crites, Mercury, Cupid) who take even less part in the world of the play than had Macilente or Carlo Buffone. In spite of a general correspondence to some late moralities, what is absent from *Cynthia's Revels* is just that feature that had given the "estates" morality its direction and vigor, the emphatic presence of the insidious, intriguing public Vice who initiated and carried out the actions which set forth the thesis of the play.

The peculiar flavor (or lack of flavor) of Jonson's play is largely a result of the absence of such action. The Prologue announces that the author's muse "shunnes the print of any beaten path; / And proues new wayes to come to learned eares" (ll. 10–11), new ways which will emphasize "words, aboue action: matter, aboue words" (l. 20). The description of priorities is quite accurate, for, as Barish points out, Jonson "seems deliberately to side-step the theatrical possibilities of the plot in favor of formal satiric comment." [26] Such intense concern with "matter" or content comes as no surprise to readers of *Every Man Out*, but here there is even less "action" and more dependence upon "words" (telling instead of showing). To extend the scope of the issues raised by the play, Jonson resorts not to representative social types (Sordido, Fungoso, Brisk, Deliro) but rather to set speeches which often provide elaborate catalogues of the various parts of society. Thus Amorphus paints for Asotus and for the audience a picture of a world that respects only surfaces by means of a lengthy disquisition on "the particular, and distinct face of euery your most noted *species* of persons, as your

26. *Ibid.*, p. 115. As Barish observes, "the undramatic nature of Jonson's procedure" (p. 114) is summed up by his having verbally described rather than enacted what might have been two good comic scenes (Asotus' first discomfiture, Crites' spoiling of Hedon's "inuention").

marchant, your scholer, your souldier, your lawyer, courtier, &c." He concludes that "(in any ranke, or profession whateuer) the more generall, or *maior* part of opinion goes with the face, and (simply) respects nothing else" (II.iii.16–19, 54–56). A similar effect is gained through the petty and selfish wish-fulfillment speeches of Moria, Philautia, and Phantaste (IV.i.140–214), which expose the hollow ideals of such false courtiers and offer a disturbing picture of the type of society that might result if figures with such limitations dominated the court. In accordance with the priorities established in the Prologue, however, such issues are largely expressed through "words" and not through comic "action." A major exception is the mannered combat between Amorphus and Mercury in Act V (which undoubtedly is meant to illustrate how trivial details and pointless mannerisms have been elevated into a hollow code), but the dramatic effectiveness of this sequence, even for an elite audience, is highly questionable.

There is no question, however, about the primacy of "matter" in *Cynthia's Revels*. Perhaps the basic premise of the play is the importance for all of society of the example set by figures such as Cynthia, Arete, and Crites. As Cynthia herself points out:

> "Princes, that would their people should doe well,
> "Must at themselues begin, as at the head;
> "For men, by their example, patterne out
> "Their imitations, and reguard of lawes:
> "A vertuous *Court* a world to vertue drawes.
>
> (V.xi.169–73)

The emphasis throughout much of the play falls upon those characters who fail to understand the true nature of the court but rather (like the analogous figures in *Every Man Out*) substitute their false worship of surface values for appreciation of true merit. To Anaides the court represents "a certaine mysterie," superior to the other "beggerly *sciences*," upon which only "wee that haue skill must pronounce" (V.iv.541–44), although the audience by this point is well aware that Anaides himself is scarcely an initiate. To demonstrate the pretenders' lack of appreciation for true courtly virtue and absolute qualities, Jonson has them first reject the plain but noble Crites as "a piece of serge, or *perpetuana*" (III.ii.30), then scornfully disdain the paragon Arete as "good ladie *Sobrietie*" (IV.v.18), and finally set themselves up as equal to Cynthia herself (V.x.42–52). The denouement can restore order and sanity by exposing such false standards and reasserting the control of Cynthia and her virtuous companions over the court and all of society.

But the efficacy of such "matter" on stage is unquestionably affected by the limitations of the comic "action." What little action the play does provide, moreover (from Mercury and Echo at the Fountain at the outset to the masques of the denouement), is highly colored by the dominant allegorical mode. Thus during the contest between Amorphus and Mercury, first Moria, then Philautia, and finally Phantaste are placed "in state" (i.e., in a canopied chair or mock throne) in front of and above the combatants and onlookers. Such a falling away from the true throne of Cynthia can demonstrate allegorically how Folly, Self-Love, and Shallowness, rather than the worthy ideals of Crites and Arete, are dominating the scene before us. Similarly, Asotus' treatment of Argurion's favors during Act IV allegorically acts out his prodigality, for the young man recklessly gives away the gifts of Money to the other ladies. Not until *The Staple of News* does Jonson again introduce allegory into dramatic comedy in so overt a manner,[27] and there one can note more effort to accommodate allegorical figures to literal comedy so that the Vices might appear as "*men and women o' the time.*" The "new wayes to come to learned eares" attempted in *Cynthia's Revels* have thus been even less successful than the "new wayes" of *Every Man Out*, for in an analogous manner Jonson's intense concern with "matter" has once again come into conflict with the basic demands of the stage. Comparison with the late morality, instead of opening up the play for further investigation, only heightens the general absence of dramatic movement and vitality. The general scholarly verdict,[28] that Jonson has here subordinated his dramatic instinct to allegory, satire, and static effects, is indeed a just one.

Poetaster

The same criticism cannot be leveled against *Poetaster*, the third of the comical satires. Although at times the play itself has been overshadowed by the stage quarrel it reflects, recent critics have demonstrated how *Poetaster*, like "Lycidas" or "In Memoriam" or "An Epistle to Dr. Arbuthnot," rises above the events that occasioned it. Comparison to the latter is particularly helpful, for Jonson, like Pope, is here going beyond a mere apology for himself to a general statement of what a poet, particularly a satiric poet, should be. Eugene Waith has shown how the poet's "moral obligations" are "brought out by Horace in the third act, by Caesar in the fourth act, and by Horace, Virgil, and Caesar in the fifth act,"

27. Interestingly, the later play also has a young man (Penniboy Junior) who acts out his prodigality during Act IV by his reckless treatment of a female figure who stands for Money (Lady Pecunia).

28. In addition to Barish, see H & S, I, 397; and Knoll, *Ben Jonson's Plays*, p. 57.

while the Ovid-Julia plot presents "the case of the morally irresponsible poet, in order to show that he is not reckoned among the good." [29] These figures, along with the poetasters (Crispinus, Demetrius) and the detractors of poets and poetry (Captain Tucca, Lupus, Ovid Senior), provide the audience with a series of positive and negative definitions of the good poet and his relationship to society.

In dramatic structure, *Poetaster* is less ambitious than the two previous comical satires, perhaps reflecting Jonson's haste in composition in order to anticipate *Satiromastix*. Instead of experimenting with an Asper-Macilente or a Fountain of Self-Love, Jonson here turns to multiple plots and analogous situations in order to consider his central question, the role of the poet, from various different perspectives. Likewise the scope sought by *Every Man Out* and to a lesser extent suggested by *Cynthia's Revels* has here given way to a more limited investigation of the precarious role of the poet. As the Apologetical Dialogue tells us, Jonson has chosen

> AVGVSTVS CAESARS times,
> When wit, and artes were at their height in *Rome*,
> To shew that VIRGIL, HORACE, and the rest
> Of those great master-spirits did not want
> Detractors, then, or practisers against them.
> (ll. 101–5)

By somewhat limiting his focus in this manner, Jonson has for the first time allowed his ambitions for comical satire to come to terms with the needs and demands of the stage, so that his third attempt is undoubtedly the most successful dramatic vehicle.

29. "The Poet's Morals in Jonson's *Poetaster*," MLQ, XII (1951), 19, 15. For a similar argument, see C. G. Thayer, *Ben Jonson: Studies in the Plays* (Norman, Okla., 1963), pp. 38–49.

Poetaster is by no means a complete success. Still it offers the first example of that step-by-step exploration of a central issue which is to be Jonson's trademark in comedy. Act I gives us Ovid, the defender of poetry against the philistines, arguing that "*heauenly* poesie *no death can feare. / Kings shall giue place to it, and kingly showes*" (I.i.74–75). With the departure of the detractors of poetry (Ovid Senior, Tucca, Lupus), Ovid again apostrophizes "sacred *poesie*," stressing "what prophane violence, almost sacriledge, / Hath here beene offered thy diuinities!" (I.ii.231–34) No longer can men appreciate

> the high raptures of a happy *Muse*,
> Borne on the wings of her immortall thought,
> That kickes at earth with a disdainefull heele,
> And beats at heauen gates with her bright hooues.
> (ll. 243–46)

Rather in venal Rome (as he envisages it):

> "No matter now in vertue who excells,
> "He, that hath coine, hath all perfection else.
> (ll. 255–56)

But the appearance of Tibullus with news of Julia evokes a different Ovid, whose love

> Shall be a law, and that sweet law I'le studie,
> The law, and art of sacred IVLIAS loue:
> All other obiects will but abiects prooue.
> (I.iii.56–58)

Ovid's ideals for heavenly poetry have been immediately called into question by his less than heavenly love for Julia, which he regards as a law unto itself, a law which throughout the play causes him to renege on his higher responsibility as a poet.

Act III, on the other hand, introduces Horace who, along with Virgil, upholds the poetic ideals set forth in Act I but so far not sustained by the behavior of Ovid and Crispinus. Horace indignantly rejects "vndermining enuie, and detraction" as "moodes, onely proper to base groueling minds" and offers instead a description of Maecenas as ideal patron (III.i.252–59). To Crispinus, such emphasis upon "merit" instead of money is "a wonder" and "scarce credible" (l. 260), as it would have been to Ovid who described Rome as a place where "he, that hath coine, hath all perfection else." The relationship between money and poetry is further explored through Demetrius and Histrio who are about to bring forth a play (*Satiromastix*, of course) which "will get vs a huge deale of money (Captaine) and wee haue need on't" (III.iv. 327–28). Although the topical reference may be obvious, Jonson is nonetheless providing another example of the debasement of poetry under various pressures (profit, love, personal rivalries). In the Folio, Act III ends with Jonson's translation of Horace's dialogue with Trebatius (*Satires* I.ii), which provides a Horatian statement of the ideal role to be played by the satirist. Act III as a whole has thereby explored the role of the poet from various vantage points in order to establish a context for understanding the fates of Ovid, Crispinus, Demetrius, Virgil, and Horace in the remainder of the play.[30]

The banquet of the gods in Act IV now displays the results of Ovid's love, which has become a law unto itself. Caesar's

30. As Waith points out ("The Poet's Morals," pp. 16–17): "Where Ovid emphasized the transcendent nature of poetry, Horace emphasizes

entrance and violent reaction emphasize the violation of degree (the presence of Julia in such debased circumstances) and, more important for the play as a whole, the degradation of the role of the poet. When Crispinus identifies himself as a parcel-poet, Caesar exclaims: "O, that prophaned name!" (IV.vi.30) and soon after provides a long diatribe against false poets (ll. 34–47). "Sacred *poesie*," which according to Ovid's earlier statement should beat "at heauen gates with her bright hooues," has here been debased by poets sacrilegiously masquerading as gods, thereby "making them like you, but counterfeits." Instead of teaching virtue and setting an example for all of society, Ovid and his companions have become abusers and profaners of the "vse-full light" of Heaven, acting as if there were "no law vnto your liues." The clear echo of Ovid's statement about his love for Julia shows us how far this false "law" has taken him from the poetic ideals announced in Act I. The presence of Chloe and Albius, moreover (suitably transformed into Venus and Vulcan), demonstrates the corruption of other parts of society occasioned by the failures of poets and courtiers. As in *Cynthia's Revels,* Jonson suggests the inevitable decay of morals and manners without a positive example from those in positions of responsibility and trust.

The presence of Caesar, Maecenas, and Horace, however, provides an alternative example within the world of the play, even though such false poets (Crispinus *and* Ovid) may

---

the value of poetry to society and the great responsibility of the poet. Both poets promise to champion virtue, but after comparing Horace with Ovid we look critically, or even skeptically, for the fulfillment of Ovid's promises." For a detailed and incisive development of this approach to *Poetaster*, see Gabriele Bernhard Jackson, *Vision and Judgment in Ben Jonson's Drama* (New Haven, Conn., and London, 1968), pp. 20–30, 145.

"thinke gods but fain'd, and vertue painted" (l. 48). Thus Caesar concludes by announcing his standards for preferment:

I will preferre for knowledge, none, but such
As rule their liues by it, and can becalme
All sea of humour, with the marble *trident*
Of their strong spirits: Others fight below
With gnats, and shaddowes, others nothing know.
(ll. 74–78)

Ovid's final remarks in the play spell out how far he is from such control; after Julia has departed he concludes: " 'The truest wisdome silly men can haue, / 'Is dotage, on the follies of their flesh" (IV.ix.108–9). Act V, on the other hand, demonstrates how Virgil and Horace *are* worthy of preferment owing to their ability to "rule their liues" by knowledge. First, we are given Caesar's discussion of true poetry which "of all the faculties on earth" is "the most abstract, and perfect; if shee bee / True borne, and nurst with all the sciences" (V.i.18–20). The heights to which poetry can aspire are then shown through the honors bestowed upon Virgil who is placed in a chair higher than Caesar himself and told: " 'Vertue, without presumption, place may take / 'Aboue best Kings, whom onely she should make" (V.ii.26–27). Ovid's claims for poetry ("*Kings shall giue place to it . . .*") are here substantiated by this ideal configuration of the virtuous poet and the enlightened prince.

Lupus' interruption of Virgil's reading can then set up the final investigation of the role of poetry. In contrast to Act IV where the ideal monarch had interrupted the activities of the false poets, here the detractor breaks off the reading of the true poet, significantly in the midst of his discussion of Fama. Although there is no mistaking the topical allusions in the arraignments that follow, such twitting of Marston and Dekker was undoubtedly meant to be subsumed in the larger issues of the play, the investigation of the ideal nature of poetry and the postulation of the need for personal responsibility among poets. According to Jonson, in a state characterized by an enlightened monarch who willingly elevates "sacred *poesie*" above himself true satire is not only permitted but welcomed. The vindication of Horace in the eyes of Virgil, Maecenas, and Caesar can thereby serve as Jonson's major defense of his own satiric art as well as one final example of what the poet should be.[31]

Poetaster provides a suggestive example of how Jonsonian comedy is already capable of exploring a central issue through a step-by-step dramatic process of posing questions and testing answers. That Jonson was not yet in complete control of his comic medium can be seen in the various limitations of the play. Thus Horace does not appear until Act III, nor Virgil until Act V, while Ovid disappears in Act IV. The curious imbalance that results perhaps reflects Jonson's haste in composition. The presence of ideal figures (Maecenas, Caesar, Virgil) with their set speeches is at times reminiscent of the author's static spokesmen of *Cynthia's Revels* (Arete, Cynthia, Crites), although here there is considerably more comic action, especially through the Ovid plot and the detractors of Horace. The relatively limited use of Chloe and Albius to demonstrate the corruption of the citizenry from above is certainly more effective than the introduction of Asotus' sister (Mistress Downfall) and her citizen husband into Act V of

31. To Waith ("The Poet's Morals," pp. 18–19), "the most famous incident of the play, the punishment of Crispinus, is a dramatic necessity but is secondary in importance to the final expression of the theme of the good poet as a bulwark of society," for "the essence of the denouement is not the incident of Crispinus' humiliation but rather the final vindication of Horace."

Cynthia's Revels, but even so these distant cousins of the morality play's "estates" figures are not fully integrated into the play as a whole. Nonetheless, in *Poetaster* Jonson was able to achieve greater theatrical control by narrowing his focus to a more specialized topic than the general deformity of the times. In his next comedy, *Volpone*, he will apply the dramatic lessons learned here to the same broad issues of *Every Man Out*.

Taken together, Jonson's five early comedies show him grappling with a basic dramatic problem: how to combine conventional comedy, satiric portraits, social criticism, and moral issues into a unified dramatic statement about society as a whole. Other dramatists were obviously content with what Madeleine Doran terms "incidental satire," in which satiric thrusts could be contained within a conventional framework such as the revenge play (*The Malcontent*) or romantic comedy (*The Fawn*).[32] Although *Every Man In* could be grouped with such plays, the subsequent comical satires strike out in bold and original directions towards "structural satire" in which the satiric conception can somehow form the basis for the entire work. But Jonson's innovations in his comical satires led him not in the direction of effective theater but rather towards the presentation of a gallery of eccentrics parading across the stage. The answer was obviously not to scrap the "humours" approach entirely, for Jonson's dramatic strength lay in his grotesque comic creations, but to find some way of using such individual aberrations as an integral part of

32. See *Endeavors of Art*, pp. 167–71. Miss Doran sees Jonson "groping after a method" of structural satire in *Every Man In* and *Every Man Out*; she also considers the "plots" of *Cynthia's Revels* and *Poetaster* as "the flimsiest excuse on which to hang satire on literary foibles and types, often scarcely disguised portraits of his contemporaries" (p. 169).

a larger whole. The use of the Fountain of Self-Love shows an initial attempt at such added coherence, while the controlling themes and analogous situations of *Poetaster* suggest further development towards a workable solution. Still, none of these plays uses the stage to full advantage in order to provide an image of the times.

Comparison between the comical satires and the Elizabethan morality has suggested one important facet of Jonson's problem.[33] Many of the late moralities use the lively combination of representative "estates," who act out the faults characteristic of various parts of society, and the public Vice, who allegorically embodies that particular failing felt to be responsible for such evils. By placing such emphasis upon the activities of the Vice, the moral dramatists are often able to move away from static allegorical summary towards action, intrigue, and literal demonstration. In spite of a heavy didactic emphasis, these plays need not sacrifice dramatic movement and vitality in their attempts to convey a thesis about society. But just such movement and vitality are often absent from Jonson's comical satires, for in spite of fine character sketches, lively dialogue, and occasional moments of effective comic business, none of these plays fully achieves Jonson's announced goal of transforming the stage into a mirror that can reflect the diseases of society. The absence of any effective equivalent for the public Vice is one reason for this deficiency. Jonson, to be sure, does provide various commentators (Macilente, Carlo Buffone, Cordatus, Crites, Mercury, Cupid, Arete, Horace, Virgil, Caesar) who in differing ways convey

33. Robert C. Jones has argued persuasively that another reason for the dramatic weaknesses of the comical satires lies in the "ambivalence of an author who wants to claim, on the one hand, that his art is too lofty to affect that bawd the world and, on the other, that he can transform the world with his art." See "The Satirist's Retirement in Jonson's 'Apologetical Dialogue'," *ELH*, XXXIV (1967), 447–67.

the point of view usually implied in nondramatic satire, but unlike the Vice these figures are often set apart from, rather than involved in, the main action. There is no central figure in *Every Man Out, Cynthia's Revels,* or *Poetaster* who stands for the central issue of the play and then acts out his significance by his effect upon other representative figures.

Investigation of Jonson's early plays has shown how his ambitious goals for dramatic satire and his intense concern with "matter" have led to effects and a distinctive tone which may well be "more then the nature of a *Comoedie* will in any sort admit." To achieve his dramatic goals, Jonson has already glanced at the dramatic possibilities available in the late morality, especially in *Cynthia's Revels.* In *Volpone,* his next effort at comedy, Jonson once again goes beyond "*the strict rigour of* comick *law*" in an attempt to anatomize on stage the time's deformity, but here he fully explores for the first time the possibilities in the Elizabethan morality.

CHAPTER 3

The Movement toward Moral Comedy: *Volpone*

BEFORE turning once again to comedy, Jonson made the first of his two ambitious attempts at neo-classical tragedy in *Sejanus His Fall.* As the Apologetical Dialogue affixed to *Poetaster* had argued, "since the *Comick* MVSE / Hath prou'd so ominous," perhaps the tragic muse might "haue a more kind aspect" (ll. 222–24). But unfortunately the audience's reaction to *Sejanus* was apparently "ominous" rather than "kind." As with *Every Man Out* and *Cynthia's Revels,* Jonson once again produced an original, and in many ways impressive, work which did not come to terms with the basic demands of the stage. Recent scholarship on *Sejanus* has called our attention to its many virtues, as a "tragic poem" if not as a tragedy, and has emphasized the depth and range of Jonson's ideas and scholarship.[1] Of par-

1. See, for example, Joseph Allen Bryant, Jr., "The Nature of the Conflict in Jonson's *Sejanus,*" *Vanderbilt Studies in the Humanities,* I (1951), 197–219; Ralph Nash, "Jonson's Tragic Poems," *SP,* LV (1958), 164–86; Daniel C. Boughner, "Sejanus and Machiavelli," *SEL,* I (1961), 81–100; and *Sejanus,* ed. Jonas Barish (New Haven, Conn., 1965), pp. 1–24 and *passim.*

ticular interest to this study, however, is the evidence in *Sejanus* of solutions to dramatic problems that had haunted the comical satires.

Several revealing differences between the early comedies and *Sejanus* in fact point the way to *Volpone*. In differing ways the earlier plays had introduced figures who could serve as norms or even ideals of behavior by which the audience could judge the world of the play (Paulo Ferneze, Doctor Clement, Cynthia, Arete, Caesar, Maecenas). Owing to the presence of such wise and judicious figures, the eccentrics or offenders in these plays (with the possible exception of *Every Man Out*) never posed too serious a threat to the health of society. But in the world of Rome set forth in *Sejanus*, the equivalent ideal figures who might serve as a standard or as a repository of values are either already dead (Germanicus) or about to be eliminated by the intrigues initiated by Sejanus (Drusus Senior, Silius, Cordus, Sabinus). Instead of an ideal ruler (Cynthia, Augustus Caesar) who represents a stable and virtuous center for all of society, Jonson gives us an enigmatic, relativistic Tiberius who at the end of the play replaces the evil Sejanus with the equally insidious Macro. Even the role of the satirist-spokesman has undergone drastic change, for in place of a Crites or a Horace we are given the outspoken but ineffectual Arruntius who classifies himself among "the good-dull-noble lookers on" that "are only call'd to keepe the marble warme" (III.16–17) and who is considered by Sejanus more valuable alive than dead (III.498–501). The various fixed points or ideal roles that had characterized the comic atmosphere of the early plays have been challenged or eliminated here.

Thus many of the concerns of the earlier comedies are explored once again in *Sejanus* in a different key and with more sinister and disturbing effects. In both *Every Man Out* and *Cynthia's Revels*, for example, Jonson could demonstrate how the absence of absolute standards among parts of society led to a preference for surface appearances over true merit. Here in *Sejanus*, on the other hand, can be found the same kind of relativism with no such alternative. So Sejanus woos Eudemus, Livia's physician, by arguing:

> Sir, you can loose no honor,
> By trusting ought to me. The coursest act
> Done to my seruice, I can so requite,
> As all the world shall stile it honorable:
> "Your idle, vertuous *definitions*
> "Keepe honor poore, and are as scorn'd, as vaine:
> "Those deeds breathe honor, that do sucke in gaine.
> (I.326–32)

According to this argument, honor is determined not by any absolute standard ("idle, vertuous *definitions*") but rather by the judgment or decree of a corrupt Sejanus (or Tiberius). The relationship between Eudemus and Sejanus, moreover, in which even "the coursest act" of "seruice" is worthy of honor, is analogous to the more important relationship between Sejanus and *his* master, Tiberius, who "requites" his favorite in much the same way. The end of the play brings out the perils and frustrations of such a situation, wherein all value is dependent upon the whim of a Sejanus or Tiberius, by showing what happens when the emperor deliberately makes ambiguous his attitude towards his favorite. Thus Laco complains: "Would he would tell vs whom he loues, or hates, / That we might follow, without feare, or doubt" (IV.424–25), an attitude that Arruntius accurately describes as heliotropic. In place of the satisfying arraignments of *Cynthia's Revels* and *Poetaster*, where the false values of the offenders are weighed in a higher scale, Act V of *Sejanus* emphasizes the absence of any such standards among the senators, who start by fawning over Sejanus and end, once Tiberius' intentions have been clarified through his letter, by shifting their seats away from the former favorite. Instead of the firm sense of justice and order characteristic of the denouements of the earlier plays, the tragic events here only reaffirm Sejanus' own relativism, which is now turned back upon him.

Structurally as well as thematically, *Sejanus* differs from the comical satires in an interesting way. The goals that Jonson announced to the reader in his preface ("truth of Argument, dignity of Persons, grauity and height of Elocution, fulnesse and frequencie of Sentence") do not leave much room for dramatic experimentation, yet there is no equivalent in the earlier comedies to the role of Sejanus himself in relation to the world of the play. At the outset, Jonson makes it quite clear that all of Roman society is diseased and corrupt; Sabinus points out that the gentry, the consuls, and the praetors all have been guilty of "sordide acts," while even the senators

> Start vp in publique *Senate*, and there striue
> Who shall propound most abiect things, and base,
> So much, as oft TIBERIVS hath beene heard,
> Leauing the court, to crie, ô race of men,
> Prepar'd for seruitude!
>
> (I.44–53)

As Arruntius points out, the fault lies in the men, not in the times:

> 'tis we are base,
> Poore, and degenerate from th'exalted streine
> Of our great fathers.
>
> (11.87–89)

Sejanus, whom Eudemus later describes as "this soule of *Rome,* / The empires life, and voice of CAESARS world" (II.55–56), thereby becomes a natural outgrowth of such a diseased society. According to K. M. Burton, Sejanus is meant to be not "a realistic picture of a vicious man" but rather "a dramatic symbol of the monstrosity which is born when a society degenerates." According to this formulation, Jonson's tragic dilemma "involves the whole city of Rome whose citizens bring evil on themselves and are directly responsible for the monster to which they give birth." [2]

Seen in this light, Sejanus' function in the play as a whole has an interesting resemblance to the analogous role played by the public Vice in the late morality. As with Haphazard, Courage, and Contempt, here again a central figure, who embodies the immoral or amoral qualities practiced or condoned by those around him, succeeds in exercising his power at the expense of the society that spawned him. Such a comparison, of course, is only admissible in the most general terms, for Jonson's antecedents and authorities for his tragedy obviously lie elsewhere. Still, for the first time Jonson has used a dramatic structure built around a series of intrigues in which the intriguer (as opposed to a Musco or even a Macilente) in some way represents an attitude or set of attitudes basic to the world of the play. In contrast to the dramatically inert Fountain of Self-Love, Sejanus can serve as an active and vital embodiment of what is wrong with Tiberius' Rome. Ironically, the first indication of what is to be Jonson's answer to one of the important unsolved problems of the earlier comedies is found here in this learned tragedy.

With the various experiments of both the early plays and *Sejanus* behind him, Jonson returned to comedy in *Volpone*

2. K. M. Burton, "The Political Tragedies of Chapman and Ben Jonson," *EIC,* II (1952), 404.

and achieved his first great success. The contrast between *Volpone* and the comical satires is immediately apparent. Gone (at least from the main plot) are the static spokesman, the conveniently formulated ideal, the easy dispensation of comic justice from a lofty vantage point. In their place is a searching, critical, and often disturbing type of comedy which in mood and effect is closer to *Sejanus* than *Every Man In*. For the first time, the author of *Every Man Out* has found a dramatic vehicle capable of conveying an anatomy of the time's deformity through comedy.

In his usual eclectic manner, Jonson has tapped many different sources for material and techniques to demonstrate how Lucre has gained control over the minds and hearts of men, even to the point of becoming "the worlds soule" (I.i.3). Obviously, the suggestion for the *captatores* is derived from the Roman satiric tradition, perhaps from Petronius specifically, while the mountebank scene exhibits the author's knowledge of contemporary Italy.[3] Rainer Pineas has added to such antecedents by noting a similarity between Volpone-Mosca and the morality Vice. To Pineas, Volpone is Vice-like because of his use of disguise and "his love of evil for its own sake rather than for any secondary cause." He finds Mosca, however, to be the true Vice of the play, because the parasite manages most of the intrigues, reminds the

3. For recent appraisals of Jonson's sources, see Freda L. Townsend, *Apologie for Bartholmew Fayre* (New York, 1947), pp. 21–22, 58–62; Madeleine Doran, *Endeavors of Art* (Madison, Wis., 1954), pp. 169–70 and *passim*; Alvin Kernan, *The Cankered Muse: Satire of the English Renaissance* (New Haven, Conn., 1959), pp. 150–91; and P. H. Davison, "*Volpone* and the Old Comedy," *MLQ*, XXIV (1963), 151–57. For an excellent discussion of how "past and present are fused" in *Volpone*, see the Introduction to *Volpone*, ed. Alvin Kernan (New Haven, Conn., 1962), pp. 4–6 and *passim*. L. C. Knights (*Drama and Society in the Age of Jonson* [London, 1937], pp. 179–227) has emphasized the continuity of the "anti-acquisitive attitude" to which Jonson adhered.

audience continually of his function, makes occasional slips of the tongue, develops a reputation for truth and honesty, and even moralizes occasionally. Pineas concludes "that in his writing of the didactic comedy *Volpone,* Jonson was influenced not only by classical models, but also by the native prototype of homiletic drama, the morality play with its immoral and moralizing Vice." [4]

Most scholars would agree that Mosca's dramatic ancestry includes the morality Vice and the wily slave of Roman comedy. But to what extent does knowledge of such antecedents help us to understand the over-all structure and effect of this distinctive play? Jonson's debt to Roman comedy in *Volpone,* for example, is undeniable but is certainly less significant than the Plautine and Terentian features of *Every Man In.* Pineas' observations about the Vice-like role of Volpone and Mosca are suggestive but take little of the play into account. His examples, moreover, are largely culled from earlier moralities (*Nature, Mankind, Respublica, Lusty Juventus*) rather than Elizabethan plays (none of the "estates" plays is included). Significantly, no attention as yet has been paid to that group of Elizabethan moralities (e.g., *Enough is as Good as a Feast, All for Money,* and *The Three Ladies of London*) which are concerned with the same issues as *Volpone* and provide a ready-made native English dramatic vehicle for any later dramatist also interested in the displacement of traditional values by the worship of gold. Discussion of some of the characteristic devices of these plays can serve as a helpful prelude to analysis of *Volpone.*

To put on stage the effects of Lucre upon society, the moral dramatists usually resorted to the thesis-and-demonstration structure already discussed at length. The use of "estates,"

4. "The Morality Vice in *Volpone,*" *Discourse,* V (1962), 451–59.

for example, can be found in the trial scene of *All for Money* or in the appearance of the artifex, lawyer, scholar, priest, and merchant in *The Three Ladies*. Some of the plays from the 1560s and 1570s, however, offer little specific demonstration of their thesis; instead they often establish their central theme by means of a speech (usually by an allegorical figure) cataloguing the various ways in which Money or Lucre can dominate society. In W. Wager's *Enough is as Good as a Feast* (ca. 1560), Covetouse (disguised as Policy) explains to Worldly Man in his major speech that

> of this world I rule the whole state,
> Yea faith I gouern all lawes, rites and orders:
> I, at my pleasure raise war, strife and debate.

He concludes:

> Power I haue lawes to alter and make,
> And all lawes made are guided by me:
> All that is doon, is doon wholly for my sake.[5]

Even more elaborate catalogues are provided at key points in *All for Money*. The Prologue provides a long list of vices and corruptions brought about by money:

> Howe many for money haue bene robbed and murthered?
> Howe many false witnes and for money periured?
> Howe many wyues from their husbands haue bene enticed? [6]

5. W. Wager, *Enough is as Good as a Feast*, ed. Seymour de Ricci, Henry Huntington Facsimile Reprints (New York, 1920), sig. D4^v.

6. *All for Money*, ed. Ernst Vogel, *SJ*, XL (1904), 147. Besides prefiguring the events of Lupton's play, this catalogue also points to many of the events of *Volpone*, e.g., the enticing of Celia away from Corvino, the perjury at the trials.

In his opening speech, Money then brags how he dwells "with euery degree," pointing out that he waxes "of such force that no earthly corse / But embraceth me out of measure." After an extensive catalogue of the various professions devoted to him (doctor, plowman, smith, shoemaker, minstrel, covetous man, usurer, among others), Money adds:

> I am worshipped and honoured, and as a god am esteemed:
> Yea manie loues me better then God.
> No sooner come I to towne, but manie bowe downe
> And comes if I holde vp the rodd.
>
> (p. 151)

As Satan later points out: "Money is so beloued, / That of manie aboue god he is esteemed and honoured" (p. 159).

By displaying or describing the behavior of representative "estates," the moral dramatists were able either to show or tell their audience how the materialism of the age had elevated gold "aboue god." Another way of making the same point was to provide various virtues or virtuous individuals as standards by which to judge the behavior of those dominated by Lucre. Sometimes the audience is presented with the parallel stories of two central figures, such as Worldly Man and Heavenly Man (*Enough*), or Lust and Just (*The Trial of Treasure*), whose respective fates spell out the author's message; elsewhere we are shown at least one figure, such as Virtuous Living (*Like Will to Like*) or Faithful Few (*The Tide Tarrieth No Man*), whose steadfastness is in contrast to the degenerate behavior caused by the pervasive influence of the Vice. Some dramatists, on the other hand, chose to employ such virtuous personae in order to portray the plight of absolute standards in a Lucre-dominated society. In *Impatient Poverty* (1547), Conscience, after an unsuccessful attempt to reform Abundance the Usurer, is persuaded by Envy (disguised as Charity) to flee the country for his own safety, thereby allegorically eliminating himself as an active force in contemporary society. In *The Tide Tarrieth No Man,* Christianity is degraded by being forced to bear the "titles" of Policy and Riches rather than those of Faith and God's Word owing to the representative behavior of such figures as Greediness and No Good Neighborhood. In *The Three Ladies,* Love and Conscience are humiliated (Love is forced to marry Dissimulation; Conscience is first reduced to beggary, then forced to keep a brothel) and even physically degraded (Conscience is literally spotted with abomination), while Simplicity, who represents unprotected humanity, is stripped, beaten, and, in general, portrayed as a helpless victim of forces beyond his control. In these latter examples, the moral dramatists have used the fates of Conscience or Christianity or Innocent Humanity as effective and often quite vivid demonstrations of the power of Lucre in contemporary society.

To turn from such late moralities to *Volpone* is apparently to enter an altogether different world. Certainly *Volpone* is not a morality play, nor does it contain allegorical personae who would appear out of place in a Jacobean comedy set in Venice. There is, for example, no Money or Covetouse to set forth in one speech the major premises of the play, nor is there a Christianity or Virtuous Living to lament the absence of absolute standards. But in many important respects Jonson's literal comedy does use means analogous to those of the late morality to achieve similar ends. Thus, our first view of Venice provides a dramatic image of the wealthy magnifico Volpone kneeling and offering a morning hymn to his gold. By placing this address to "the worlds soule, and mine" in such a commanding position at the outset of the play, Jonson is deliberately shocking his audience by providing "a new metaphysic and a new ethic, almost point for point the reverse of the Christian." [7] At the same time, he is offering a series of hyperbolic statements about the power of gold over society, statements which set up some extreme propositions that will be tested by the subsequent action. Volpone claims, for example, that the pleasures derived from gold far transcend "all stile of ioy, in children, parents, friends, / Or any other waking dreame on earth"; gold, he postulates, "giu'st all men tongues," "mak'st men doe all things," and can even purchase "vertue, fame, / Honour, and all things else!" (I.i.17–18, 22, 23, 25–26) With superb dramatic ingenuity, Jonson has here catalogued the potential power of this "dumbe god" (l. 22) and shown how men worship "with adoration" (l. 12) at its "shrine" (l. 2), thereby achieving and far surpassing the effect sought by Lupton in the opening scenes of *All for Money* without sacrificing the literal surface of his play.

The remainder of Act I develops Jonson's thesis about Lucre and society by showing how Volpone's gold, in the form of a legacy, can function as a weapon against the venal elements in Venice (or London), appropriately represented by a merchant, a miser, and a lawyer who possess respectively a young wife, a son, and a reputation for forensic ability in the Venetian courts. Without resorting to an obvious thesis-and-demonstration structure built around allegorical personae, Jonson is indirectly yet effectively setting up a dramatic proposition for the audience: how will the bait of money dangled before these *captatores* affect such basic concerns as the ties between husband and wife, the ties between father

7. Edward B. Partridge, *The Broken Compass* (London, 1958), p. 76. For excellent discussions of the issues raised by *Volpone,* see Partridge, pp. 70–113; and Kernan, *Cankered Muse,* pp. 164–91 and Introduction, pp. 1–26.

and son, and, by Act IV, the very fabric of justice in Venice? Or, to put the question in slightly different terms, how much truth lies behind the hyperboles in Volpone's hymn to gold?

To provide the audience with answers to such propositions Jonson in his main plot employs three sets of characters, all of whom show marked similarity to comparable figures in the morality tradition. In *The Cobbler's Prophecy,* the duke, the priest, the scholar, the soldier, the courtier, and the country gentleman act out the effects of the ascendancy of Contempt in Boeotia; in *A Knack to Know a Knave,* the courtier, the coneycatcher, the farmer, and the priest display the faults inherent in four major areas of English society; similarly in *Volpone,* Corvino the merchant, Corbaccio the miser, and Voltore the lawyer function as "estates" which provide specific demonstration of Jonson's thesis about gold and society. Celia and Bonario, like Heavenly Man or Just or Faithful Few, function as virtuous figures whose behavior provides a standard by which to judge the world of the play, and, even more important, their fates, like those of Conscience or Christianity or Simplicity, vividly suggest the perilous situation confronting innocent humanity. And perhaps most interesting, Volpone and Mosca, who victimize both the "estates" and the virtues, provide Jonson's Venetian equivalent for the vices who traditionally impose their will upon a world which by its acquiescence and complicity has granted them power. Without the obtrusive commentary necessary in the 1620s, Jonson has here *"attir'd"* his vices, virtues, and "estates" as *"men and women o' the time."*

Such a process of transformation, needless to say, produced a work of art far removed from the limitations of the late morality. Still, with this structural breakdown of the play in mind, the modern reader can appreciate the manner in which situations and blocks of action in *Volpone* provide comic or satiric equivalents for characteristic morality devices. Act I introduces the Vice-like powers of Volpone and Mosca by demonstrating the ease with which they can control a lawyer, a miser, and a merchant. The widespread power of gold and those who know how to use it is further emphasized through Mosca's remarks about the venality of various professions, such as law (I.iii.52–66) and medicine (I.iv.20–35). In contrast to *Cynthia's Revels,* these set pieces (which all relate to a central theme) are successfully integrated into the larger fabric of the play. Mosca's machinations, particularly his planting in Corbaccio's mind of the idea to disinherit Bonario, can then show how effectively such representative victims can be corrupted from within. Given the iterated dramatic image of Volpone's groping hands, reaching out of his sick bed for material possessions (especially Corvino's pearl), there can be little doubt of the central disease in Venice and its potential effect upon society as a whole.

During Acts II and III, Jonson concentrates upon the campaign against Corvino and Celia. After Celia has volunteered her handkerchief to Volpone disguised as a mountebank, her jealous husband treats the audience to an entire scene of hysterical rant about the "death of mine honour" (II.v.1). Although the comically outrageous portrait of the merchant-husband is certainly delightful in its own right, Jonson has simultaneously set up an interesting question: how will this absurdly jealous husband, here outraged by a trifle, react to an offer to buy his wife for a very high price? Since Corvino is the merchant of the play, the question can be stated in even broader terms: how will his traditional values, such as those associated with matrimony or his own honor, stand up against his business ethics, which are based upon a monetary standard?

The outcome of this particular test case becomes clear almost as soon as Mosca baits the trap. The comic hyperbole of Act II, scene v now serves to heighten the effect of

Corvino's reaction to Mosca's request for a young woman "lustie, and full of iuice" (II.vi.35) for Volpone. Not only does the businessman quickly volunteer his own wife, but he also curses the "conscience" and the "scrupulous doubts" (ll.89–90) which earlier had stopped Mosca from smothering Volpone in order to protect his investment (I.v.68–74). The merchant can now inform his bewildered wife that he had not really been jealous at all ("a poore, vnprofitable humour" II.vii.7). Without having Conscience go into voluntary exile or having Mercatore gladly forswear his principles for the favors of Lady Lucre, Jonson has made his point about business ethics and the power of gold in Venice by means of this rapid and effective (and literal) *volte-face* from the comically outraged husband to the eager and willing purveyor of his wife.[8]

Act III provides further demonstration of the effects of gold upon both the corrupt and the innocent. First, Mosca extols the fine art of being a parasite in a speech which sums up his insight into the science of controlling others. To be successful, the "fine, elegant rascall" (III.i.23) must

> be here,
> And there, and here, and yonder, all at once;
> Present to any humour, all occasion;
> And change a visor, swifter, then a thought!
>
> (ll. 26–29)

8. For an equivalent scene in the late morality, see *The Three Ladies,* where Mercatore swears to "forsake a my fader, moder, king, country, and more dan dat" and to "lie and forswear meself," for, "What is dat for love of Lucre me dare, or will not do? / Me care not for all the world, the great devil, nay, make my God angry for you" (Dodsley, VI, 275–76). Although Corvino's rapid change of mind is a standard comic device (witness the similar exposures of Bobadilla and Shift), it is here integrated (like the scenes involving Mercatore) into a larger thesis-and-demonstration structure rather than remaining a discrete comic moment.

To show again Mosca's powers, Jonson introduces the virtuous but naïve Bonario, whose "simple innocence" and "pietie" (III.ii.56–57) are no match for the parasite's crocodile tears. Although Bonario starts off with an accurate appraisal of Mosca's methods and qualities (flattery, baseness, sloth), he is soon deceived by this elegant rascal's ability to "change a visor, swifter, then a thought" ("What? do's he weepe? the signe is soft, and good!" or "This cannot be a personated passion!" ll. 18, 35). To demonstrate how grossly Bonario has been deceived, Jonson has Mosca accurately describe his activities in the play while apparently disclaiming any such role:

> but that I haue done
> Base offices, in rending friends asunder,
> Diuiding families, betraying counsells,
> Whispering false lyes, or mining men with praises,
> Train'd their credulitie with periuries,
> Corrupted chastitie, or am in loue
> With mine owne tender ease, . . .
> Let me here perish, in all hope of goodnesse.
>
> (ll.25–31, 34)

Without recourse to a Macilente or a Crites or a Horace, Jonson has here summed up Mosca's role in the play even though the innocent Bonario and the corrupt *captatores* are blind to such truths. Dramatic irony has replaced the author's commentary as a guide for the audience's reaction to the events on stage.

Bonario's helplessness against Mosca's "visor" is followed by Celia's plight during the lengthy rape and rescue sequence lasting from scene vi to scene ix. In his pursuit of Volpone's gold, Corvino assumes that his wife's first obligation is to her husband's business interests, not to any abstract standard of conduct. Therefore he tells Celia: "if you bee / Loyall, and mine, be wonne, respect my venture" (III.vii.36–37), which he describes as "a pious worke, mere charity, for physick, / And honest politie, to assure mine owne" (ll. 65–66). The final phrase effectively sums up the mercenary assumptions of this merchant who is subordinating honor and matrimonial loyalty to the success of the present business "venture."[9] In the midst of such venality and moral expediency, Celia remains the spokesman for Christian virtues with her pointed yet unsuccessful questions ("Are heauen, and saints then nothing?" l. 53) and reminders ("thinke / What hate they burne with, toward euery sinne" ll. 55–56). After Corvino has been led off by Mosca, her lament (which could have been spoken by Heavenly Man or Just or Faithful Few) underscores the point of the previous action:

> O god, and his good angels! whether, whether
> Is shame fled humane brests? that with such ease,
> Men dare put off your honours, and their owne?
> Is that, which euer was a cause of life,
> Now plac'd beneath the basest circumstance?
> And modestie an exile made, for money?
>
> (ll. 133–38)

After appealing to an eternal and fixed order above this corrupt world of Venice, Celia provides a list of the various examples of base human conduct to which she has been exposed, a list, moreover, which is syntactically arranged so that the horror and disbelief grow until the final question: and all this was done only "for money?"

9. Jonson reinforces this effect by having Mosca, in a mellifluous speech, tell his master that Corvino has come "to offer, / Or rather, sir, to prostitute . . . his owne most faire and proper wife" (III.vii. 74–75, 78), for which speech the merchant thanks him (l. 75).

Unfortunately for this innocent Christian wife, the phrase "for money?" which sums up her horror at such a state of affairs simultaneously acts as a tonic for the supposed invalid who, at the sound of the magic word "money," "*leapes off from his couch*" (139.s.d.). In place of such "a base husband" as Corvino, Volpone offers himself as "worthy louer" seeking "the true heau'n of loue" who has the power to make Celia a Queen, "not in expectation, / As I feed others" but in reality (ll. 140, 186–87, 189–90). The imaginative flights of the subsequent seduction speeches with their emphasis upon exotic delicacies and Protean shapes seem to break free of all mortal limitations, thereby brushing aside any inconvenient moral considerations like honor (ll. 174–75) or sin (ll. 180–83). By the end of the song, in fact, the *carpe diem* spirit of Catullus' lyric has been transformed into a moral relativism worthy of a Sejanus, for according to Volpone the only crime is "*to be taken, to be seene.*" Celia, however, like Wager's Heavenly Man, opposes her worldly antagonist:

> Good sir, these things might moue a minde affected
> With such delights; but I, whose innocence
> Is all I can thinke wealthy, or worth th'enioying,
> And which once lost, I haue nought to loose beyond it,
> Cannot be taken with these sensuall baites:
> If you haue conscience—
>
> (ll. 206–11)

Volpone, who could understand almost any attitude except this one, here interrupts, defining "conscience" as "the beggers vertue, / If thou hast wisdome" (ll. 211–12). The "wisdome" to which Volpone is referring is that worldly wisdom of which he has proved himself master (as in his control of Corvino to get Celia into this situation) but to which Celia's innocence and conscience can never be reconciled. Her kneeling and her repeated appeals to Heaven are in ironic contrast to the earlier kneeling of Volpone during the opening scene at the shrine of a quite different god. Although Celia's faith remains steadfast, her arguments only succeed in increasing Volpone's desire for possession. In keeping with the animal emphasis of the play, moreover, the seducer now descends from verbal appeals directed at reason and worldly wisdom to brute force. The results to come, barring intervention, are obvious.

Such intervention, of course, is supplied in the person of Bonario who "*leapes out from where Mosca had plac'd him*" (267.s.d.). Unfortunately, the dialogue at this point cannot be accepted at its face value by a modern audience:

> Yeeld, or Ile force thee. CEL. O! iust God. VOLP. In
> vaine—
> BON. Forbeare, foule rauisher, libidinous swine,
> Free the forc'd lady, or thou dy'st, impostor.
> (ll. 266–68)

Despite the post-Jonsonian clichés evoked by both the terminology and the situation, the dialogue here is in keeping with the major issues of the play. Celia, the helpless innocent, has only one possible appeal in such a situation, to "iust God," an appeal which Volpone, the worldly realist, immediately points out to be "in vaine." Bonario then forces the audience to face squarely the reality that lies beneath the aura cast by Volpone's words. Volpone *is* a ravisher, a swine, and an impostor; the place *is* a "den of villany" (ll. 273–74). From Bonario's Christian point of view, Volpone's "gold becomes dross; his god, an idol; his gorgeous room, only the den of a fox." [10] The worldly wisdom and moral relativism which had

10. Partridge, *Broken Compass*, p. 97.

appeared to be the controlling force in this corrupt world have suddenly been confronted and thwarted by an opposing force that both rescues the innocent and promises "iust reward" (l. 275) for the guilty.

Before objecting to Bonario as "the hero leaping through the door to save the little seamstress from the clutches of the villain,"[11] the modern reader should both recognize the traditional dramatic formulas and appreciate how they are being transformed. Jonson's audience would not have been aware of the conventions of nineteenth-century melodrama but would have had as part of their dramatic heritage various contests between Heavenly Man and Worldly Man or various stock situations in which Good Conscience or God's Merciful Promises rescues Innocent Humanity or Youth from the clutches of the Vice. This rape and rescue sequence is, in fact, closer to the morality tradition in spirit and technique than any other part of the play (an affinity which may explain much of the adverse critical reaction). Even though Corvino, Celia, Bonario, and Volpone fit appropriately into the literal world of Venice established by the play, they simultaneously embody ideas or attitudes which Jonson can play off against one another in order to bring moral issues to the attention of his audience, albeit in a manner far more sophisticated than that of Wager or Wilson. Although Celia, for example, as a "character" has been disparaged by modern critics,[12] her prime function is to represent not a psychologi-

11. Wallace A. Bacon, "The Magnetic Field: The Structure of Jonson's Comedies," *HLQ*, XIX (1956), 137. For other adverse reactions, see Davison, "*Volpone* and the Old Comedy," p. 156; and C. G. Thayer, *Ben Jonson: Studies in the Plays* (Norman, Okla., 1963), p. 53.

12. Thus Herford states that Celia and Bonario "as characters" are "almost as insipid as they are innocent" (H & S, II, 63–64); Rufus Putney argues that to present them "realistically would be disastrous;

cally realized individual but rather, like Simplicity in *The Three Ladies* or Christianity in *The Tide Tarrieth No Man* or Piers Plowman in *A Knack to Know a Knave*, a helpless victim whose plight can suggest the effects upon society of Volpone's way of life. To see a completely successful synthesis of literal and allegorical elements for such a purpose one must turn to Desdemona or Cordelia, but Jonson's figure of Innocent Humanity, even though somewhat pale in comparison to vivid and realistic "characters" such as Volpone and Corvino, still effectively fulfills her role in the play. The language and imagery of the scene, moreover, help to enforce this effect. Jonson certainly does not present a figure named Conscience reduced to begging and selling brooms as in *The Three Ladies*, but he makes the same point—that "conscience" has no place in a Lucre-dominated society—by having *his* successful Worldly Man cut off Celia's appeal by defining "conscience" as "the beggers vertue." Similarly, the highly ironic nature of Volpone's announced quest for "the true heau'n of loue" becomes apparent when we remember the name of the character whom he is addressing and the "heau'n" with which she is continually associating herself.[13]

---

humans cannot be that inane" ("Jonson's Poetic Comedy," *PQ*, XLI [1962], 199); Thayer describes Celia as a "simpering parody of heavenly beauty" who "turns out to be nothing but a humorless, prim, fatuous girl without a brain in her head and nothing but clichés in her mouth" (*Ben Jonson*, p. 62); and the most astute critic of the play, Alvin Kernan, laments that "on the whole these examples of virtue are too placid and lifeless to save themselves or make us very concerned about whether they are saved" (*Cankered Muse*, p. 185). Such reactions have been reinforced by the often produced Stephan Zweig adaptation of *Volpone* which turns Celia into Columba who *is* "a humorless, prim, fatuous girl without a brain in her head."

13. Jonson's use of "heaven" imagery, needless to say, is not confined to this scene. Volpone established his position at the outset when he said of his gold: "euen hell, with thee to boot, / Is made worth heauen" (I.i.24–25). Corvino, according to Volpone, "would haue sold

With the various tools at his disposal Jonson is raising and developing the type of moral issue characteristic of the late morality within the limitations of Jacobean literal comedy.

A mere listing of affinities with the morality tradition, however, certainly does not tell the entire story, for Jonson has added several ironic twists. This sequence, for example, does not end with the rescue of Celia and the thwarting of Volpone, for Mosca quickly turns Corbaccio, who has already drawn up the new will, against his supposedly unnatural son (completing the husband-wife, father-son parallel perversion effected by Volpone's treasure) and then further adapts the story to enlist Voltore in the cause. Despite Bonario's platitudes about gold being "this drosse, thy idoll" (III.vii.272), such "drosse" has lost none of its efficacy in controlling most men.

Even more significant are the reasons for Bonario's opportune presence in the first place. Mosca, with his usual manipulative skill, had placed Bonario in hiding so that the son could hear himself being disowned and perhaps help his father to an untimely end (III.ix.28–35). Although Bonario refers to "the hand of iustice" (l. 270) and the "iust reward" awaiting the wicked, his opportunity to help Celia is not the direct result of a providential plan but rather is made possible by the complicated machinations of Mosca and, most important, by the lust for gold (and cuckoldry) of Corvino who arrived well before his appointed hour on the timetable. Only Mosca's underestimation of the real depths of villainy and corruption in the world of Venice has saved Celia, the heavenly innocent, from Volpone, the worldly realist. The

---

his part of paradise / For ready money" (III.vii.143–44) if he had had an offer. See the discussion of the trial scenes for Celia's iterated appeals to Heaven, below, pp. 95–96.

rescue does follow a familiar didactic pattern which could have conceivably detracted from the literal effect of the scene, but Jonson's ironic twists have forestalled any melodramatic effect by calling into question Bonario's assumptions and have underscored the continuing power of Lucre and the continuing helplessness of those who trust in conscience and innocence.

These issues are further explored in the first trial of Act IV where Jonson, like many of the moral dramatists, uses the corruption of Justice as the central symbol of the pernicious effect of Lucre upon society. Throughout the morality tradition the lawyer or justice, like the merchant, the usurer, and the miser, appears as a worshipper of gold. One of the Vice's favorite vaunts in the Lucre plays, in fact, is how he has bribed witnesses, lawyers, or judges in order to subvert justice.[14] The most elaborate dramatic rendition of the inroads made by Lucre upon Justice occurs in the scene from *All for Money* described in Chapter 1. All for Money, acting as magistrate, proclaims that "*All maner of men*" will prosper in his court "*be their matter neuer so wrong*" as long as "*they come from money*" (p. 171). A series of petitioners then parades before this corrupt figure of justice, getting favorable results so long as they fill his purse. Only poor Moneyless-and-Friendless is refused, showing us "without a man haue money / He shalbe cast away for a tryfell we see" (p. 174). As an epilogue to this dramatic sequence (the major demonstration in the play of the power of Lucre in society), Sin concludes: "Doo you not see howe all is for money, masters?

14. See Covetouse's speech quoted above (p. 77) or Money's speech (*All for Money*, pp. 168–69) in which he provides a series of examples of how he has "made manie a crooked matter straight" by his power. In *Impatient Poverty* the hero is arrested by the Summoner while Abundance manages to bribe his way free.

/ He helpes to make good all wrong and crooked matters" (p. 182).

Jonson's trial scene achieves the same goal as Lupton's by means suitable to literal comedy. To establish the rationale of his trial Jonson does not need an allegorical proclamation but rather employs a brief yet effective scene before the arrival of the judges. Although Voltore begins with a pompous reference to "the carriage of the businesse" and the "constancy" of the witnesses (IV.iv.1–3), Mosca punctures such euphemisms with his question:

> Is the lie
> Safely conuai'd amongst vs? is that sure?
> Knowes euery man his burden?
>
> (ll. 3–5)

The Venetian court, as Jonson is telling us, will now have to choose between the honesty of the innocent and the concerted lying of the guilty and implicated, a situation further enforced by the entrance lines of the Avocatori (IV.v.1–11), who at the outset have the entire story as it actually happened.[15]

Voltore now announces what he intends to "prove":

> I must now
> Discouer, to your strangely'abused eares,
> The most prodigious, and most frontlesse piece
> Of solid impudence, and trecherie,
> That euer vicious nature yet brought foorth
> To shame the state of *Venice*.
>
> (IV.v.29–34)

15. For an interesting parallel to *Sejanus* see III.1–12 where Sejanus, like Mosca, instructs Varro and Afer in the roles they are to play in the false accusations against Silius before the Senate. Act III of *Sejanus*, like Act IV of *Volpone*, enacts the power of the intriguers over justice.

The audience is well aware that the impudence, treachery, and shame are to be found not in Celia and Bonario but rather in the group appealing to the "strangely'abused eares" of the judges. Although the Avocatori are at first incredulous (ll. 59–60), the testimony of Corbaccio and Corvino eventually turns the court against the two innocents, for both father and husband are quite willing to commit perjury and bring shame upon themselves for the sake of the legacy. Bonario and Celia, moreover, are hampered by their own virtues. Hearing Corbaccio denounce him, Bonario decides that he would "rather wish my innocence should suffer, / Then I resist the authority of a father" (ll. 113–14). The helpless Celia, maligned for her lewdness by Corvino, can only faint, leaving an impression that she is a suspicious woman of "too many moodes" (l. 142). Against the weight of purchased evidence and concerted lying, the two innocents can offer as "witnesses" only their "consciences" and "heauen, that neuer failes the innocent," which, as the fourth Avocatore bluntly points out, "are no testimonies" in this court (IV.vi.15–18). Like Simplicity or Lupton's Moneyless-and-Friendless, Celia and Bonario here act out the plight of the innocent and virtuous in a Lucre-dominated society.

The arrival of Volpone "*as impotent*" (IV.vi.21.s.d.) now provides the climax to this disturbing scene. As with Mosca's crocodile tears in Act III, scene ii, Volpone's apparent helplessness (as opposed to the real helplessness of Celia and Bonario) only serves as a "visor" to cloak the greatest display of his power, for Jonson is showing us how the disease which until now had been largely confined to Volpone's chambers is literally being carried in to infect the halls of justice. Voltore's subsequent speech then makes clear the implications of the events on stage through dramatic irony. Again, as with Mosca's handling of Bonario, almost every statement made by the advocate presents the truth as the audience knows it but is meant (and is taken by the court) as sarcasm or intentional irony. The Avocatori, for example, are offered a sarcastic yet accurate description of Volpone as "the rauisher, / The rider on mens wiues, the great imposter, / The grand voluptuary!" (ll. 23–25) but like Sir Pol in the mountebank scene or Bonario faced with Mosca, Voltore's audience on stage rejects the truth at hand in favor of the "visor."

As the speech swells and expands, the advocate, albeit indirectly and ironically, raises perhaps the most significant question in the entire play:

> O, my most equall hearers, if these deedes,
> Acts, of this bold, and most exorbitant straine,
> May passe with sufferance, what one citizen,
> But owes the forfeit of his life, yea fame,
> To him that dares traduce him? which of you
> Are safe, my honour'd fathers?[16]
>
> (ll. 38–43)

According to Voltore's argument, if crimes such as those of Celia and Bonario are not controlled, no one in Venice is safe. Such obvious crimes cannot "haue any face, or colour like to truth," for even "vnto the dullest nostrill, here" they must smell of "rancke, and most abhorred slander" (ll. 45–47). The audience, of course, is well aware of what is slander and what is truth. Their realization of the helplessness of the innocent and the imminent victory of the opposition is brought to a head by Voltore's ironically pointed question: who is safe if such perjury, venality, and corruption go unpunished? Celia and Bonario, who have trusted in innocence and conscience, are about to be led off for sentencing,

16. Later Jonson adroitly calls attention to the importance of Voltore's question by having Volpone mimic it in V.ii.33–36 ("If these strange deeds / May passe, most honour'd fathers").

while Voltore, who has led the assault on truth and justice, is to be commended for his "worthy seruice to the state" (l. 60). Here, as with Mosca's "visor" speech, Jonson's technique recalls the traditional vaunt of the Vice or lament of a virtue,[17] but it is through dramatic irony, not didactic zeal, that the audience is being forced to face up to the subjection of Innocent Humanity and the ascendancy of Lucre over Justice. As in *All for Money*, the propositions about gold and society set up at the outset of the play lead with inexorable dramatic logic to the conclusions in this scene in which justice itself is on trial.

Jonson, however, is writing a sardonic comedy, not a morality play or a tragedy. Act V, as a result, moves to a comic climax in the second trial, which serves as denouement. Still, the issues raised in the first trial and in the play as a whole are not resolved in the tidy and expeditious manner one might expect on the basis of the earlier comedies. Jonson, for example, carefully manipulates the events so that the first movement towards the expected resolution of the comedy is a false start. Voltore, whom Volpone in his comic *hubris* has pushed too far, betrays the cause before the Avocatori, admits his "couetous endes" (V.x.9), and begs pardon. Although Celia, equating the advocate's conversion with a providential plan set in motion to save the faithful, exclaims: "O heau'n, how iust thou art!" (l. 13), such exegesis is not borne out by subsequent events. Voltore's revelations, for example, implicate Mosca, not Volpone, whom the advocate believes dead. But the court now regards Mosca as "a man, of great estate" (l. 39) who must be treated accordingly. Even at this point in

17. See, for example, the long lament of Conscience in *The Three Ladies* (Dodsley, VI, 325–26) which elaborately demonstrates that there exists no place in society where "conscience" is welcome. See also n. 14 above.

the play, with the Avocatori in possession of the incriminating evidence from Voltore's papers (Celia chimes in: "How ready is heau'n to those, that pray!" V.xii.5), the promise of Volpone's treasure can still turn the advocate away from his present course of "conscience." Once again Jonson, in his own literal fashion, banishes Conscience from the stage and suggests that gold will once more defeat justice.

Mosca's subsequent arrival keeps the issue in doubt, for his refusal to admit that Volpone is still alive once more jeopardizes the cause. The various interchanges that follow emphasize in a highly effective dramatic manner the nonjudicial nature of the Venetian justice that is about to sentence Celia and Bonario. While the first three Avocatori puzzle over the conflicting statements, the fourth is thinking of Mosca as "a fit match for my daughter" (l. 51) and instead of cross-examining him for the truth only asks: "Sir, are you married?" (l. 83) Volpone and Mosca meanwhile are carrying on a running bargaining session to determine the price of allegiance. Even here, moments away from the resolution of the play, the power of gold is still much in evidence.

Mosca, however, like Volpone has overplayed his hand. Faced with the bleak prospect of both the loss of his wealth and a whipping, Volpone discovers himself in order to prevent that wealth from benefitting someone else. Only by such a "miracle" (l. 95) is the insidious knot of intrigue undone and the innocent spared an unjust fate. "Heauen could not, long, let such grosse crimes be hid" (l. 98), concludes Bonario, echoing Celia's confidence in the imminence of divine justice. Despite the abundance of such ex post facto comments, however, the weight of the dramatic action and the nearness of victory for Volpone's forces militates against any easy explanation of either the role of Heaven or the failure of Lucre as a controlling force. As with Bonario's rescue of Celia in Act III, a reprieve for the innocent is achieved not through the direct intervention of Providence but rather through Mosca's inability to gauge accurately the depths of depravity in his victim (here Volpone instead of Corvino). Although the first Avocatore in the closing lines of the play describes, in Alvin Kernan's terms, a "natural process" in which "a defect inherent in vice and folly . . . leads them to overreach themselves,"[18] this concluding scene leaves the audience with one final question in a play of many such questions. Can the villains and fools be counted upon continually to destroy each other, thereby releasing from bondage the innocent and virtuous who are otherwise helpless? Does the denouement of the play represent a "natural process" (Kernan's term) or a "miracle" (the immediate reaction of the first Avocatore in V.xii.95)? The question is and is meant to be left unanswered. As such, it represents an integral part of the complex response demanded by the final scene and by the play as a whole.[19]

Another feature of this thought-provoking denouement that requires further comment is the sham dispossession of Voltore, an event which takes on added significance when viewed in the light of the morality tradition. The first three acts of *Volpone* demonstrate how Corvino, Corbaccio, and Voltore are obsessed (to the exclusion of almost all other considerations) with the hope of gaining Volpone's treasure.

18. *Cankered Muse*, pp. 187, 191.

19. For a morality equivalent to this "miracle" aspect of Jonson's denouement, see the arraignment of Love, Conscience, and Lucre by Judge Nemo in the resolution of *The Three Ladies.* Earlier in the play Sir Nicholas Nemo had been the only one to offer Sincerity any help, and, although the implications of the denouement are by no means clear, it is quite possible that the author is again using the "Nemo" technique to bring out the continuing power of Lucre and the probability that "nobody" will ever be able to remedy the situation.

In Act III, Jonson specifically calls our attention to this obsession through a speech by the foolish Lady Wouldbe who points out:

> in politique bodies,
> There's nothing, more, doth ouer-whelme the iudgement,
> And clouds the vnderstanding, then too much
> Settling, and fixing, and (as't were) subsiding
> Vpon one obiect. For the incorporating
> Of these same outward things, into that part,
> Which we call mentall, leaues some certaine *faeces*,
> That stop the organs, and as PLATO sayes,
> Assassinates our knowledge.
>
> (III.iv.104–12)

Although the physiological argument and the general tone illustrate Lady Wouldbe's brand of folly, the idea of fixation or obsession as a major cause of the overwhelming of judgment has still been introduced into the dramatic context. The subsequent arrival of Corvino bringing Celia to Volpone provides a specific example of how the "subsiding vpon one obiect" can cloud the understanding.

After the first trial, the concept is again explicitly introduced. In answer to Volpone's query about why the dupes did not perceive the elaborate deception, Mosca replies:

> True, they will not see't.
> Too much light blinds 'hem, I thinke. Each of 'hem
> Is so possest, and stuft with his owne hopes,
> That any thing, vnto the contrary,
> Neuer so true, or neuer so apparent,
> Neuer so palpable, they will resist it—
> VOLP. Like a temptation of the diuell.
>
> (V.ii.22–28)

The dupes, according to Mosca, were "so possest" with their hopes for Volpone's gold that they were impervious to any other influence, even, as Volpone mockingly adds, temptation by the devil. Ironically, direct diabolic interference is unnecessary in a world in which a man, "stuft with his owne hopes" for Lucre, will willingly resist the truth and in the process destroy himself. In contrast, the success of Volpone and Mosca at the first trial had demonstrated their ability to recognize and use the obsessions of others to satisfy their own.

The themes of obsession, possession, and temptation are then fully explored during the second trial. When Voltore in his fit of "conscience" decides to confess his duplicity, Corvino at first claims that the advocate is distracted, next argues he must be envious, and finally exclaims: "The deuill ha's entred him!" (Bonario adds: "Or bides in you" V.x.35.) According to the merchant, the Avocatori should "credit nothing, the false spirit hath writ: / It cannot be, but he is possest" (ll. 49–50). Jonson then takes us briefly to Volpone who is cursing the "dull deuill" (V.xi.4) in his brain that had caused him to feast upon the discomfiture of the *captatores*, thereby jeopardizing his various successes. Next we are brought back to the courtroom where Corvino is arguing that Voltore "is possest; againe, I say, / Possest: nay, if there be possession, / And obsession, he has both" (V.xii.8–10). Once more Jonson is using the comments of a fool and a dupe rather than a set speech by a Crites or a Horace to call our attention to an important question. In reality, Voltore has momentarily dispossessed himself of his obsession with Volpone's gold and is acting out of "conscience." To Corvino, on the other hand, such behavior based upon principles and not upon materialism can only be explained by reference to diabolic possession.

Voltore's fit of "conscience" is short-lived. Once the bait of

Volpone's treasure is again dangled before him, the advocate recants his confession and, with Volpone acting as prompter and stage manager, acts out in high comic fashion the part of a man possessed by the Devil. With Volpone pointing out the symptoms as they occur and Corvino chiming in to reinforce the effect, the audience is treated to one of the funniest scenes in the play, culminating in the final lurid description of the spirit emerging "in shape of a blew toad, with a battes wings" (V.xii.31). Now that Voltore has been "dispossessed," he can conveniently deny the validity of his papers and statements that would otherwise incriminate the conspirators. His supposed "possession," in other words, has been overcome so that his obsession with Volpone's gold can reassert itself.

But to see only such ironies is to miss the full force of Jonson's dramatic image. Volpone, who supposedly is helping to "dispossess" the advocate, is in reality offering the audience a final and summary demonstration of his Vice-like ability to control a representative figure (here a lawyer in a courtroom) by playing upon his particular weakness or obsession. The visual impact of this scene is more important than what is actually said. What we *see* is an erect figure (Volpone) standing over (and visually exercising control over) a victim who is groveling on the floor of the stage in a fit (a comic analogue for Iago's quite similar relationship to Othello in Act IV, scene i). Like Sir Pol (who had been forced to crawl into his tortoise shell), Voltore too in visual terms is being degraded to the level of an animal crawling on the ground. The effect is even more striking when one recalls the earlier trial scene. The imposing advocate, who had dominated and controlled the innocent and guilty alike with the power of his rhetoric, has been reduced to this groveling and writhing figure now that the supposedly "impotent" Volpone has exercised his true power. Rather than driving a devil out of Voltore, the

Vice-like Volpone in reality is banishing that "conscience" or principle that had caused the advocate, even for a moment, to give up his obsession and self-interest. In keeping with the animal imagery that permeates the play, those qualities that separate man from beast (conscience, principle, reason) are here driven out of a representative figure so that his obsession with the false promises of his tempter can reassert itself. With the resolution of the comedy almost at hand, Jonson has summed up Volpone's function and significance by showing us how the power of gold and worldly wisdom can defeat law and conscience. In addition, we are offered the best example in the play of how the corruptive powers of the public Vice and the representative quality of an "estates" figure can be metamorphosed into literal comedy.

Jonson's earlier comedies had also presented characters who embodied a particular affectation, humour, or aberration which to some extent posed a threat to the health of society. But in the attempt to use such personae to create an image of the times, the comical satires had often lacked coherence and unity of effect, producing an impression of a gallery of individual eccentrics rather than a unified statement about society as a whole. But here in *Volpone* Jonson has introduced through the comments of Mosca and the fatuous Lady Wouldbe an explanation of aberrant moral behavior related to the humours theory and has exhibited that obsessive behavior within a thesis-and-demonstration structure comparable to that of the late morality but centered around two pseudo-Vices, Volpone and Mosca. By introducing Voltore's supposed dispossession before the final reversal, Jonson has provided one last dramatic image to sum up the power of Volpone and the attitudes he represents over his victims or, to extend the metaphor of the Vice (as set up by Jonson himself), the power of man's own greed and baser nature in general to "cloud the vnderstanding" and "ouer-whelme the iudgement." In contrast to the comical satires, *Volpone* does achieve unity and coherence through its controlling thesis (established by the hyperboles and inverted religion of the opening scene) and its intriguers, who embody that thesis. As opposed to the disparate effect created by the many different offenders in *Every Man Out*, the behavior of the *captatores* (whether Corvino's *volte-face* or Corbaccio's disinheriting his son or Voltore's dispossession) acts out for the audience one central truth about the power of gold and the nature of man. The result is a disturbing yet brilliantly entertaining spectacle of man's ability to destroy or degrade himself.

Other steps forward from the earlier plays can also be noted. Not only has the satirist-spokesman (Macilente, Crites, Horace) given way to the pseudo-Vice, but the intrusive commentary practiced by such spokesmen has been replaced by effective use of dramatic irony. When Mosca defines himself in front of Bonario, or Voltore describes Volpone before the Avocatori, the audience can gain the full impact of Jonson's intended point even though the characters on stage are blind to such truths. Again, the providential intercession of Paulo Ferneze to rescue Rachel from the clutches of Angelo (significantly occurring in Act V) can be compared to Bonario's rescue of Celia in Act III. The difference between the analogous events lies not only in Jonson's ironic handling of Celia's plight and its aftermath but also in the continuing perilous situation faced by both victim and rescuer in the subsequent two trials. In place of elaborate verbal descriptions or catalogues of man's depravity (as in Crites' lengthy discourse at the end of Act I), the characters in the animalistic world of *Volpone* exhibit in a series of telling scenes the depths to which man is capable of sinking. As in *Sejanus*, moreover, the ideal figures of the early comedies who had confidently meted out appropriate justice have given way to the severely limited Avocatori who start with the truth and end up condemning the innocent.

Volpone, of course, is not a morality play. Jonson has not introduced a contest between Heavenly Man and Worldly Man as Wager might have done, nor has he shown Innocence brought to her knees by Worldly Wisdom until rescued by God's Merciful Promises. Rather he has presented the same conflict between expediency and eternal values within the world of Volpone's Venice by means of characters who participate in that world in recognizable positions (*"attir'd like men and women o' the time"*) yet at the same time personify the relevant qualities or attitudes. Presentation of evidence from the late morality (the three types of personae, the over-all thesis-and-demonstration structure, the trial scene of *All for Money*) has been vital to an assessment of this Jonsonian comedy, not because Jonson was slavishly following a particular play or set of plays as sources but because such moralities, even with their many limitations, are closer in over-all structure and intent to *Volpone* than most conventional comedies. To view the Elizabethan morality as the only source for *Volpone* would be to deny the obvious importance of classical and Renaissance elements, but to ignore the morality antecedents would be to miss an essential key to the play's distinctive nature.

To be the *"charitable critick"* sought by Jonson, the modern reader must therefore appreciate how this learned popular dramatist has blended comedy, satire, and morality into "his own style, his own instrument." Instead of providing a comfortable vantage point from which to view assorted eccentrics and knaves, Jonson has presented a searching examination of the causes of such follies and crimes and an unsettling view of the effects, especially the narrow escape of Celia and

Bonario. Our moral sensibilities may be satisfied by the punishments meted out at the end or by the summary comment of the first Avocatore ("these possesse wealth, as sicke men possesse feuers, / Which, trulyer, may be said to possesse them" V.xii.101–2), but the final disposition of knaves and dupes cannot blot out the disturbing power of gold depicted by the play as a whole. Here are the first signs of that characteristic Jonsonian assault upon an audience uncomfortably involved with the events on stage, particularly with the central Vice-like figures who cannot be readily dismissed or forgotten. In short, in *Volpone* we can see the birth of Jonson's moral comedy.

CHAPTER 4

Comic Synthesis: *The Alchemist*

ALTHOUGH *Volpone* is the first major achievement of Jonson's dramatic art, it is by no means the culmination. Certainly, many of the problems that had beset the earlier comedies have been overcome, but the play still lacks that total unity of effect of which this dramatic craftsman was capable. Even though the subplot has been astutely defended and justified by Jonas Barish,[1] one cannot help seeing in Peregrine and Sir Pol that combination of "presenter" and eccentric which Jonson was leaving behind him. The subplot and the various entertainments offered by Nano, Androgyne, and Castrone do relate thematically and symbolically to the main action, as Barish and Harry Levin[2] have demonstrated, but at the cost of slightly blurring the dramatic focus. The presence of Celia and Bonario in the midst of the animalistic world of Venice, moreover, although an integral feature of the play, still produces some jarring effects

1. "The Double Plot in *Volpone*," *MP*, LI (1953), 83–92.
2. "Jonson's Metempsychosis," *PQ*, XXII (1943), 231–39.

of which Jonson, as subsequent practice indicates, was aware. The arguments and tone of the dedicatory letter indicate that its author was conscious of potential objections on various counts and may not have been wholly satisfied with his work. *Volpone* thus represents an impressive first step toward, but not the culmination of, Jonson's moral comedy.

Ironically, Jonson's great success with *Volpone* (both artistic and popular) was followed by a three-year absence from the stage. During this period he established himself as the premier writer of court masques, a role that gave him his opportunity to serve as Crites or Horace for James I. Given the intensity of the probing and questioning found in *Volpone,* his return to the stage in 1609 with *Epicoene* or *The Silent Woman* comes as somewhat of a surprise. What most readers have seen as "an abrupt reversion to the *gaudeamus igitur* note"[3] of *Every Man In* may be a result of a return to the child actors and their elite audience (from which *Volpone* had been a departure), but, even so, *Epicoene* is in various ways quite different from *Cynthia's Revels* and *Poetaster,* the two previous plays written for children. For the first time since *Every Man In,* there is little evidence of Jonson's characteristic assumption that his audience must be bullied out of their complacency and stupidity into a realization of the truths he is about to offer; instead he announces that "Our wishes, like to those (make publique feasts) / Are not to please the cookes tastes, but the guests" (Prologue, ll. 8–9). Since the "guests" in this case are presumably from the upper strata of society, the emphasis is upon the fashionable world (wits, ladies, fops) rather than the more sweeping view of all

3. H & S, II, 74. For valuable discussions of this play, see Edward B. Partridge, *The Broken Compass* (London, 1958), pp. 161–77; and Ray L. Heffner, Jr., "Unifying Symbols in the Comedy of Ben Jonson," *English Stage Comedy*, ed. W. K. Wimsatt, Jr., English Institute Essays, 1954 (New York, 1955), pp. 74–88.

of society provided by *Every Man Out* or *Volpone* (both, significantly, written for the popular stage). Like *Every Man In, Epicoene* exposes for comic censure various social affectations that are not presented as serious threats to the welfare of society but rather are viewed from a comfortable vantage point embodied in the young wits of the play (Dauphine Eugenie, Clerimont, Truewit), a vantage point apparently not to be questioned or endangered (perhaps analogous to the roles of Cynthia and Augustus Caesar). As in *Every Man In,* moreover, the framework for the exposure of the foolish or affected characters (Jack Daw, Sir Amorous LaFoole, the Otters, the Ladies Collegiate) consists of an intrigue in which again a young man (Dauphine) is pitted against the older generation (Morose).

This similarity between the intrigue comedy found in *Every Man In* and *Epicoene* is surprising considering what their author has written in between. In *Sejanus,* the central intriguer (Sejanus himself) had represented an insidious evil force which Rome had brought upon itself, so that his various plots could constitute a distinct threat to the health of society. Similarly in *Volpone,* the successful intrigues carried out by Volpone and Mosca had established the power of gold over the *captatores,* the innocent, and justice itself. But in *Epicoene,* there is no such menace associated with the central intrigue; rather, the name of its prime mover (Dauphine Eugenie or "wellborn heir") suggests a rightful claim to his intended goal. As opposed to Sejanus or Volpone, moreover, there is no equivalent thesis or set of attitudes behind the witty intriguers here, unless one assumes that they represent the values of the "guests" in contrast to the affected and foolish characters. The far from insidious intrigue found in *Epicoene,* in fact, serves to heighten the distinctive nature of the central situation of *Volpone* with its overtones of the Vice's campaign against representative "estates."

To see the difference between the searching moral comedy of *Volpone* and the lighthearted exposés of *Epicoene* one need only compare the respective third acts. In the rape and rescue sequence of *Volpone,* Jonson had used the intrigue against Corvino and Celia to examine the plight of innocent humanity in a world corrupted by money. The equivalent part of *The Silent Woman* is primarily concerned with the discomfiture of Morose after his marriage, a discomfiture brought about by a growing crescendo of "noise" that starts with the bride's unexpected pronouncements in Act III, scene iv, and ends with the drums and trumpets of Act III, scene vii. This highly entertaining spectacle, like the combat between Daw and LaFoole or the tribulations of Captain Otter, is much closer in tone and effect to the treatment of Bobadilla, Mattheo, Stephano, and Thorello than to the sardonic and disturbing scenes of *Volpone.* Equally revealing is Jonson's decision to keep Epicoene's true sex a secret from the audience until the final unraveling (although various hints are dropped along the way). Some of the most telling moments in *Volpone,* particularly during the first trial, grow out of the audience's insight into truths to which the characters on stage are blind (hence the impact of Voltore's question about who is safe). But such sardonic effects are out of place in *Epicoene* where even Truewit, who at times appears to be the *raisonneur* of the play, is unaware of Epicoene's secret. In tone, scope, and method, then, *Epicoene* is a marked departure from *Volpone.*

Jonson's next play, *The Alchemist,* signals a return both to the adult companies and to moral comedy. Again, as in *Volpone,* elements from disparate sources ranging from Plautus' *Mostellaria* to Renaissance alchemical treatises[4]

4. See, for example, H & S, II, 88–98; and Edgar H. Duncan, "Jonson's *Alchemist* and the Literature of Alchemy," *PMLA,* LXI (1946), 699–710.

have been adapted and contained within a larger structure comparable to that of the late morality. Again, no allegorical personae intrude into the literal Jacobean scene. Rather, Jonson embodies the antisocial forces to be found in London in Subtle, Face, and Dol, a highly realistic group of conspirators out to make a profit by exploiting the weaknesses of the Jacobean public. As victims for these Jacobean pseudo-Vices, moreover, Jonson has provided a group of dramatis personae who form a cross section of contemporary society reminiscent of the "estates" plays. In order of appearance we are presented with: (1) Dapper, the young law clerk and incipient fop; (2) Abel Drugger, the young tobacconist; (3) Sir Epicure Mammon, the knight and supposed social reformer; (4) Ananias and Tribulation Wholesome, the Faithful Brothers of Amsterdam; and (5) Kastril, the young heir from the country. The types thus include a young lawyer, a young merchant, a knight, two men of religion, and a young country gentleman. In place of the lawyer, miser, and merchant of *Volpone,* Jonson has here supplied six characters who represent different social stations, different professions, and different age groups but who possess one common denominator, a susceptibility to the wiles of Subtle, Face, and Dol. Again, without the obtrusive commentary of *The Staple of News*, Jonson has effectively "*attir'd*" his Vices and representative figures "*like men and women o' the time*" in order to make his statement about his society through literal comedy.

The "venter *tripartite*" of Subtle, Face, and Dol provides a good point of departure for more detailed discussion of *The Alchemist*. Like Volpone and Mosca, these three conspirators gain their power from an ability to recognize and exploit the weaknesses of those around them. Jonson, moreover, has endowed this realistic triumvirate with terminology and pretensions that establish their affinity to contemporary Jacobean figures, particularly businessmen. The business imagery in the play is apparent from the outset, for both The Argument and the opening scene introduce such terms as "contract," "share," "company," "trades," "credit," and "house to practise in."[5] Such terminology, repeatedly used by the rogues as a euphemistic cloak for their various practices, also calls our attention to the disturbing analogy between business and cheating. In Act IV, scene iii, for example, when Don Diego is about to be turned away unsatisfied because Dol is busy with another "client," Face suggests that Dame Pliant be employed in her stead. Although both Face and Subtle had wanted the widow and her dowry for themselves, "all our venter now lies vpon't" and "the credit of our house too is engag'd" (ll. 65–66, 70). A business decision (one that will be based upon mutual self-interest, not morality) is needed, and Face's ethics, by implication, are no worse than standard business ethics.

The opening scenes of the play carefully establish the basic operating principles of this businesslike "venter." Both Subtle and Face in their expository argument claim to have "alchemized" the other into his present state from a previous base condition. Thus Subtle claims to have had Face "by my meanes, translated suburb-Captayne" (I.i.19), later adding:

> Thou vermine, haue I tane thee, out of dung, . . .
> *Sublim'd* thee, and *exalted* thee, and *fix'd* thee
> I' the *third region*, call'd our *state of grace?*
> Wrought thee to *spirit*, to *quintessence*, with paines
> Would twise haue won me the *philosophers worke?*
> (ll. 64, 68–71)

5. For detailed discussion of the business imagery, see Partridge, *Broken Compass*, pp. 139–44.

The real "base metal" upon which this modern "alchemy" will practice is clearly man himself.[6] When Face later defends his role in this newly formed corporation ("You must haue stuffe, brought home to you, to worke on?" I.iii.104), he rests his case upon his abilities as a procurer of the raw material, man.

Much of the action of the play can then be devoted to examples of the alchemical transmutation of that base metal, the Jacobean public, into gold or profit. The gulling of Dapper, the first dupe introduced and the last disposed of, supplies a representative example, for his progress and fate, evenly spaced throughout the play, epitomize the process undergone by all the dupes. In Act I, scene ii, Dapper asks Subtle only for a "fly" or minor spirit to assist him in his small-time gambling, but the Alchemist quickly provides more grandiose possibilities. First, Subtle offers a tantalizing hint (that much greater gains would be possible if Dapper only knew the truth) which is soon expanded into a prediction that this nephew of "the Queene of *Faerie*" could easily "draw you all the treasure of the realme" (I.ii.102). Although Face emphasizes that Dapper "knowes the law" (ll. 20,54) and is well aware of the "*statute*" (l. 22) against necromancy, the dupe is quite willing to "leaue the law" (l. 91) in the hope of gain. Man's persistent dreams of wealth and satisfaction, which he is willing to pursue at the expense of laws (whether civil or moral), make him potential base metal for Subtle's alchemical process. Knowledge of such human weakness, moreover (along with the ability to use that knowledge to control his victim), becomes a source of power and profit for the Vice-like manipulator.

6. For discussion of this point, see Duncan, "Jonson's *Alchemist*," pp. 701–2; Partridge, *Broken Compass*, pp. 126–27; Alvin Kernan, *The Cankered Muse: Satire of the English Renaissance* (New Haven, Conn., 1959), p. 177.

When in the middle of the play Dapper reappears for his expected interview with his gracious aunt, he is literally blinded before the eyes of the audience (III.v.15.s.d.) and then instructed to "throw away all worldly pelfe, about him" (l. 17). Both actions epitomize the behavior of all the dupes who, in the hope of gaining the elusive goals promised them, are submissively and willingly "blinded" and then relieved of their "worldly pelfe." Since the Fairy Queen is in reality Dol Common, Dapper's interview is forestalled by the arrival of Mammon, who demands her services elsewhere. In place of his grandiose expectations he is instead hustled into "*Fortunes* priuy lodgings" (l. 79) where "the Fumigation's somewhat strong" (l. 81). Typically, striving for the dream offered by the Alchemist yields only degradation and loss. When Dapper's great moment finally arrives at the end of the play, the still blindfolded "nephew" is forced to kneel, "wriggle" across the floor, and kiss Dol's skirts (V.iv.21, 28–29). Such degradation has no effect upon his blindness, however, for at the end of the scene he departs to "fetch the writings" that will transfer his "fortie marke a yeare" to his "aunt" (ll. 58–60).

The "venter *tripartite*" has thus been able to take advantage of man's universal dreams of success, power, and satisfaction, thereby turning such base metal as Dapper into gold or profit for themselves. In *Sejanus*, the corruption and decadence of Rome had been vividly expressed through the monster which society had created and condoned. In *Volpone*, the power of gold in Venice had been set forth through the successful machinations of two rogues who exploited the weaknesses of both representative figures and Venetian justice itself. Here in *The Alchemist*, the antisocial forces that offer a potential threat to Jonson's own society have been embodied in Subtle, Face, and Dol whose businesslike quest for profit feeds upon acquiescent victims who are willingly blinded and milked of their resources. Significantly, the "fly" which Dapper is eventually granted is to feed upon his own blood (ll. 35–38), just as this "modern" alchemy nourishes itself upon human beings. As in *Sejanus* and *Volpone*, the success of the Vice-like central figures of *The Alchemist* is only made possible by the greed, sensuality, and gullibility of the Jacobean public which, by giving up "law" and dignity in the hope of gain, is unwittingly creating and nourishing from within itself forces that can prey upon it. Although the tone here is admittedly not as dark as that of the two earlier plays, the issues and implications are much the same.

Dapper, of course, is a relatively minor figure in the play. To see Jonson's adaptation of the "estates" technique on a grander scale, one need only turn to perhaps his most highly esteemed creation, Sir Epicure Mammon. In his opening speech, Mammon presents in a series of "No more's" a panoramic picture of the various vices and abuses that will be eliminated once he has been granted the philosopher's stone. His magic words, *"be rich"* (II.i.7,24), a parody of the *fiat lux* of Genesis, will cure such social evils as gambling, quarreling, overindulgence, and timeserving. Prodded on by Surly's disbelieving comments, Mammon expands upon both the beneficial powers of gold and the related powers of the philosopher's stone until by the end of the scene he has reached the heights of comic absurdity. Along with such amusing effects, however, Jonson at the outset of the play has endowed Sir Epicure with various pretenses to social reform worthy of his "estate" of knighthood even though obviously based upon a naïve faith in the power of gold.

The scenes that follow reveal the reality beneath Sir Epicure's pretensions. When Face as "Lungs" asks for more material to "project upon," Mammon quickly assents to using "the couering of o' churches" (II.ii.14). News of the progress and near completion of the projection then prompts the knight to promise Face his reward as "the master of my *seraglia*" (ll. 32–33). This new emphasis upon sensuality and sexuality is developed in a series of long and justly praised speeches which clearly convey Mammon's basic interests. Instead of a knightly quest for the improvement of society, we are presented with a "sustained lyrical drool" [7] with the emphasis upon "wiues, and concubines, / Equall with SALOMON" (ll. 35–36) and various epicurean delights fitting for Sir Epicure. The stone, rather than being an instrument of social reform, has become the means to achieve this character's view of heaven on earth.

To bring Mammon down from his heights, Surly poses an astute question. For one to possess the stone, he points out:

> Why, I haue heard, he must be *homo frugi*,
> A pious, holy, and religious man,
> One free from mortall sinne, a very virgin.
> MAM. That makes it, sir, he is so. But I buy it.
> My venter brings it me, He, honest wretch,
> A notable, superstitious, good soule,
> Has worne his knees bare, and his slippers bald,
> With prayer, and fasting for it: and, sir, let him
> Do it alone, for me, still.
>
> (II.ii.97–105)

Besides demonstrating Mammon's credulity, this exchange makes explicit one of the knight's basic tenets; as Cyrus Hoy has pointed out, Mammon here offers an ingenious distinction between production and ownership of the stone.[8] Even

7. Wallace A. Bacon, "The Magnetic Field: The Structure of Jonson's Comedies," *HLQ*, XIX (1956), 144.
8. "The Pretended Piety of Jonson's *Alchemist*," *Renaissance Papers, 1956*, pp. 15–19.

though he admittedly cannot measure up to that ideal man, that "*homo frugi*," who alone could produce the stone, the knight is confident that by means of this "venter" he can "buy it." By parlaying Subtle's supposed piety into his own profit, Sir Epicure expects to satisfy the rigorous Christian requirements and reap the subsequent benefits (thereby serving both God and Mammon) without any real discomfort. "Good soules," it is assumed, can be hired to perform such necessary but unpleasant tasks as praying and fasting; faith, integrity, and sacrifice cease to be important since, given sufficient funds, they can be supplied by paid subordinates. As with the "venter *tripartite*," Jonson is demonstrating how businesslike assumptions are undermining that personal responsibility or integrity necessary for the health of society.

With the subsequent entrance of Subtle, before whom Mammon must conceal any "importune, and carnall appetite" (II.iii.8), Jonson's point becomes even clearer, for the Alchemist, posing as that ideal *homo frugi*, points out that his efforts

> Haue look'd no way, but vnto publique good,
> To pious vses, and deere charitie,
> Now growne a prodigie with men. Wherein
> If you, my sonne, should now preuaricate,
> And, to your owne particular lusts, employ
> So great, and catholique a blisse: be sure,
> A curse will follow, yea, and ouertake
> Your subtle, and most secret wayes.
>
> (II.iii.16–23)

This speech and the subsequent appearance of Dol as a great lady set up the machinery of righteous punishment that will be used successfully to gull Sir Epicure. Equally important, moreover, is the proper use of wealth and resources for the good of society established here, albeit indirectly. Mammon's pretensions to social reform, obviously a mere pretext to cloak his desire for the gold necessary to satisfy his "owne particular lusts," represent a serious falling away from the social concerns suggested by this speech ("publique good," "pious vses," "deere charitie") which would be appropriate for one of his "estate." Similarly, to cover a slip that had revealed his true interests, the knight promises:

> I shall employ it all, in pious vses,
> Founding of colledges, and *grammar* schooles,
> Marrying yong virgins, building hospitalls,
> And now, and then, a church.
>
> (ll. 49–52)

Although the obvious pretense of such protestations (effectively set forth in the anticlimax of the last line) makes us laugh, the ends themselves are certainly not laughable. Jonson, in fact, is exposing the hollowness of Sir Epicure's pretensions in an amusing way, while at the same time suggesting that charity, piety, and philanthropy *have* "growne a prodigie with men" owing to attitudes and actions analogous to those displayed here by this knightly pretender. To see Mammon as only a laughable fraud is to overlook the larger implications for the "publique good" in the *homo frugi* passage and his false conception of knighthood.

These social issues are, for the most part, submerged during Mammon's next appearance in Act IV, for here the knight and potential reformer argues for "a perpetuitie of life, and lust" by means of gold and the elixir (IV.i.165–66), thereby reminding us that he is no more than a fool and a lecher. The mock-righteous agency that brings about his punishment in Act IV, scene v, then calls attention to Mammon's "voluptuous mind," his "base affections," and "the curst fruits of vice, and lust" (ll. 74–77), which have replaced even the pretense of concern for "publique good." During Sir Epicure's final appearance in Act V, however, Jonson returns to these issues. After twitting the knight on his gullibility, Lovewit points to the "great losse in hope" Mammon has sustained (V.v.75).

> MAM. Not I, the common-wealth has. FAC. I, he would ha' built
> The citie new; and made a ditch about it
> Of siluer, should haue runne with creame from *Hogsden:*
> That, euery sunday in *More*-fields, the younkers,
> And tits, and tom-boyes should haue fed on, *gratis*.
> (ll. 76–80)

Face's lines, a *reductio* of the knight's original hopes and pretensions, provide the final pronouncement in Jonson's exposé of Sir Epicure Mammon. In a sense, however, his statement here *is* true and "the common-wealth" *has* suffered, because of him, "a great losse in hope." Although we cannot help laughing at Mammon's naïve belief that piety and integrity can be purchased from others or his obvious pretenses about social reform and public weal, such muddled thinking is far less comical when seen as typical of those in positions of responsibility. That the concern for "publique good" as displayed by Mammon and Subtle is only a comic pretense is in itself a disturbing fact of which Jonson makes good use. "The common-wealth" in the long run *is* the loser, as Mammon suggests, for such obvious misdirection of energy and resources can only be detrimental to society as a whole. Even though Sir Epicure Mammon is undeniably an exceptionally fine comic figure whose pretensions and affectations are exposed in a manner worthy of the author of *Every Man Out,* he also functions, by virtue of his "estate" and his various assumptions and pretensions, as a symbolic embodiment of the failure of social obligation and personal responsibility in a world dominated by gold.

A similar combination of comic exposé and symbolic failure is to be found in the two Faithful Brothers of Amsterdam, Ananias and Tribulation Wholesome. Jonson, in fact, quickly sets up a parallel between Ananias and Mammon. When Subtle, looking for additional profits, attempts to resell Mammon's pewter and brass as "some orphanes goods" (II.v.52), Ananias asks if the orphans' parents were *"sincere professors."*

> SVB. Why doe you aske? ANA. Because
> We then are to deal iustly, and giue (in truth)
> Their vtmost valew. SVB. 'Slid, you'ld cossen, else,
> And if their parents were not of the *faithfull?*
> (ll. 57–60)

Clearly Ananias is more concerned with his one sect than with any abstract values or principles of conduct, thereby transforming Mammon's concern with "particular lusts" at the expense of his "estate" into an obsession with his particular sect at the expense of true religious feeling. Like Sir Epicure, Ananias here is comical insofar as his narrow mind becomes an object of derisive laughter but far less amusing when seen as representative of at least one strain of contemporary religion. Certainly Ananias does not represent all Jacobean religious attitudes (he is not an Anglican) any more than Mammon stands for all knights. Rather, Jonson in both instances has chosen to include in his play timely examples of failures within two major "estates" (the clergy, the knighthood) that are necessary for the health of society.

The failings of the Brethren as men of religion become clearer with the reappearance of Ananias with Tribulation Wholesome. Both of the Brethren consider the Alchemist to be "a *heathen*" and "a prophane person," viewing "his *Stone*" as "a worke of darknesse" which "with *Philosophie*, blinds the eyes of man" (III.i.5, 7, 9–10). Yet despite such rejection in principle of the man and his methods, Tribulation, the arch-equivocator, can still argue that "we must bend vnto all meanes, / That may giue furtherance, to the *holy cause*," for, as he assures Ananias: "The children of perdition are, oft-times, / Made instruments euen of the greatest workes" (ll. 11–12, 15–16). Like Mammon, Tribulation is quite willing to distinguish between production and ownership of the stone if such a distinction suits his ends. His goal, the restoration of "the *silenc'd Saints*," as he realizes, "ne'er will be, but by the *Philosophers stone*" (ll. 38–39):

> *Aurum potabile* being
> The onely med'cine, for the ciuill *Magistrate*,
> T'incline him to a feeling of the cause:
> And must be daily vs'd, in the disease.
>
> (ll. 41–44)

Although Tribulation recognizes the corrupt state of the money-dominated society depicted by Jonson, this man of religion does not, as one might expect, attempt to cure the "disease" embodied in the venal "ciuill *Magistrate*" but rather seeks to avail himself of the benefits of such corruption. Hence follows his need for the stone and his willingness to ignore any contradictions that might arise while pursuing it. The importance of the stone to the Brethren is made even clearer by Subtle who, upon his arrival in Act III, scene ii, provides a long discourse upon "the good that it shall bring your cause" (l. 21), stressing in particular "the med'cinall vse" (l. 25) as a means to win friends and influence people. Once more a worthy end, the curing of disease, is valued only as a means to personal or party advantage With recourse to unlimited funds, all things are possible, for: "What can you not doe, / Against lords spirituall, or temporall, / That shall oppone you?" (ll. 49–51). With possession of the stone, all the "singular arts" (l. 92) or low practices now engaged in by the Brethren (which Jonson lists at length) "for propagation of the *glorious cause*" (l. 99) can be given up. Both Subtle and Tribulation prove to be well aware of the power of money in this society; the supposed man of religion, moreover, is obviously prepared to act in accordance with this knowledge with little heed to any religious principles.

While Tribulation, the epitome of expediency and equivocation, is demonstrating his understanding of the way of the world, Ananias speaks out only to quibble about subjects or terminology raised in the discussion (Christmas, bells, starch, traditions). Each time Subtle pretends to be angry at the interference, forcing Tribulation to mollify the Alchemist and rebuke the overzealous Brother in order not to jeopardize the enterprise. Ananias' final objection is the most revealing:

ANA. I hate *Traditions:*
I do not trust them—TRI. Peace. ANA. They are *Popish*, all.
I will not peace. I will not—TRI. ANANIAS.
ANA. Please the prophane, to grieue the godly: I may not.
SVB. Well, ANANIAS, thou shalt ouer-come.
TRI. It is an ignorant zeale, that haunts him, sir.
But truely, else, a very faithful *Brother*,
A botcher: and a man, by reuelation,
That hath a competent knowledge of the truth.
(ll. 106–14)

Having demonstrated at length Tribulation's willingness to compromise any or all of his principles, Jonson is here showing us the little that remains of the doctrine of the Brethren. Ananias functions in this scene as an overzealous conscience that offers "precise" objections to the issues at hand but is ridiculed and easily held in check by the hope for money and power. In this world, Jonson is telling us, principles exist only as amusing obstacles to satisfaction or success. But Ananias, as we realize from the passage above, does at least firmly believe in something, even though his "ignorant zeale" and "competent knowledge of the truth" are made ludicrous by Subtle. His unwillingness to "please the prophane" so as "to grieue the godly" is as close as he or Tribulation comes to true religious conviction that rises above personal or party advantage. Ananias' discomfiture may be highly entertaining, but it is also quite disturbing in its disclosure that such scruples in this world are only worthy of our laughter.

Both the Faithful Brethren and Sir Epicure Mammon are successful comic creations who provide a source of laughter yet at the same time prove to be significant failures in their respective "estates." The other three dupes, Dapper, Drugger, and Kastril, do not function in quite the same way. Drugger, who seeks Subtle's help in order to "thrive" more quickly, epitomizes the naïve young tradesman or merchant who expects to profit from propitious signs rather than from the gullibility of his clients. Dapper, on the other hand, who seeks help in his small-time gambling, is trying to cut a good figure in his particular milieu. And Kastril, the young heir up from the country, is seeking to learn the fashions of London, especially the quarreling and swaggering of the "angry boys." Like the foolish young men of *Every Man In*, this trio of youths can scarcely be seen as a threat to the health of society as can Mammon and the Brethren. None of the three, for example, is seeking the philosopher's stone to achieve some supposedly important goal. Rather, their naïveté and gullibility are shown to be helpless before the antisocial forces embodied in the "venter *tripartite*" which can prosper unchecked owing to the failure of figures in positions of responsibility such as the knight and men of religion to provide help or insight. Jonson's basic principle of dramatic operation, as a result, is analogous to that found in *The Three Ladies of London* or *A Looking Glass for London and England*. In the former the situation in London had been defined by the corruption of Love and Conscience by Lady Lucre and by the ascendancy of the four knaves, while the effects of such evil conditions had been spelled out by the fates of Simplicity, who represents helpless humanity, and "estates" figures such as an artisan, a lawyer, a scholar, a priest, and a merchant. In the latter play the situation in Nineveh had been defined by the evil conditions in Rasni's court, while the inevitable effects upon the rest of society had been demonstrated through the fates of Thrasibulus, Alcon, and the clown. Here in *The Alchemist,* with means and tone suitable to the literal world of Jacobean comedy, Jonson is providing his own presentation of the inevitable degradation of simple humanity in a world in which both religion and social obligation have lost their true meaning. The symbolic failures of Mammon and the Brethren define the nature of the London of *The Alchemist* (just as the degradation of Love, Conscience, and Lucre had defined the London of *The Three Ladies* or the corruption in Rasni's court had defined the Nineveh of *A Looking Glass*), while the fates of Dapper, Drugger, and Kastril spell out the inevitable effects. Jonson has provided his audience with both a thorough analysis of why Subtle, Face, and Dol have been granted their power and a specific demonstration of how they will inevitably use it.

In his adaptation of this popular dramatic structure, however, Jonson has not drawn upon a third potential set of figures, the virtues or virtuous individuals. The early plays, as we have seen, had introduced figures like Crites and Horace who clearly upheld the author's values, while Celia and Bonario had provided a standard by which to judge the Venetian jungle of *Volpone.* Dame Pliant, on the other hand, unlike Celia, stands for no definable attitude but rather functions as "a ball whose various movements serve to exhibit the quality of the players and mark the progress of the game." [9] The outcome of the struggle to possess her is one indication of who is the strongest and shrewdest in this world of knaves, for along with the money and Mammon's brass and pewter she is part of the spoils of this particular war.

The contrast between Surly and Bonario is even more revealing. Although scarcely the embodiment of virtue or conscience, Surly is used by Jonson to introduce as an issue the concept of honesty. From the outset this gamester is the only one tough enough and shrewd enough to refuse to be treated as "base metal" and be alchemized by Subtle; as he tells us: "Faith, I haue a humor, / I would not willingly be gull'd. Your *stone* / Cannot transmute me" (II.i.77–79). It is Surly, as a result, who raises the *homo frugi* issue, recognizes Subtle's "braue language" as canting, and foresees the temporary hitch in the operation that requires more capital from Mammon. It is Surly who attacks the linguistic fraud that is being perpetrated in Subtle's lecture on alchemy and, with the appearance of Dol, correctly labels the place as a "bawdy-house." And finally, after Mammon refuses to accept the truth, it is Surly who points out that the knight "with his owne oathes, and arguments" is making "hard meanes / To

9. H & S, II, 106.

gull himselfe" (II.iii.281–82). Although admittedly no paragon of virtue, this gamester is nonetheless established as the single voice of truth and sanity in the midst of a world of lies and self-deceptions.

Surly next appears in Act IV as Don Diego, the Spaniard, where, disguised as a dupe and setting up a language barrier of his own, he proves to be the only character to deceive the deceivers before Act V. After Mammon, who has ignored Surly's advice, has been gulled, the gamester appears, telling the truth about this "nest of villaines" (IV.vi.2) to Dame Pliant. He then asks her to consider "whether, I haue deseru'd you" as a wife (l. 15), for, as he points out, "I might haue wrong'd your honor, and haue not" (l. 10). Although Surly's confession here is part of his own calculated attempt to win the widow (and her money), the audience can at least distinguish such admitted self-interest from the totally amoral and cleverly concealed self-interest of the rogues. With the reappearance of Face and Subtle, the gamester confronts them with the truth about their operations, a discovery which would seem to assure the end of the "venter *tripartite*." But the rogues, true to form, are more than a match for this attempted exposure of their duplicity; by adroitly involving Kastril, Drugger, and finally Ananias in the argument they successfully produce an uproar of fools and rascals that proves too much for the simple unadorned truth.

Surly reappears in Act V only to find Dame Pliant married to Lovewit and therefore lost to him. Like the other gulls, he has his final speech:

> Must I needs cheat my selfe,
> With that same foolish vice of honestie!
> Come let vs goe, and harken out the rogues.
> That FACE I'll marke for mine, if ere I meet him.
> (V.v.83–86)

Since Face has literally ceased to exist, Surly's position at the end of the play is only slightly less ridiculous than that of his companion, Sir Epicure, who announces: "I will goe mount a turnep-cart, and preach / The end o' the world" (ll. 81–82). Surly's "honestie" not only goes unrewarded but turns out to be as foolish and self-defeating as the folly and gullibility of the dupes. His scruples in his treatment of Dame Pliant (effectively satirized by Lovewit in V.v.54–58), turn out to be just as comical and ineffectual in this corrupt world as the precise scruples of Ananias. Through Surly, Jonson is clearly and unambiguously depicting the fate of a man seeking success and satisfaction who makes the fatal mistake of acting, even for a moment, out of principle and not out of expediency. Rather than introducing an Honesty or Good Counsel figure from the morality tradition or even a virtuous figure like Bonario to serve as a reference point, Jonson has provided a shrewd and cynical gamester whose fate provides a dramatic *exemplum* that, given this corrupt society, honesty is merely a "foolish vice" and good counsel a vain undertaking. By means of Jonson's adept manipulation and inversion, the "virtue" of honesty in this "modern" world has become laughable.

Throughout *The Alchemist*, Jonson presents us with comic situations which force us to consider significant and often unsettling issues. Consider the role played by religion in the play.[10] Along with the failure of the Brethren, Jonson provides various other examples of false religion, ranging from the rites prescribed for Dapper to prepare him for the Queen of Faerie to the alchemical ideal propounded to Mammon and the "heretic" Surly. Significantly, religion is the forbidden subject in Sir Epicure's dealings with Dol, just as true religion, in a sense, has been banished from the play. In

10. For a full discussion of religious imagery, see Partridge, *Broken Compass*, pp. 127–32.

place of the voice of Celia in *Volpone*, the audience is left with only the equivocations of Tribulation Wholesome, the hypocritical piety of Subtle, the fraudulent righteous punishment visited upon Sir Epicure, and the word-chopping of Ananias, who concludes that "coining" may be illegal but "casting" may be permitted. Through an array of characters and a wealth of incidents, Jonson is stressing the absence of any absolute standards in contemporary London.

Nowhere is this emphasis clearer than in the sequence of scenes in Act IV which provides this play's equivalent to the first trial of *Volpone*. Instead of a public display of the failure of justice (as in both *Sejanus* and *Volpone*), Jonson here uses the fates of both Mammon and Surly within Lovewit's house to act out the implications of the triumph of the knaves over their victims. First we are shown in Act IV, scene v, the explosion *in fumo* of Mammon's hopes. Dol's feigned madness has brought "close deeds of darknesse" (l. 34) to the attention of Subtle, the supposed *homo frugi*, deeds which therefore must account for the "check in our *great worke* within" (l. 40). Mammon's patently false defense of his conduct with Dol ("our purposes were honest") is countered by Subtle's rejoinder: "As they were, / So the reward will proue" (ll. 54–55). The test case having been set up, Jonson immediately provides "*a great crack and noise within*" (55.s.d.), whereupon Face rushes in to announce:

> O sir, we are defeated! all the *workes*
> Are flowne *in fumo*: euery glasse is burst.
> Fornace, and all rent downe! as if a bolt
> Of thunder had beene driuen through the house.
> *Retorts, Receiuers, Pellicanes, Bolt-heads,*
> All strooke in shiuers!
>
> (ll. 57–62)

At the news of the descent of such a heavenly "bolt of thunder," Subtle "*falls downe as in a swoune*" (62.s.d.). When the Alchemist revives, he castigates "the curst fruits of vice, and lust!" and, in righteous indignation, calls out: "Hangs my roofe / Ouer vs still, and will not fall, ô iustice, / Vpon vs, for this wicked man!" (ll. 77–80) Mammon, who *has* been guilty of vice, lust, deeds of darkness, and a voluptuous mind, is then "iustly punish'd" (l. 74), not only by Subtle's strictures but, far more painfully, by his enforced departure with no "reward," no returns upon his investment, no fulfillment of his dreams of satisfaction and success. "Is no *proiection* left?" he asks—"All flowne, or stinks, sir" is the answer (l. 89).

But Mammon, of course, has only lost those visionary goals that he had no chance of gaining in the first place (the philosopher's stone, Dol as a great lady); such visions of power and satisfaction have been encouraged by the conspirators only so long as they prove profitable (to them). Even though the explosion of the projection has accurately "judged" Sir Epicure's "honesty," the audience is aware that the figure of judgment, the supposed *homo frugi,* is as corrupt as his chastened victim. In a play replete with vice, crime, and stupidity, here we have been offered the sole example of the just retribution of the heavens upon man's deeds of darkness, but such retribution turns out to be only another fraud perpetrated by the rogues to ensure their profit. That heavenly intervention continually requested by Celia does appear in *The Alchemist* but under rather dubious auspices. The implication left with the audience is that those who wait passively for such a heavenly thunderbolt may be playing into the hands of Subtle and Face.

In contrast to Mammon's acquiescence, Jonson next presents the attempt of Surly, a human counterpart to the bolt of thunder, to uncover the deeds of darkness committed by the rogues. Our first impression is that the gamester's combination of shrewdness and indignation may actually triumph. When Subtle appears, expecting to pick the pockets of Don Diego, he is instead struck down and forced to "reele" by an angry Surly (IV.vi.26–28). The staging establishes a parallel to Mammon's discomfiture, for, in contrast to the pretended swoon used in the previous scene, the Alchemist is truly struck down by an equally shrewd individual who has learned the truth (elaborately catalogued in ll. 35–53) and has acted on the basis of that truth. The gamester's intervention here, to save Dame Pliant's virtue and confront the rogues, is analogous to the fortuitous appearance of Bonario in Volpone's chambers, but Surly's opportune presence is a result of his own plan, not the errors of a Mosca or the venality of a Corvino. Here if anywhere is the hope for that moral ordering so speciously applied to Sir Epicure.

But Face, unlike the chastened Mammon, is unwilling to accept his just rewards passively. In *Volpone,* Jonson had waited until the first trial of Act IV to reverse the gains achieved by Bonario over Volpone in Act III. Here in *The Alchemist,* however, only moments elapse between the blow struck against Subtle and Face's reentry with allies against Surly and his truth. The central figure in the comic chaos that follows is Kastril, the nascent "angry boy," who is urged to exercise his newly acquired art of quarreling upon Surly who is described as a spy "employ'd here, by another coniurer, / That dos not loue the Doctor" (IV.vii.9–10). Although exact stage directions are lacking, the disposition of the various figures on stage can be pieced out from the text. On one side of Kastril is Face, who successfully primes the youth with false information (ll. 8–11, 17–19, 20–22, 27–31) while urging him: "Doe not beleeue him, sir: / He is the lying'st

Swabber!" (ll. 24–25) On the other side is Dame Pliant, who tries to whisper the truth in her brother's ear (l. 23) but is rejected, even though "all is truth, she saies" (l. 24). The audience is thereby presented with a dramatic image of a figure, faced with an important decision, who is being bombarded by opposing versions of "truth." Certainly Face and Dame Pliant should in some way be physically involved with this young man, either by pulling him in opposite directions or wrestling over his sword or any other such stage business. Regardless of the exact staging, the central situation is highly reminiscent of the morality conflict of a vice and a virtue over a fateful decision to be made by mankind. Like the good and evil angels of Doctor Faustus (who had just been mentioned in IV.vi.46), Face and Dame Pliant are here playing roles analogous to figures in the *psychomachia* conflict.

Kastril, needless to say, chooses Face over his sister and with the help of Drugger and Ananias drives Surly off the stage. As in the first trial of *Volpone,* truth and righteous indignation have little chance against concerted lying, self-deception, and comic confusion. As with Voltore's sham dispossession, moreover, Jonson is giving us a summary presentation of the nature and source of the power invested in his Vice-like figures. To drive away Surly's unwelcome truth, Face and Subtle have played upon the particular weaknesses of their victims (Kastril's desire to "give the lie," Drugger's dreams of winning Dame Pliant, Ananias' zeal). Significantly, the arrival of Ananias with his tirade against "*Spanish* slops," "ruffe of pride," "*Sathan,*" and "*Antichrist*" has sealed Surly's doom, for before such false religion the truth "must giue way" (ll. 48–56). There is no Honesty or Truth here to be thrust off by Youth under the influence of Hypocrisy and False Religion, nor is there a Una to be abandoned by Red Cross Knight owing to the machinations of Archimago.

Rather, within the bounds of literal comedy Jonson has explored the same theme, man's vulnerability to error and self-deception, by means of this amusing yet disturbing exhibition of folly and blindness.

Surly's ejection is one of the most revealing moments in the play, especially insofar as it brings out the hollowness of the moral framework invoked against Sir Epicure. The shrewd gamester, who has literally brought the false Alchemist to his knees, is the sole hope, before Lovewit's return, for any just retribution within the world of the play. Obviously no thunderbolt carefully aimed from Heaven is going to eliminate Subtle, Face, and Dol. Any such ordering must come from the responsible actions of individuals acting on the basis of those principles so conveniently rejected in practice by Mammon and the Brethren. But Surly, who in his own qualified way has attempted such an ordering, has here been driven off the stage. Not only has direct heavenly intervention been exposed as a sham, but even this limited attempt to "show the Heavens more just" (*King Lear,* III.iv.36) in the manner of an Edgar or Cordelia has been rejected by the combined uproar of fools and rascals. The ejection of Surly can thereby serve as a vivid demonstration of the moral climate of contemporary London.

The appearance of Lovewit now provides the second major threat to the "venter *tripartite*" and the second opportunity for ordering and retribution. Hearing Dapper's voice, the master of the house confronts his servant, asking for "the truth, the shortest way" (V.iii.74). But again Face is not daunted. If the master, who is "wont to affect mirth, and wit," will cooperate, he will gain "in recompence" a widow who "will make you seuen yeeres yonger, and a rich one" (ll. 80–86). In typical Vice-like fashion, Face gains his end by working upon an individual's particular weaknesses, here love of wit, fear of age, and desire for money. " 'Tis but your putting on a *Spanish* cloake" (l. 87) to grasp a diminished yet real version of Mammon's grandiose dreams of wealth and "a perpetuitie of life, and lust."

After Jonson has shown us the dissolution of the alchemical corporation, Lovewit reappears, still wearing the Spanish cloak and ruff (V.v.8). The last figure to appear as a Spanish Don had used that disguise in an attempt to confront the knaves and educate the dupes, but Lovewit has put on the same costume, not for retribution or ordering or education, but to cash in on the spoils available from the activities of the rogues, particularly the widow whom he has just married. Instead of opposing Face (as had Surly), this version of Don Diego accepts the shrewdest of the conspirators as his "braine" (l. 7), later adding: "I will be rul'd by thee in any thing, IEREMIE" (l. 143). In place of a moral ordering of the events of the first four acts, Jonson is offering a "venter *bipartite*" in which Face as Jeremy is granted a place in the normal order of society.

Lovewit's handling of the dupes can then demonstrate how the methods of this new corporation are merely a refinement upon those of the old. Earlier Subtle had observed to Dol that to deceive a knave like Face was "no deceipt, but iustice" (V.iv.103). This same type of justice through deceit is now visited upon Mammon, Drugger, the Brethren, and even Surly, all of whom in some way have been deceiving themselves. Each rebuff, moreover, is carefully tailored to fit the particular individual. Mammon, for example, is told that he may reclaim his pewter and brass provided he can "bring certificate, that you were gull'd of 'hem, / Or any formall writ, out of a court, / That you did cosen your selfe" (V.v.68–70). Sir Epicure, who would rather lose his goods than make any such public confession, bequeathes the spoils to the master of the house. By successfully playing upon such individual weakness, Lovewit brings to a profitable close the venture started in Act I.

The discomfitures undergone by Surly, Mammon, and the Brethren demonstrate that no ordering or retribution can be expected through them. Subsequently, Drugger and Kastril are no match for the combination of witty master and clever servant. The final speeches of the play then underscore the implications of the previous action. First Lovewit, who unlike Plautus' Theopropides has proved himself equal to Tranio-Face, announces to the audience:

That master
That had receiu'd such happinesse by a seruant,
In such a widdow, and with so much wealth,
Were very vngratefull, if he would not be
A little indulgent to that seruants wit,
And helpe his fortune, though with some small straine
Of his owne candor.

(V.v.146–52)

Lovewit places no stigma upon his having attained "such happinesse" by the duplicity just displayed and therefore offers only a token defense of the dishonesty in "that seruants wit" that made possible the acquisition of "such a widdow" and "so much wealth." The spoils, it is assumed, belong to the victor, not to the virtuous. Since Lovewit, unlike Surly, has no intention of succumbing to the "foolish vice of honestie," the "small straine" upon his "candor" is a bargain price for such a profitable operation. Like Tribulation Wholesome, who had no qualms about using venal civil magistrates, the master of the house sees no need to reform the world around him but rather takes full advantage of this businesslike opportunity.

Face's subsequent address to the audience, significantly the final speech in the play (the last word, so to speak) is even more explicit in its implications.

> And though I am cleane
> Got off, from SVBTLE, SVRLY, MAMMON, DOL,
> Hot ANANIAS, DAPPER, DRVGGER, all
> With whom I traded; yet I put my selfe
> On you, that are my countrey: and this pelfe,
> Which I haue got, if you doe quit me, rests
> To feast you often, and inuite new ghests.
>
> (ll. 159–65)

Here Jonson turns the epilogue with its conventional appeal for applause into a highly effective speech with implications both disturbing and insulting. The audience, about to applaud (or so Jonson hopes) following the final speech of the play, find themselves by that very action condoning Face's operations, past, present, and future. It is the Jacobean audience, that representative mass of London humanity, who embody Face's true "countrey," his "nation to be exploited." [11] The attitude of this pseudo-Vice toward his future dupes, moreover, has not changed in the least. "To the very end he remains the business man, giving the monthly report of the companies with whom he has 'traded', and keeping a sharp eye on those with whom he will trade in the future." [12] Although Subtle and Dol have fled over the back wall, Lovewit's continued possession of "this pelfe," Face's freedom from punishment, and the promise of similar operations in the future demonstrate that, as Alvin Kernan has suggested, "there is no sense of a better and more stable society having evolved," [13] but rather an implication that more of

11. Partridge, *Broken Compass*, p. 155.

12. *Ibid.*, pp. 154–55.

13. *Cankered Muse*, p. 190. For another persuasive rendition of this view of *The Alchemist*, see Gabriele Bernhard Jackson, *Vision and*

the same is yet to come. The folly, amorality, and irresponsibility found in the dramatis personae and in their counterparts, the audience or Jacobean public at large, have enabled Face and his like to be "quit" of any control or punishment and, in fact, have enabled them to "inuite new ghests." The audience's applause that would naturally and unthinkingly follow the above speech represents one of Jonson's most effective and devastating strokes. Such applause, in fact, may signal the creation of a new "venter *tripartite*": Lovewit, Face, and the audience.

Face's epilogue calls attention to the most interesting feature of this play, the manner in which Jonson has involved his audience in the action. Although Sejanus had represented a monster created by the acquiescence of the people of Rome, the action of that classical tragedy had been conveniently distanced from the Jacobean public. In *Volpone,* events in the world of Venice had left unsettling issues and implications with the English spectators. But Face, in his final speech, steps forth as a successful rogue whose behavior is condoned by the very audience before him. The blindness to truth, the absence of absolute standards, and the failure of social conscience which have permitted the events of *The Alchemist* have not been associated with a historically distant Rome or an analogous Venice but rather are firmly connected with the minds and hearts of those in the theater at this moment. To reinforce this identification, Jonson has placed the action of the play in the Blackfriars district (adjacent to the theater itself) and timed Lovewit's return after the plague to coincide with the similar return of his audience.[14]

Judgment in Ben Jonson's Drama (New Haven, Conn., and London, 1968), pp. 67–69, 90–92.

14. See H & S, II, 87–88; and C. G. Thayer, *Ben Jonson: Studies in the Plays* (Norman, Okla., 1963), pp. 108–9.

A basic danger inherent in satire, as Swift has ironically pointed out, is its tendency to become *"a sort of Glass, wherein Beholders do generally discover every body's Face but their Own."* [15] Jonson's play, particularly in its denouement, avoids such a pitfall. Rather than being allowed to regard the dupes and knaves from the comfortable vantage point of a Crites, a Horace, or a Dauphine Eugenie, the viewers of *The Alchemist* are themselves involved in and affected by what has happened on stage, both by their acquiescence to Face's activities and their presence as future Dappers, Druggers, and Kastrils for such rogues to "practise" upon. Instead of allowing the detachment found in the comical satires, Jonson has here involved his audience in the moral and ethical issues of the play in such a way that their laughter now turns back upon themselves.

Two interesting analogues can be noted for such manipulation of an audience. On the one hand, Jonson is making use of what had been implicit in the role of the public Vice of the late morality. So in *King Darius,* the virtues address Iniquity in such a way as deliberately to confuse him with the values of the audience who represent the public at large. The power of the Vice on stage is thereby an outgrowth of the moral failings of the spectators. A similar device from the opposite end of the allegorical spectrum can be found in the general practice of the masque with which Jonson at this time was fully engaged. As Stephen Orgel has pointed out, the masque

> attempted from the beginning to breach the barrier between spectators and actors, so that in effect the viewer became part of the spectacle. The end toward which the

15. "The Preface of the Author" to *Battle of the Books* in *A Tale of a Tub With Other Early Works 1696–1707,* ed. Herbert Davis (Oxford, 1957), p. 140.

> masque moved was to destroy any sense of theater and to include the whole court in the mimesis—in a sense, what the spectator watched he ultimately became. The most common method of effecting this transformation was to have the production culminate, dramatically and literally, in the revels, the dance between the masquers and members of the audience.[16]

The dance extends the meaning or harmony of the masque "beyond the confines of dramatic fiction into the world of the audience and the realities of the court."[17] But so does the ending of *The Alchemist.* Here, as in the morality play or the masque, Jonson has projected his final effect beyond the fictive world on stage into the lives that must be led by the audience after the performance.

As in *Volpone,* Jonson has skillfully and ingeniously adapted and reshaped the crude base metal of the morality tradition into his own unique comic synthesis. Recognition of the morality basis for the general structure and parts of the action, however, only heightens the disparity between Face's London and the divinely ordered world of the earlier didactic tradition. Thus Jonson's treatment of Ananias' scruples or Surly's honesty suggests that, as matters now stand, convictions or virtues are only a fit subject for laughter. Lovewit, on the other hand, who is not addicted to such a foolish vice as honesty, can emerge as the most successful rogue in a world of knaves and fools. Here is the individual who will inevitably prosper in a society where religion and social obligation have lost their true meaning and where truth is driven off the stage. The "guests" to whom Jonson had been catering in *Epicoene,* moreover, have become the "ghests" that Face is eying as prospective customers for the future.

16. *The Jonsonian Masque* (Cambridge, Mass., 1965), pp. 6–7.
17. *Ibid.,* p. 32.

In general structure, *The Alchemist* has many interesting connections with the late morality. In tone, however, it is farther removed from the didactic tradition than *Volpone.* The movement from Celia and Bonario to Dame Pliant and Surly, for example, has achieved a more successful blending of comic surface and moral purpose. The slight blurring of the dramatic focus caused by the subplot in *Volpone* has here given way to a total unity in which all events and characters are integrally related to a central satiric and moral conception. Jonson, in addition, has found more ways to establish indirectly his own standards and point of view without recourse to spokesmen and set speeches; so the implied ideal behind the knight and men of religion, the *homo frugi* passage, and the fate of Surly help us to understand what is lacking in the world of the play. Again and again Jonson has provided thought-provoking comedy that simultaneously directs our laughter not merely at distant eccentrics but back at ourselves. Even more than in *Volpone,* the resolution of the complex plot does not leave the audience with a convenient ordering of the forces that have run wild for five acts but rather plants the disturbing suggestion that, owing to our own culpability, there is only limited hope for improvement in the world outside the theater. *The Alchemist,* particularly in its last two acts, is the culmination of Jonson's moral comedy.

CHAPTER 5

The World in Panorama: *Bartholomew Fair*

FROM *The Alchemist,* his greatest achievement for the popular stage, Jonson moves to his greatest debacle, *Catiline His Conspiracy.* Even the modern reader sympathetic to Jonson's goals and ideals can hardly view this tragedy as a dramatic success, especially when he considers the lengthy and static orations that form the bulk of Act IV. Herford argues that "to Jonson the possession of so ample and indubitable an historical document as the Catilinarian orations was an irresistible bait, and he flooded the later acts with Cicero's eloquence, even in the original too voluble for our taste." [1] Still one can at least appreciate the purpose behind Act IV and the play as a whole. As in *Sejanus, Volpone,* and *The Alchemist,* Jonson has chosen a situation in which a conspiracy identified with an individual (or group of

1. H & S, II, 124. For valuable discussions of the play, see Joseph Allen Bryant, Jr., "*Catiline* and the Nature of Jonson's Tragic Fable," *PMLA,* LXIX (1954), 265–77—especially on the role of Caesar; and Robert Ornstein, *The Moral Vision of Jacobean Tragedy* (Madison, Wis., 1960), pp. 97–104.

individuals) forms a threat to the health of the kingdom. In the earlier Roman tragedy, the destruction of Sejanus had resulted in a new and equally dangerous villain as his replacement. In *Catiline,* on the other hand, the activities of one good man, Cicero, thwart the conspiracy and restore some semblance of order to the state. Cicero's orations against Catiline, moreover, upon which Jonson drew so heavily, were commonly regarded as the ultimate example of the power of eloquence to move men to virtuous action.[2] In place of the disturbing culminations of *Sejanus* and *The Alchemist,* Jonson begins *Catiline* by frightening his audience with the horrors associated with a successful conspiracy (see especially I.465–80 in which Rome is seen as "a field, to exercise your longings in"), only to leave them with a sense of relief at the triumph of Cicero and all he represents (although admittedly the sparing of Caesar has ominous implications for the future). Unlike *Sejanus, Volpone,* and *The Alchemist,* then, *Catiline* presents a dramatic picture of moral relativism and antisocial forces to some extent controlled and subdued by the efforts of alert and committed individuals. A shrewd, eloquent statesman has for the moment been able to save the kingdom.

The importance Jonson attaches to Cicero's role is clearest in a key scene in the middle of the play. In Act I, Catiline had shown a Vice-like ability to play upon the particular weaknesses of disaffected individuals (e.g., the bloodthirsty

2. Quintilian, for example, in a discussion of eloquence asks: "Did not the divine eloquence of Cicero win popular applause even when he denounced the Agrarian laws, did it not crush the audacious plots of Catiline and win, while he still wore the garb of civil life, the highest honour that can be conferred on a victorious general, a public thanksgiving to heaven?" *The Institutio Oratoria of Quintilian,* trans. H. E. Butler, Loeb Classical Library (London and Cambridge, Mass., 1958), I, 321.

nature of Cethegus, the patrician pride of Lentulus), thereby turning base metal into conspiracy. But in Act III, Cicero is forced to form a counterconspiracy out of equally questionable raw material. Hearing from Fulvia about Catiline's plot, Cicero first reacts (for her benefit) with a speech that assumes a direct relationship between the Heavens and the evils of man.

> Is there a heauen? and gods? and can it be
> They should so slowly heare, so slowly see!
> Hath Iove no thunder? or is Iove become
> Stupide as thou art?
>
> (III.235–38)

But in spite of the monstrous nature of this plot (elaborately set forth in ll. 258–81), Cicero realizes that no such thunderbolt is forthcoming from Heaven or Jove, any more than one had been available in *The Alchemist.* To preserve Rome, he is therefore obliged to use his most persuasive rhetoric to exploit the weaknesses of a prostitute (Fulvia) and conspirator turned counterspy (Curius). As part of his argument, Cicero even cites the inevitable reaction of the Heavens who must surely come to the aid of the Rome they have so carefully nourished (ll. 388–94). But after Fulvia and Curius have been won over, Cicero in an important soliloquy sums up his true feelings. The "sicknesse" (l. 438) into which Rome has fallen is characterized as especially insidious because the city maintains an illusion of security. Ironically, "the first symptomes" of Rome's "maladie" have been disclosed not through "any worthy member" but through "a base / And common strumpet, worthlesse to be nam'd / A haire, or part of thee" (ll. 448–52). The important role played by such base instruments indicates

how much the gods
Vpbraid thy foule neglect of them; by making
So vile a thing, the author of thy safetie.
They could haue wrought by nobler wayes: haue strooke
Thy foes with forked lightning; or ramm'd thunder;
Throwne hills vpon 'hem, in the act; haue sent
Death, like a dampe, to all their families;
Or caus'd their consciences to burst 'hem. But,
When they will shew thee what thou art, and make
A scornefull difference 'twixt their power, and thee,
They helpe thee by such aides, as geese, and harlots.
(ll. 454–64)

If he wishes to save Rome, Cicero cannot await the descent of the divine thunderbolt nor even the appearance of human agents who might better suit his ideals and sensibilities. To achieve his ends, he can permit himself no illusions about the role of Heaven or the nature of mankind (" 'Tis well, if some men will doe well, for price: / So few are vertuous, when the reward's away" ll. 479–80), but must seize any available opportunity. Although some critics (e.g., Robert Ornstein) have concluded that Cicero's nobility is tainted by such compromise, there is no viable alternative, given the diseased world of the play, if any semblance of order is to be restored. Unlike Surly, Cicero both uncovers the plot that threatens society *and* brings about some degree of retribution and ordering. Not the intervention of the Heavens (so speciously applied to Sir Epicure) but rather the committed actions of this virtuous figure distinguish the Rome of *Catiline* from the Rome of *Sejanus* or the London of *The Alchemist.*

Catiline provides yet another example of Jonson's dramatic investigation of a diseased society. Such analyses are not limited to his plays. In "An Epistle to a Friend, to perswade him to the Warres" (*Underwoods*, xv), for example, society is described as being so "bogg'd in vices" (l. 30) that man's only choice is to flee.

> The whole world here leaven'd with madnesse swells;
> And being a thing, blowne out of nought, rebells
> Against his Maker; high alone with weeds,
> And impious ranknesse of all Sects and seeds:
>
> (ll. 31–34)

The madness of the world is linked to the decay of virtues, institutions, and absolutes:

> what we call
> Friendship is now mask'd Hatred! Justice fled,
> And shamefastnesse together! All lawes dead,
> That kept man living! Pleasures only sought!
> Honour and honestie, as poore things thought
> As they are made!
>
> (ll. 38–43)

A discussion of the vices and affectations found at court leads to the question: "And are these objects fit / For man to spend his money on? His wit? / His time? health? soule?" (ll. 101–3), for the pursuit of "Bravery" (l. 110) yields only disease, surfeit, quarrel, even damnation (ll. 114–16). Jonson concludes by urging his friend to flee from this "hell on earth" dominated by flatterers, spies, informers, and slanderers "where the envious, proud, / Ambitious, factious, superstitious, lowd / Boasters, and perjur'd, with the infinite more / Praevaricators swarme" (ll. 162–70).

Such decay of justice, friendship, law, honor, and honesty is associated with the failure of the court and others in positions of responsibility to provide a proper example of behavior and "manners" for the remainder of society. After citing examples of lechery at court, for example, Jonson asks: "Who can behold their Manners, and not clowd- / Like upon them lighten?" (ll. 60–61). The false titles sought by the great ("woman of fashion" or "Lady of spirit") are linked to the general decay of morals (here expressed in terms of adultery), just as other false goals lead to the wasting of "our states, strength, body, and mind" and the ultimate loss of the "formes, and dignities of men" (ll. 133, 146). Even allowing for Jonson's satiric persona, this picture of "hell on earth" provides ample evidence of his pessimistic vision of the future, given a society unable to control its madness and disease.

"An Epistle to a Friend" is but one example of Jonson's continuing concern both in his plays and his nondramatic poetry with the causes and effects of contemporary vice and folly. The antidote to such diseases of society, according to Jonson's formulation, is always available, if men only know how to take advantage of it. So we are told that "*Good men* are the Stars, the Planets of the Ages wherein they live, and illustrate the times. *God* did never let them be wanting to the world" (*Discoveries*, ll. 1100–1102). He also states: "But they are ever good men, that must make good the times: if the men be naught, the times will be such" (ll. 247–48). Although Jonson's early plays, even at the expense of dramatic movement, do present such "good men" (Crites, Horace), the mature plays depict a world where for the most part "the men be naught" (Corvino, Voltore, Mammon, Ananias) and "the times" suffer. In *The Alchemist* in particular, the absence of good men to make good the times allows Face at the end of the play to "invite new ghests." In *Catiline*, on the other hand, the times clearly benefit from the activities of Cicero, regardless of his various compromises.

The nondramatic poetry offers numerous straightforward examples of such good men. "To William Earle of Pembroke" (*Epigrams,* cii), for example, places its eulogy in a larger context. To write an epigram on Pembroke, we are told, is to write "an *Epigramme,* on all man-kind" (l. 2). In the midst of the venal contemporary world in which all things are "at a price" (l. 11), Pembroke's noble example provides the antidote:

But thou, whose noblêsse keeps one stature still,
 And one true posture, though besieg'd with ill
Of what ambition, faction, pride can raise;
 Whose life, eu'n they, that enuie it, must praise;
That art so reuerenc'd, as thy comming in,
 But in the view, doth interrupt their sinne;
Thou must draw more:

(ll. 13–19)

and the poem concludes significantly:

and they, that hope to see
The common-wealth still safe, must studie thee.

(ll. 19–20)

Here Pembroke and his "one true posture" of "noblêsse" embody those qualities necessary for the safety of the commonwealth. Although Jonson is certainly interested in eulogy of the individual, the poem also comments upon contemporary society and helps to spell out what the author found lacking in the Venice of *Volpone* or the London of *The Alchemist.*

A similar point of view is expressed in "To Sir Thomas Overbvry" (*Epigrams,* cxiii). Since Overbury has come to court, "what ignorance, what pride is fled! / And letters, and humanitie in the stead!" (ll. 7–8); Overbury's presence at court is necessary so that "the wit there, and manners might be sau'd" (l. 6). Again it is "good men, that must make good the times." Jonson, moreover, is once more using the term "manners" to sum up those intellectual and social attainments of the upper classes necessary for the maintenance of a civilized society.[3] In his dedication of *Cynthia's Revels* to "THE SPECIALL FOVNTAINE OF MANNERS: The Court" (which first appeared in 1616), Jonson states:

> *Thou art a bountifull, and braue spring: and waterest all the noble plants of this* Iland. *In thee, the whole Kingdome dresseth it selfe, and is ambitious to vse thee as her glasse. Beware, then, thou render mens figures truly, and teach them no lesse to hate their deformities, then to loue their formes:*
>
> (ll. 5–10)

The point is stressed heavily in Jonson's epistle to Sir Edward Sackville (*Underwoods*, xiii). After arguing for the necessity of continual improvement in virtue, he concludes:

> 'Tis by degrees that men arrive at glad
> Profit in ought; each day some little adde,
> In time 'twill be a heape; This is not true
> Alone in money, but in manners too.
>
> (ll. 131–34)

3. Among the definitions of "manners" the *O.E.D.* lists: "A person's habitual behaviour or conduct, esp. in reference to its moral aspect; moral character, morals"; or: "In a more abstract sense: Conduct in its moral aspect; also, morality as a subject of study; the moral code embodied in general custom or sentiment." See James D. Redwine, Jr., "Beyond Psychology: The Moral Basis of Jonson's Theory of Humour Characterization," *ELH*, XXVIII (1961), 332–33.

After equating "manners" with the over-all attainments of virtuous men, Jonson continues:

> Yet we must more then move still, or goe on,
> We must accomplish; 'Tis the last Key-stone
> That makes the Arch. The rest that there were put
> Are nothing till that comes to bind and shut.
> Then stands it a triumphall marke! then Men
> Observe the strength, the height, the why, and when,
> It was erected; and still walking under
> Meet some new matter to looke up and wonder!
> Such Notes are vertuous men! they live as fast
> As they are high; are rooted, and will last.
>
> (ll. 135–44)

Such "vertuous men," who "are rooted, and will last," become, as in the case of Pembroke, models of "manners" who can provide a standard necessary for the general welfare of the rest of society.

The epistle to Lady Aubigny (*Forest,* xiii) makes the same point with regard to women. Here Lady Aubigny is praised for her choice to stay away "from the maze of custome, error, strife" (l. 60) of the world with its false concern with "fashions, and attyres" (l. 71) which can only result in the wasting of both "body, and state" (l. 81). She, on the other hand, represents "that rare wife, / Other great wiues may blush at: when they see / What your try'd manners are, what theirs should bee" (ll. 110–12). A model of "try'd manners" is thereby held up as one constant in the midst of "the maze of custome, error, strife" which is "the turning world" (l. 64).

Jonson's treatment of the court in general and Pembroke, Overbury, and Lady Aubigny in particular shows us how important he considered the power of good example set by those in high positions in society. As a satirist, moreover, he was even more effective in portraying the "manners" of individuals like Sir Epicure who fail to measure up to such responsibilities and obligations. In "A Speech according to Horace" (*Underwoods*, xliv) Jonson attacks national degeneracy by first praising the amateur Artillery Company of London (to whom national defense has been entrusted now that the aristocrats have given up the use of arms) and then providing the indignant response of the "Tempestuous Grandlings" (l. 64) to the suggestion that they might learn something from these commoners. Jonson's aristocrat, who asks: "Why are we rich, or great, except to show / All licence in our lives?" (ll. 69–70), eschews such concerns as the "Arts, the Lawes, the Creed" (l. 74) or service to the state "by Councels, and by Armes" (l. 85) and prefers pursuits more befitting "the Gallants" (l. 89) such as whoring, mastering "the Hawking language" (l. 72), or cultivating various affectations. After presenting this biting satire on the irresponsible nobility, Jonson breaks off:

> I may no longer on these pictures stay,
> These Carkasses of honour; Taylors blocks,
> Cover'd with Tissue, whose prosperitie mocks
> The fate of things: whilst totter'd vertue holds
> Her broken Armes up, to their emptie moulds.
> (ll. 98–102)

The failure of such nobles to live up to the obligations of their rank has resulted in the tottering of virtue and the weakening of the entire fabric of society. The absence of good men in positions of responsibility and eminence yields disastrous consequences.[4]

4. See also *A Panegyre* addressed to King James in 1603 (H & S, VII, 111–17), where Jonson observes that "kings, by their example, more

Given this pessimistic appraisal of society and its diseases, the reader may be somewhat surprised by the generally accepted interpretation of Jonson's next play, *Bartholomew Fair.* According to most of the critics, Jonson here is concerned with "the mere follies of a fair,"[5] not with "improving moral studies"[6] or "extraneous moral issues."[7] The most thorough critic of the play, Jonas Barish, argues that "the dominant spirit" here is one "of warmth and animal appetite," so that "one chief office of the Fair is to lure or coerce back into the human fold the numerous kill-joys who threaten it." According to this interpretation, Jonson is here relinquishing his characteristic moral position in favor of an indulgent attitude towards "irredeemable human weakness" and "is content to cry 'Duc-dame,' place himself in the center of the circle, and let it go at that."[8] The Fair, to Barish, represents the world as Jonson finds it, and the objects of his satiric wrath become not the rogues and fools who inhabit that world but rather the reformers or "kill-joys" who attempt to change it or control it.

Such a position on Jonson's part, as these critics would probably admit, represents a departure from the "impersonal

---

doe sway / Then by their power" (ll. 125–26). In his *Discoveries* he states: "*When* a vertuous man is rais'd, it brings gladnesse to his friends: griefe to his enemies, and glory to his Posterity. Nay, his honours are a great part of the honour of the times: when by this meanes he is growne to active men, an example; to the sloathfull, a spurre; to the envious a Punishment" (ll. 1292–97).

5. E. A. Horsman, Introduction to his Revels Plays edition of *Bartholomew Fair* (London, 1960), p. xiii.

6. Muriel Bradbrook, *The Growth and Structure of Elizabethan Comedy* (London, 1961), p. 146.

7. John Enck, *Jonson and the Comic Truth* (Madison, Wis., 1957), p. 194.

8. *Ben Jonson and the Language of Prose Comedy* (Cambridge, Mass., 1960), pp. 222, 225. For an interesting recent essay, much closer to this study, see Jackson I. Cope, "*Bartholomew Fair* as Blasphemy," *Ren D*, VIII (1965), 127–52.

severity" and "censorious sternness"[9] of much of his work. There is likewise a departure from Jonson's use elsewhere of the image of the Fair. Thus, in one of his most extended discussions of contemporary folly he states:

> *What* petty things they are, wee wonder at? like children, that esteeme every trifle; and preferre a *Fairing* before their Fathers: what difference is betweene us, and them? but that we are dearer Fooles, Cockscombes, at a higher rate. They are pleas'd with Cockleshels, Whistles, Hobby-horses, and such like: wee with Statues, marble Pillars, Pictures, guilded Roofes, where under-neath is Lath, and Lyme; perhaps Lome. Yet, wee take pleasure in the lye, and are glad, wee can cousen our selves.
>
> (*Discoveries,* ll. 1437–45)

After carefully establishing the analogy between a child's concern for trifles at a Fair and man's pursuit of possessions and false ideals, Jonson demonstrates that "all that wee call happinesse, is meere painting, and guilt: and all for money" (ll. 1446–47). As analysis of *Volpone* has shown, such concern for money at the expense of honor or "true reputation" (l. 1449) represents one of Jonson's major indictments against his society. That he should use the analogy of a child or foolish individual in a Fair as part of his criticism of materialism is one indication that moral issues may not be "extraneous" in a play about Bartholomew Fair.

A similar indication can be found in "To the World. A farewell for a Gentle-woman, vertuous and noble" (*Forest,* iv). Here the speaker whose "part is ended on thy stage" (l. 4), apostrophizes the "false world" (l. 1) in which "all thy good is to be sold" (l. 16).

9. H & S, II, 132–33.

I know thou whole art but a shop
  Of toyes, and trifles, traps, and snares,
To take the weake, or make them stop:
  Yet art thou falser then thy wares.

(ll. 17–20)

After listing the various ways in which she has been betrayed by society, the speaker presents a graphic picture of this toyshop world where pride, ignorance, and rumor reign supreme and "where euery freedome is betray'd. / And euery goodnesse tax'd, or grieu'd" (ll. 51–52). This description of "the World" as "but a shop / Of toyes, and trifles, traps, and snares" shows us Jonson once more using the superficial attractions of a Fair to symbolize those false appeals of contemporary society which can lead the helpless individual to his destruction.

Such use of fair imagery outside of *Bartholomew Fair* proper, although suggestive, is not conclusive evidence that "the crude jollities of Fair and carnival" do not "belong under the trusteeship of the festival spirit, and satisfy a legitimate craving for joy." [10] To test such an hypothesis requires a thorough reading of the play, and an excellent point of departure is provided by the three "kill-joys" whom the Fair supposedly coerces "back into the human fold," Humphrey Wasp, Zeal-of-the-Land Busy, and Adam Overdo.

Men in Authority

The first of these three figures to appear is Cokes's guardian and counselor, Humphrey Wasp, whom Barish considers a "frenzied busybody" who must "be shaken to his senses" so that he may "become a participant in pleasure instead of an

10. Barish, *Ben Jonson*, p. 236.

enemy of it." [11] Although Wasp's failings may be obvious, his role was considered quite important by his creator. In his *Discoveries,* Jonson dwells at length on the requisites for one who is "to counsell others" (l. 74). Such a person "must be cunning in the nature of Man" (l. 78), must have wisdom and honesty, must be able "to beget love in the persons wee counsell" (l. 93), must season "all with humanity and sweetnesse" (ll. 97–98), and must not "counsell rashly, or on the suddaine, but with advice and meditation" (ll. 99–100).[12] He concludes:

> For many foolish things fall from wise men, if they speake in haste, or be *extemporall.* It therefore behooves the giver of counsell to be circumspect; especially to beware of those with whom hee is not throughly acquainted, lest any spice of rashnesse, folly, or self-love appeare, which will be mark'd by new persons, and men of experience in affaires.
> (ll. 100–106)

From the outset of *Bartholomew Fair,* however, Wasp displays the rashness that should be eschewed in a good counselor. When told that he already knows the price for the license, he replies:

> I know? I know nothing, I, what tell you mee of knowing? (now I am in hast) Sir, I do not know, and I will not know, and I scorne to know, and yet, (now I think on't) I will, and do know, as well as another;
> (I.iv.19–22)

11. *Ibid.*, pp. 215–16, 237.

12. Jonson is quite emphatic about the need to eschew rashness in wise speech. Later in his *Discoveries* he lashes out against "the rashnesse of talking" as not befitting a "*wise tongue*" which "should not be licentious, and wandring; but mov'd, and (as it were) govern'd with certaine raines from the heart, and bottome of the brest" (ll. 330–42). See also ll. 1015–19.

Such a passage not only establishes Wasp's characteristic speech pattern with his "jabs of language" that verge on the meaningless,[13] but also, as suggested in *Discoveries*, sets up a connection between "wantonnesse of language" and "a sick mind" (ll. 957–58).[14] The symptoms of Wasp's "sick mind" are such lapses into meaninglessness owing to haste and perversity, qualities, as Jonson points out, unsuitable for a good counselor.

Wasp's limitations, like those of Mammon or Ananias, become important as a key not only to his personal eccentricity but also to his symbolic failure in the role he has undertaken. Ideally, he should be guardian and protector to Cokes; as Wasp himself points out, "the whole care of his well doing, is now mine" because the youth's "foolish scholemasters" have "almost spoyled him" so that "he has learn'd nothing" (I.iv.71–75). Instead of fulfilling such a role, however, Wasp has great difficulty controlling both his charge and himself. So even the foolish Mrs. Overdo can observe that she, for one, is willing to "be gouern'd by you; . . . but 'twill be expected, you should also gouerne your passions" (I.v.21–23). As guardian to Cokes, Wasp is quickly forced to make a concession about looking at the license. He admits to Winwife and Quarlous that "a man must giue way to him a little in trifles," but hastily adds that Cokes's juvenile whims are only "errors, diseases of youth: which he will mend, when he comes to iudgement, and knowledge of matters" (I.v.42–45). Rather than living up to his role of good counselor or educator, Wasp passively places his trust in a long-range

13. See Barish, *Ben Jonson*, pp. 213–15, for an excellent analysis of Wasp's speech patterns.

14. Jonson also tells us that "no glasse renders a mans forme, or likenesse, so true as his speech," and adds, "Negligent speech doth not onely discredit the person of the Speaker, but it discrediteth the opinion of his reason and judgement" (ll. 2033–35, 2151–53).

process which will perhaps cure Cokes of his present failings.

In the Fair, Wasp's limitations are even clearer. Throughout Overdo's tirade against ale and tobacco, Wasp rails against the Fair and attempts to pull Cokes away. Finally and belatedly Cokes's governor takes action, stating: "By this light, I'le carry you away o' my backe, and you will not come" (II.vi.97–98); the stage direction tells us: "*He gets him vp on pick-packe.*" The stage business is amusing, but, if one remembers the literal meanings of "charge" and "burden," it also comments upon the relationship between Wasp and Cokes. A figure with a similar role in the morality tradition (Good Nurture in *The Marriage of Wit and Wisdom*) laments, while searching for his "charge," young Wit:

> To them whose shoulders doe supporte
> the charge of tender youth,
> One greefe fales on anothers neck,
> And youth will haue his rueth.[15]

Wasp's comic yet meaningful assertion of his proper role, however, comes too late, for Cokes's next speech reveals that "one o' my fine purses is gone" (ll. 100–101).

When this group next appears in Act III, scene iv, the manner in which Cokes has spent his time is visually summed up by the toys and other purchases from the Fair with which the supposed protector and guardian is burdened. In his new role of beast of burden (ll. 67–70), Wasp is unable to prevent Cokes from spending his money foolishly on the wares of Leatherhead and Trash but can only offer advice, which is ignored or misunderstood, or lapse into petulance, perversity, and "selfe-affliction" (l. 46). Although he tries again, as in

15. Ed. J. O. Halliwell (London, 1846), p. 54.

Act II, scene vi, to get the young man to "fasten your selfe to my shoulder" (ll. 16–17), he is here unable to assert even that small degree of control over his charge but rather must bear the goods of the Fair, a visual image which calls attention to the course that the foolish young man is taking. Mere words without decisive action have no efficacy whatsoever for Cokes, who only tells his mentor to "hold that little tongue o' thine, and saue it a labour" (ll. 40–41). Clearly Wasp has been "ouerparted" or given too difficult a role to play in his "Protectorship" of "this plague of a charge" (ll. 52–54).

The implications of Wasp's failure soon become apparent. Although the guardian recognizes a danger in the ballad man (III.v.17–19), he is unable to protect Cokes from this particular snare, once more offering only advice, not effective action. The ballad itself is excellent evidence that mere good counsel will have no effect on Cokes, for it contains a pertinent warning (the danger of cutpurses) which the youth is unable to appreciate. After Cokes has again demonstrated his folly by losing his second purse, Wasp "*takes the Licence from him*" (214.s.d.), suggesting that "now you ha' got the tricke of losing, you'ld lose your breech, an't 'twere loose" (ll. 217–19). The closing lines of this important speech point out:

> An' there were no wiser then I, Sir, the trade shoud lye open for you, Sir, it should i'faith, Sir. I would teach your wit to come to your head, Sir, as well as your land to come into your hand, I assure you, Sir.
>
> (ll. 223–27)

Hazelton Spencer has paraphrased lines 223–24 as follows: "If it weren't that wiser heads than mine would not permit it, I would turn you loose to ply your trade of creating cutpurses."[16] Through Jonson's adroit handling of this speech, however, Wasp is also ironically revealing to the audience that, given the presence of no wiser and more competent authority than his own demonstrably incompetent self to guide the fortunes of such young men, both Cokes's "trade" of breeding cutpurses and Edgworth's "trade" of cutting purses would "lye open." Both the need for and the lack of an authority "wiser then I" to guide and protect these outsiders to the Fair is thereby postulated for the audience. Ideally Wasp's task would be, like the Good Counsel or Charity figure of the morality tradition, to rise above temporary setbacks and educate Cokes so that this particular youth could achieve his proper goals (e.g., marriage to Grace Wellborne) and take his place in society. But this particular protector or good counselor can only postulate the role he would like to play ("I would teach your wit to come to your head") and take back the license, transferring the responsibility for Cokes's future back to his own questionable shoulders.

A similar failure in authority is provided by Rabbi Zeal-of-the-Land Busy, who, like Ananias and Tribulation Wholesome, acts out the inadequacy of one form of contemporary religion. Busy's faults are analyzed by Quarlous who describes the preacher as one who "stands vpon his face, more then his faith" and who exhibits "a most *lunatique* conscience" and "the violence of *Singularity* in all he do's" (I.iii.136–39):

> by his profession, hee will euer be i' the state of Innocence, though; and child-hood; derides all *Antiquity;* defies any other *Learning,* then *Inspiration;* and what discretion

16. *Elizabethan Plays,* ed. Hazelton Spencer (Boston, 1933), p. 444.

soeuer, yeeres should afford him, it is all preuented in his *Originall ignorance.*

(ll. 142–46)

So when Dame Purecraft asks Busy whether Win should be allowed to visit the Fair, the preacher at first refuses to allow it, but, when he finds out that she wants him to "make it as lawfull as you can" (I.vi.60–61), he equivocates in a masterly fashion. Even though such an action may have "a face of offence, with the weake," still "that face may haue a vaile put ouer it, and be shaddowed" (ll. 68–70), and Busy quickly finds specious arguments to provide just such a hypocritical "vaile."

Jonson's broad comic effects here should not obscure the significant issues being raised. Like Tribulation Wholesome, Busy is subordinating his sense of what is "lawfull" to his own particular interests or appetites (his gluttony, his desire for Dame Purecraft's money). His strictures against the idolatry of the Fair (ll. 54–55) and his comments about "the tents of the wicked" (ll. 71–72) had made clear his interpretation of the Fair's significance before self-interest caused him to place a "vaile" over the "face of offence." Not all his remarks, moreover, here or later, can be dismissed as comic bombast. His castigation of "vanity of the eye, or the lust of the palat" (ll. 77–78), for example, is really quite relevant to the main action of the play, for these are the motives that draw Cokes and Win and their respective groups into the Fair. Even such limited insight into the appeals and wiles of the Fair helps to emphasize the importance of the role that this man of religion fails to play. Not only is Jonson offering us a "complete linguistic impostor" who employs "sham biblicality"[17] for

17. Barish, *Ben Jonson*, pp. 203–4, 201.

his own ends, but he has also placed the welfare of three other individuals in the hands of that "impostor" and has demonstrated how the "biblicality" which might have provided a stable point of reference is instead subject to false inspiration, "a most *lunatique* conscience," and self-interest.

Once Busy has indulged his desire for "pigge," he acts out his obsession in his attack upon "the foule abuses" (III.vi.89) around him, particularly the idolatry of the Fair. So he characterizes Leatherhead's toys as "Apocryphall wares" (l. 54), describes the hobbyhorse as an idol, and then glosses in turn each of the toys so that, for example, a drum can become "the broken belly of the Beast" (l. 67). After providing a summary of his rationale ("the sinne of the *Faire* prouokes me, I cannot bee silent" ll. 77–78), he identifies the target of his zeal as "the peeping of *Popery* vpon the stals, here, here, in the high places" (ll. 92–93) and, in the *reductio ad absurdum* of the entire tirade, exclaims: "See you not *Goldylocks*, the purple strumpet, there? in her yellow gowne, and greene sleeues?" (ll. 93–95) Busy's "victory" over popery and idolatry is then acted out by his overthrowing of Trash's gingerbread.

Busy's zeal, however, is more than merely comic noise. Although Jonson often exaggerates to the point of caricature, he also puts into Busy's mouth observations and admonitions relevant to the main action of the play. So Busy's attack upon the hobbyhorse as a "feirce and rancke Idoll" set up "for children to fall downe to, and worship" (ll. 56–59) may act out his comic obsession with idolatry but, given the behavior of Cokes in Act III, scene iv, is also a meaningful analysis of those superficial appeals of the Fair which can draw in the naïve or foolish individual as prey. Similarly, Busy's warning that Win should "fly the impurity of the place, swiftly, lest shee partake of the pitch thereof" (III.vi.43–44) turns out to be excellent advice, as shown by what happens when the Littlewits ignore it.

Most significant are Busy's comments on the vices of the Fair:

> But the fleshly woman (which you call *Vrsla*) is aboue all to be auoyded, hauing the marks vpon her, of the three enemies of Man, the World, as being in the *Faire;* the Deuill, as being in the fire; and the Flesh, as being her selfe.
>
> (ll. 33–37)

Once again in high comic fashion Busy is exhibiting the allegorical lens through which he views the world. His exegesis, however, is not as ridiculous as it first appears. As pointed out earlier, Jonson has elsewhere used the analogy between the Fair and the World, and in many ways Bartholomew Fair, with its superficial appeals and dangerous snares, is an apt symbol for Jonson's contemporary society.[18] Many of the appeals of the Fair, moreover, especially those connected with "pigge" and prostitution, come under Ursula's jurisdiction; taking into account also her enormous bulk, there is some justification in Busy's typing her as the Flesh. The identification of Ursula's fire with the Devil is more tenuous but does derive some support from other passages in the play which associate fire with sexuality and, in general, with the forces of disorder and anarchy.[19] Although ridiculous in its

18. Busy is thus agreeing with the speaker in "To the World" (see above p. 150), who identifies the "false world" as "a shop / Of toyes, and trifles, traps, and snares, / To take the weake, or make them stop."

19. See, for example, I.iii.75; II.ii.44, 92–93; II.v.59.s.d., 155.s.d. For further discussion of "the Devil," see the analysis below of the loss of Cokes's second purse. See also Busy's remarks about "the wares of diuels" and "the shop of *Satan*" (III.ii.41–42). For a somewhat different treatment of this same question, see Cope, "*Bartholomew Fair*," pp. 142–43.

overstatement, nonetheless Busy's allegorical gloss calls attention at this mid-point in the play to the manner in which Jonson is providing an equivalent for "the three enemies of Man," the World, the Flesh, and the Devil, suitable to the literal world of Jacobean comedy.

Busy's zeal, as a result, may be misguided, but the role he fails to perform (as the partial relevance of such remarks indicates) is an important one. His obsession with idolatry and his allegorical interpretations have brought out the dangers in such a self-appointed authority; meanwhile the reaction of the spectators and officers to his zeal and "sanctified noise" (III.vi.104) has spelled out the inefficacy of such attitudes and behavior. Jonson is not only holding up gluttony and hypocrisy for derisive laughter but is also dramatizing the dangers inherent in a "flesh and blood" authority which has been divorced from traditional sanctions and norms. As a result of such "*lunatique* conscience" and "violence of *Singularity*," the man of religion, like the good counselor, has ceased to be a source of support for his group in the chaotic world of the Fair but instead is dragged off to the stocks, leaving Littlewit and his "fraile wife" to face the Fair alone.

The third of the supposed "kill-joys," Justice Adam Overdo, does not, like Busy and Wasp, accompany a group for which he is responsible into the Fair, but rather, as his "overdone" opening speech makes clear, has taken on a disguise "for the publike good" (II.i.10). He cites as a "worthy president" for "all men in authority" that earlier "worthy worshipfull man" who successfully disguised himself in order to uncover vice and corruption in the city (ll. 26–27, 13). Like his model, Overdo has resolved "to spare spy-money hereafter, and make mine owne discoueries" about the "enormities of this *Fayre*" (ll. 40–42). This statesmanlike pose is immediately called into question by his obvious self-intoxication, his concern for triviality and needless elaboration, and his misuse of classical sources.[20] Despite such evident failings, Overdo's motives for being in the Fair are worthy of his role in society. Like Honesty in *A Knack to Know a Knave* or Middleton's Phoenix or Shakespeare's Duke Vincentio, Overdo is seeking to bring to justice various vicious and corrupt elements by means of undercover work. Although in this case Justice is appearing "in the habit of a foole" (l. 9), still the aim is "publike good" and the "detection of those foresaid enormities" (ll. 44–45).

Analysis of Jonson's dramatic work has brought out his continuing concern with justice from the arraignments of *Cynthia's Revels* and *Poetaster* to the disturbing trial scenes of *Sejanus* and *Volpone* and the denouement of *The Alchemist*. In his *Discoveries*, moreover, Jonson announces that "Justice is the vertue, that *Innocence* rejoyceth in" (ll. 1202–3), and later asks: "if *Piety* be wanting in the *Priests*, *Equity* in the Iudges, or the *Magistrate* be found rated at a price; what Iustice or Religion is to be expected?" (ll. 1286–88) The most revealing analogue to Overdo's pursuit of justice, however, can be found in *Catiline* where Jonson chose a historical situation in which one "worthy worshipfull man" had saved the commonwealth by pitting his virtue and judgment against the forces of evil, corruption, and decadence. Overdo, in fact, who claims to be acting "in Iustice name, and the Kings; and for the common-wealth" (ll. 1–2, 48–49), sees himself as "Cicero reincarnate" and, as a result,

20. For discussion of Overdo's speech patterns see Barish, *Ben Jonson*, pp. 204–11; and Alexander Sackton, *Rhetoric as a Dramatic Language in Ben Jonson* (New York, 1948), pp. 105–6 and *passim*. Barish (pp. 208–9) points to Overdo's misuse of the allusion to the Epidaurian serpent. For a treatment of Overdo as "the drama's deity" see Cope, "*Bartholomew Fair*," *passim*.

"has confected for himself a language bulging with the devices of classic oratory."[21] Such pretensions, like Busy's "sham biblicality," not only provide a standard by which to judge Overdo's ineptitude but suggest indirectly that ideal role of Justicer necessary to bring under control the chaotic forces of the Fair. The disparity between the short-sighted Overdo and his Ciceronian prototype provides a revealing insight into the world of Bartholomew Fair.

Overdo's search for "enormities" is not entirely fruitless, for he finds out the ingredients of the gingerbread ("stale bread, rotten egges, musty ginger, and dead honey" II.ii.9–10) and recognizes Ursula who has "beene before mee, *Punke*, *Pinnace* and *Bawd*, any time these two and twenty yeeres" (ll. 72–73). Upon hearing Ursula's lecture to Mooncalf on the various techniques of shortchanging the customer, Overdo exclaims: "This is the very *wombe*, and *bedde* of enormitie!" (l. 106) He sums up in Ciceronian terms:

> *O Tempora! O mores!* I would not ha' lost my discouery of this one grieuance, for my place, and worship o' the *Bench*, how is the poore subiect abus'd, here!
>
> (ll. 113–15)

Overdo's reaction appears at first to be excessive; at worst, he has stumbled upon an example of Jacobean sharp business practice in the spirit of *caveat emptor*.[22] His tag phrase from Cicero's first oration against Catiline, however, is, in a deeper sense, quite relevant to the main action of the play. In his rendition of this passage in *Catiline*, Jonson has Cicero cry out:

21. Barish, *Ben Jonson*, p. 204.

22. Alfred Harbage points out that Ursula "was a profiteer, but, except that her tobacco was mixed with coltsfoot, her charge for this item was not above average" (*Shakespeare's Audience* [New York, 1941], p. 58, n. 12).

"O age, and manners!" (IV.190), thereby expressing his dismay at the decay of virtue and public conscience in a Rome in which the Senate and the Consul can know the truth about Catiline and his conspiracy "yet this man liues!" (l. 191) By means of this allusion, this "modern" version of Cicero is calling attention to the disparity between the great moment of that "worthy worshipfull man" and his own questionable "discouery." In addition, through his emphasis upon the general decay in the "*mores*" or "manners" of "the times," he is introducing, albeit ironically and indirectly (as had Busy), a larger perspective for the audience. The various reasons why "the poore subiect" can be successfully "abus'd" or exploited are basic concerns of this play (and of *Volpone* and *The Alchemist*). Overdo's lament, although obviously overstated as a description of this particular situation, provides an epigraph for *Bartholomew Fair* and indeed for Jonson's moral comedy in general.

Posing as the mad Arthur of Bradley, Overdo begins his series of foolish errors and misapprehensions. Thus, with the arrival of Edgworth the cutpurse, Overdo comments: "What pitty 'tis, so ciuill a young man should haunt this debaucht company? here's the bane of the youth of our time apparant" (II.iv.30–32). Overdo therefore decides to devote "this daies trauell, and all my policy" to an attempt to "rescue this youth, here, out of the hands of the lewd man, and the strange woman" (ll. 64–66), even though the "youth" singled out for this special project is the source of one of the main "enormities" of the Fair. At the outset of his oration against ale and tobacco,[23] he asks Edgworth to "stay" and "despise not the wisedome" about to be offered in his behalf (II.vi.2–3). Such remarks are juxtaposed with the arrival of

23. For an excellent discussion of this entire speech, see Barish, *Ben Jonson*, pp. 205–7.

Cokes, another young man, who *is* in need of the protection and guidance of "men in authority." Edgworth, ironically, does decide to stay to take advantage of a situation which, as he accurately predicts, "will call company, you shall see, and put vs into doings presently" (ll. 9–10). The oration which follows is specifically directed at "youth" or "children of the *Fayre*" or "you sonnes and daughters of Smithfield" (ll. 66, 68), but the audience is constantly reminded of the distinction between Overdo's object of concern, who is successfully stealing Cokes's purse, and the other young man, who is impressed by the "braue words" but is helpless before the forces of the Fair. In his "overdone" tirade against two relatively minor vices, this supposed champion of justice fails to notice the successful commission of a major crime before his eyes.

Like Busy's allegorical glosses, however, Overdo's oration cannot be completely dismissed as a misapprehension of the realities of the Fair. Both the man of religion and the justice provide comical tirades against exaggerated pitfalls (idolatry, ale and tobacco) but at the same time cite real dangers facing the unprotected individual in the world of the Fair. Overdo's oration, especially his defense of "the poore innocent pox" (l. 52), can be highly amusing while at the same time it calls attention to "the diseases of the body" (l. 65) and the consequent "mallady" of "the minde" (l. 69) brought about by immersion in vice, a connection basic to the play, particularly to the "vapours" scene (IV.iv). Overdo's various strictures, like those of Busy and Wasp, reveal his limited insight into the world around him and, more important, emphasize the need for just that role he is incapable of playing. As with Voltore in the first trial scene of *Volpone,* issues central to the play are being raised by a character incapable of grasping the full significance of his own words.

In his next appearance, Overdo recalls his beating at the

hands of Wasp in a speech which sets forth the ideal by which we are to judge him and his failure. He tells us:

> I had thought once, at one speciall blow he ga' me, to haue reuealed my selfe; but then (I thanke thee, fortitude) I remembred that a wise man (and who is euer so great a part o' the Common-wealth in himselfe) for no particular disaster ought to abandon a publike good designe.
>
> (III.iii.21–26)

Overdo concludes:

> come what come can, come beating, come imprisonment, come infamy, come banishment, nay, come the rack, come the hurdle, (welcome all) I will not discouer who I am, till my due time; and yet still, all shall be, as I said euer, in Iustice name, and the King's, and for the Common-wealth.
>
> (ll. 36–41)

Jonson's delightful presentation of misguided Stoicism should not obscure the larger issue here. Despite the "particular disaster" he has suffered at the hands of Wasp, Overdo is still determined to play the part of the "wise man" whose role is "so great a part o' the Common-wealth" and continue his "publike good designe" in behalf of justice, the king, and the commonwealth. Even though this particular justicer, unlike Honesty or Phoenix or Duke Vincentio, is falling far short of such a goal, Jonson has still suggested the ideal role necessary to bring under control the Fair and all it represents.

The limitations of this justice figure become even clearer during the second purse-cutting scene. Overdo observes:

> I Cannot beget a *Proiect*, with all my politicall braine, yet; my *Proiect* is how to fetch off this proper young man,

> from his debaucht company: I haue followed him all the Fayre ouer, and still I finde him with this songster: And I begin shrewdly to suspect their familiarity; and the young man of a terrible taint, *Poetry!* with which idle disease, if he be infected, there's no hope of him, in a state-course. *Actum est*, of him for a common-wealths-man: if hee goe to't in *Rime*, once.
>
> (III.v.1–9)

Nowhere is Overdo's wrongheadedness more evident. Not only does he choose the wrong "proper young man" who is in danger from "debaucht company," but he identifies poetry as that "terrible taint" or "idle disease" which will destroy the youth's value as a potential "common-wealths-man." Although the dangers of disease and debauchery in the Fair are a central concern of the play, Overdo has no better grasp of such diseases than of the young man who might benefit from his "*Proiect*." The remainder of the scene acts out the effects of Overdo's lack of judgment and perception, for the "proper young man" for whom the Justice is concerned successfully steals the second purse from the naïve and foolish Cokes. Nightingale's ballad, moreover, appeals to Overdo almost as much as it does to the young man (ll. 112–13), so that the Justice can agree with Wasp's rebuke of Cokes for his interruptions. Such agreement underscores a lack of taste and the failure to grasp the true function of poetry, themes which Jonson will develop in his denouement, and demonstrates how both "men in authority" are not only unable to help Cokes but are themselves drawn in and duped. Overdo's misguided project only succeeds in bringing about his incarceration; he, like Wasp, is clearly "ouerparted" as an opponent of the enormity of the Fair.

Each of the three "men in authority" has been entrusted with a role necessary for the health of society, but each has been endowed with a "sick mind," a set of personal symbolic failings which prevent the execution of his proper function. Wasp has his rashness, perversity, and lapses into meaninglessness; Busy his "*lunatique* conscience" and reliance upon personal inspiration; and Overdo his self-intoxication and blindness to what is happening around him. Through the combination of personal exposé and symbolic failure found earlier in *The Alchemist,* Jonson is demonstrating how figures associated with education, religion, and justice fail to come to grips with the Fair.

The Representative "Estates"

To demonstrate the effect of such failures upon "the man in the street" Jonson uses an even larger cross section of representative figures than in *The Alchemist.* Instead of Dapper, Drugger, and Kastril who had taken over the function of Wilson's Simplicity and the "estates," *Bartholomew Fair* presents the fates of Littlewit, Win, Cokes, Mrs. Overdo, and Dame Purecraft in the world of the Fair.

The best example of this technique can be seen in Jonson's use of Bartholomew Cokes. The concern with youth and education is central to Renaissance humanism and is often expressed in dramatic form, but the moralities dealing with youth are particularly enlightening as background to Cokes's part in this play. The standard pattern of action of this "morality of youth" is aptly summed up on the title page of *Lusty Juventus* which, we are told, will portray "*the frailtie of youth: of natur prone to vyce: by grace and good counsayll traynable to vertue.*"[24] Since youth is conceived of

24. Dodsley, II, 42.

as a state "unstable" and "evermore changeable," [25] man is considered to be "prone to evil from his youth" [26] unless he benefits from the governance or direction of some worthy authority. In the simplest form of this dramatic pattern, a figure such as Good Counsel or Discipline or Good Nurture or Instruction will attempt to protect Youth or Wit from a Vice such as Idleness or Inclination or Hypocrisy which is trying to lead him towards Wrath, Wantonness, Vanity, Lechery, Treasure, or Riot.

The fate of youth in such plays, moreover, is important not only in terms of his individual salvation but also in terms of the future health of society. This Renaissance commonplace is spelled out in the prologue to *Lusty Juventus:*

> Give him no liberty in youth, nor his folly excuse,
> Bow down his neck, and keep him in good awe,
> Lest he be stubborn: no labour refuse
> To train him to wisdom and teach him God's law,
> For youth is frail and easy to draw
> By grace to goodness, by nature to ill:
> That nature hath ingrafted, is hard to kill.
> Nevertheless, in youth men may be best
> Trained to virtue by godly mean;
> Vice may be so mortified and so suppress,
> That it shall not break furth, yet the root will remain.[27]

Youth is pictured as a critical period of life during which the presence or absence of proper training will have a significant effect upon the caliber of future members of society; "children, brought up in idleness and play, / Unthrify and dis-

25. *Youth* (Dodsley, II, 28).
26. *Nice Wanton* (Dodsley, II, 164).
27. Dodsley, II, 45–46. Jonson, it should be noted, refers to the stock figure of Lusty Juventus in *The Devil is an Ass*, I.i.50.

obedient continue alway."[28] In *The Longer Thou Livest,*[29] for example, after Moros, the foolish young man, departs with Idleness and Wrath, Discipline comments:

When fooles are suffred in folly,
And youth maintained in theyr will,
When they come vp to mans state wholy,
Fooles they be, and so they continue still.
One writteth thus among many thinges,
Neuer shall you haue good men and sapient,
Where there be no good children and yonglinges.
(ll. 1003–9)

The fate of youth thereby has a direct bearing upon the ultimate presence or absence of "good men and sapient" in positions of responsibility in society.

Unlike Youth or Lusty Juventus or Moros, however, Bartholomew Cokes of *Bartholomew Fair* is not the central *Humanum Genus* figure in his play. Rather, Jonson, like some of the late moral dramatists, is using the fate of youth (or, in general terms, the fate of the unprotected and helpless individual) as one part of a larger thesis-and-demonstration structure. In Fulwell's *Like Will to Like,* for example, the widespread effect of the Vice, Nichol Newfangle, is demonstrated by means of several pairs of characters, including two youths (Cuthbert Cutpurse and Tom Tosspot) who hold themselves up as an object lesson:

O all ye parents, to you I do say:
Have respect to your children and for their education,

28. *Nice Wanton* (Dodsley, II, 166).

29. Ed. A. Brandl, *SJ,* XXXVI (1900), 1–64. The name of the central figure of this play, Moros, is quite similar in meaning to that of Jonson's young man; Pug, in *The Devil is an Ass,* defines "an absolute fine *Cokes*" as "a solemne, and effectuall Asse" (II.ii.105, 107).

Lest you answer therefore at the latter day,
And your meed shall be eternal damnation.
If my parents had brought me up in virtue and learning,
I should not have had this shameful end;
But all licentiously was my up-bringing,
Wherefore learn by me your faults to amend.[30]

Similarly, as pointed out in Chapter I, one example of the effect of "Corage" upon contemporary society in Wapull's *The Tide Tarrieth No Man* is the corruption and degradation of the youthful couple, Wastefulness and Wantonness, while Wilson's use of Simplicity in both *The Three Ladies* and *The Three Lords* provides an even later example of how an earlier pattern of action could be incorporated into a larger and more comprehensive total structure. In the use of *his* young man (and also the Littlewits, Mrs. Overdo, and Dame Purecraft), Jonson adapts such representative figures into his own thesis-and-demonstration structure in order to show the effect of corrupt society upon average humanity.

The opening lines of the first scene establish Cokes's betrothal to Grace Wellborne as the first dramatic premise of the play. Although the movement of a young couple through various complications towards marriage is perhaps the most common of all patterns in comedy, Cokes's situation is particularly reminiscent of the "morality of youth." In the educational delinquency plays, Wit at the outset is promised the hand of Lady Science or Lady Wisdom provided he can perform the necessary allegorical tasks. Marriage in such plays represents the ultimate goal for the hero, a goal that must be earned by conquering both external and internal

30. Dodsley, III, 349. A little later Cuthbert Cutpurse tells the audience: "Note well the end of me therefore; / And you that fathers and mothers be, / Bring not up your children in too much liberty" (p. 354).

obstacles. So the hero of Redford's *Wit and Science* is told by his bride: "Yf ye vse me well in a good sorte / then shall I be youre Ioy & comfort." [31] Although well-born grace has been substituted for Wisdom or Science, Jonson's figure of youth has been provided with a literal equivalent for the ideal symbolic marriage of the allegorical tradition.

Wasp's elaborate analysis reveals that his young master, who is "now vpon his making and marring," has been taught nothing except "to sing *catches*, and repeat *rattle bladder rattle*, and *O, Madge*" (I.iv.70–76). In addition to Cokes's fondness for "vile tunes, which hee will sing at supper, and in the sermon-times" (ll. 77–78), we are also told about his addiction to what Busy would label "vanity of the eye":

> why, we could not meet that *heathen* thing, all day, but stayd him: he would name you all the *Signes* ouer, as hee went, aloud: and where hee spi'd a *Parrat*, or a *Monkey*, there hee was pitch'd, . . .
>
> (ll. 112–15)

Through such introductory remarks, Wasp is quite effectively performing the function of a Good Counsel or Discipline

31. Ed. Arthur Brown, W. W. Greg, and F. P. Wilson for the Malone Society (Oxford, 1951), ll. 1061–62. Redford's play provides the earliest extant example of what may have been a familiar pattern of action. Here Reason promises the hand of Lady Science to Wit, provided he can overcome Tediousness and make a journey to Mount Parnassus. As Reason points out: "Thende of hys iornay wyll aprove all / yf wyt hold owte no more proofe can fall" (ll. 31–32). The allegorical journey culminating in marriage thereby represents the proper form of education for Wit and for youth in general. See Werner Habicht, "The *Wit*-Interludes and the Form of Pre-Shakespearean 'Romantic Comedy,' " *Ren D*, VIII (1965), 73–88. In a later development of this dramatic pattern, the two contrasting heroes (Lust and Just) of *The Trial of Treasure* (Dodsley, III, 261–301) each find an appropriate female companion (Lady Treasure and Trust) who embodies the particular attitude they have embraced with regard to this world and the next.

figure of the "morality of youth." If one were to destroy Jonson's comic synthesis and restore this speech to the doggerel level of the morality, the result would be as follows. Good Nurture or Good Counsel or Discipline would enter, *solus*, and, directly addressing the audience, would (1) reveal his name and his role (which would be mutually explanatory); (2) describe his charge, including a list of characteristics to identify the particular state of that Youth; and (3) give some idea of what was at stake for Youth in this play. Although Jonson is certainly not writing such a morality play, he is, here as elsewhere, using comparable techniques to achieve many of the same ends, although without violating the literal surface of Jacobean comedy.

Wasp's prefatory remarks deal primarily with Cokes's education and upbringing, which have been neglected by "his foolish scholemasters," a conventional starting point in the "morality of youth." To describe the effects of such neglect, Wasp points to the young man's propensity for picking up "vile tunes" and remembering the words, usually nonsense syllables, of the burden or chorus. Such use of the fondness for song to typify the carefree nature of youth can be seen in the song "In Youth is Pleasure" in *Lusty Juventus*,[32] while the particular emphasis of Wasp's caustic remarks can best be annotated by the opening stage direction for Moros in *The Longer Thou Livest* who is to enter "*synging the foote of many Songes, as fooles were wont.*"[33] Wasp's description of Cokes's "vanity of the eye," moreover, is an accurate appraisal of one of his charge's major failings, a concern for ephemeral and vain objects characteristic of youth. Thus, in the so-called

32. Dodsley, II, 46–47. This song, moreover, is incorporated into the interlude played in *Sir Thomas More*, which is discussed below.

33. In the ensuing scene, the "childishness" that Discipline is trying to get Moros to forsake is embodied in the "Twentie mo songs yet" that the fool wishes to sing (l. 114).

play of *Wit and Wisdom* (really *Lusty Juventus*) played by the visiting troupe in *Sir Thomas More*,[34] Good Counsel (played extempore by More) points out to a stubborn Wit that the latter has chosen not Wisdom, the ideal female figure for whom he is intended, but rather Lady Vanity in disguise. Good Counsel moralizes:

> *Witt*, iudge not things by the outwarde showe,
> the eye oft mistakes, right well you doo knowe.
> Good councell assures thee vppon his honestie,
> that this is not *Wisedome*, but Lady *Vanitie*.
>
> (ll. 1131–34)

When Cokes appears in Act I, scene v, he quickly substantiates Wasp's description. Even though the young man asks to see "the length and the breadth" of the license (I.v.37), he is soon satisfied by looking upon the black box, thereby accepting the outside rather than the meaningful inside in which he had not really been interested. The contents of this particular box symbolize Cokes's prospective marriage to Grace Wellborne, but the young man indicates his lack of understanding of the significance of his betrothal. The references to "seeing," moreover, are so numerous as to imprint the image indelibly upon the audience (ll. 86–89). Both the simple satisfaction and the inherent meaninglessness involved in Cokes's "seeing" have here been clearly established.

Cokes's next desire is to "see" the Fair. Wasp had just remarked that one must give way with regard to such "trifles" as "seeing" the box which represent merely "errors, diseases of youth: which he will mend, when he comes to iudgement, and knowledge of matters" (ll. 43–45). By means of such

34. Ed. W. W. Greg for the Malone Society (1911).

"trifles," "errors," and "diseases of youth," Jonson is providing his equivalent for the traditional theme that "Youth by nature is prone to vice," but significantly the second half of the formula has been omitted. Instead of training and guiding this youth, Wasp can only hope that in the natural course of his life he will "mend" his errors. Such failure on the part of authority results in permission for Cokes to "see" the Fair and the entrusting of the box and its contents to the young man. Jonson has defined for his audience the state of this particular youth, put the responsibility for his fate (represented by his projected marriage) into his own hands, and then sent him forth upon his journey into the Fair, a Jacobean equivalent to Wit's allegorical journey into the world.

The failure of Overdo to help Cokes is soon added to that of Wasp, for throughout the justice's appeal to youth (directed at Edgworth) Cokes is fascinated by the "braue words" (II.vi.23, 25) but oblivious to their meaning. When the young man discovers the theft, he merely puts his second purse in the same place and dares the cutpurse to try again. Cokes, to be sure, is still in possession of the license and still in the company of his original companions, but he has learned nothing from the advice given him or from his own experience. This "prologue o' the purse" (III.ii.1–2) has established this youth's helplessness in a world of cutpurses and left small hope for any further education.

The next bait for Cokes's eyes is "more fine sights" (III.iv.1–2), the wares of Leatherhead and Trash. The significance of the toys and trifles which enthrall this young man can best be glossed by the passage already quoted in which Jonson observed: "*What* petty things they are, wee wonder at? like children, that esteeme every trifle; . . . They are pleas'd with Cockleshels, Whistles, Hobby-horses, and such like." Cokes's purchasing of such "petty things" demonstrates how this youth, lacking the proper guidance or control, is squandering his resources in a misguided attempt to put his childish view of the world into action. His vision of his forthcoming marriage (ll. 156–65), with its toys and gingerbread gloves, resembles a children's party rather than that ideal union with Grace Wellborne, while his motto, "*For the best grace*," underlines the contrast by calling attention to the meaning latent in his fiancée's name. This particular figure of youth is moving farther and farther away from the ideal goal represented by marriage to a symbolic figure. Meanwhile, those "men in authority" who should be helping him get back on the proper path are shown to be ineffectual and, in Wasp's case, weighted down with the goods of the Fair.

At this point Cokes is attracted by Nightingale's song and by the desire to "see" ("let me see, let me see my selfe" III.v.16). He adds: "I would faine see that *Daemon*, your Cutpurse, you talke of, that delicate-handed Diuell; they say he walkes hereabout" (ll. 35–37). The marginal note, "*He show's his purse boastingly*," indicates Cokes's emblematic action for this scene as he continues to flaunt his purse and call for the cutpurse (who is already on stage) to appear (ll. 114–16, 132–34). The subsequent caveat in Nightingale's song, not against ale and tobacco but against cutpurses themselves, only emphasizes Cokes's separation from even the possibility of good counsel (a term he himself invokes in l. 71). The song, which like Overdo's oration is directed at youth, describes the spread of the operations of the cutpurse to more and more areas of society; after presenting a panoramic picture of corruption at almost all possible levels, it reaches its climax in the description of England as "*you vile nation of cutpurses all*." By means of Jonson's indirect statement, the cutpurse, whom Cokes like a simple-minded Faustus considers to be a "*Daemon*" or "delicate-handed

Diuell" who can be "raised" (l. 40), becomes a real and insidious manifestation of that Devil which Busy locates (along with the World and the Flesh) in the Fair. Once more Jonson's dramatic rhetoric allows an obtuse character to act out his own folly yet still convey to the audience more than he himself realizes.

The fate of youth in the world described in Nightingale's song without the benefit of the traditional "grace and good counsayll" (here approximated by Grace and Wasp) is quite clear. While Cokes again turns a serious situation into a child's game ("here's for him; handy-dandy, which hand will he haue?" ll. 116–17), Edgworth easily makes off with both the purse and Grace's handkerchief,[35] with neither Wasp nor Overdo offering any protection. Once the theft is discovered, Cokes vents his righteous indignation on the hapless Overdo, accusing him of enticing forth and debauching his purse (ll. 209–10). Such reproach is not only directed at the wrong agent but grossly misrepresents what we have just seen, for the youth's flaunting of the purse has scarcely kept it "at quiet" in his pocket during this scene. Pointing out the meaninglessness of such "fine *Bartholmew*-termes" (ll. 211–12), Wasp takes back the box and the license, explaining that since Cokes has discovered "the tricke of losing," he can no longer be responsible for anything of value.

> I know you, Sir, come, deliuer, you'll goe and cracke the vermine, you breed now, will you? 'tis very fine, will you ha' the truth on't? they are such retchlesse flies as you are,

35. Grace's handkerchief is Jonson's equivalent for the "token" of the symbolic fiancée carried by the hero of the educational delinquency plays. Thus in Redford's *Wit and Science*, Instruction tells Wit that the latter lacks "wepons of science" which are explained to be "a token from ladye science wherbye / hope of her favor may spryng" (ll. 93, 95–96). The loss of Cokes's "token" can thus symbolize his loss of Grace and all she represents.

that blow cutpurses abroad in euery corner; your foolish hauing of money, makes 'hem.

(ll. 219–23)

The loss of the second purse and Grace's handkerchief has proved, even to Wasp, that his charge is incapable of bearing the responsibility for his own marriage and all it represents. In addition to such a personal failure, moreover, Wasp states that Cokes's "foolish hauing of money" is the real cause of the "vermine" or cutpurses who have been blown "abroad in euery corner" of the kingdom. Cokes's folly and the "diseases" of his youth are not merely personal failings detrimental to his welfare alone but help to create a specific evil that can eventually threaten everyone.[36] That England, as analyzed in Nightingale's ballad, is becoming "*a vile nation of cutpurses all*" is shown to be a result of the representative folly displayed by Cokes along with the failures of "men in authority" who are unable to control or eliminate such folly.

A second representative "estate" is Cokes's sister, Mistress Overdo, whom Wasp aptly describes as "a *Iustice* of *Peace* his wife, and a Gentlewoman o' the hood" (I.iv.83–84). From her first appearance in Act I to the "vapours" scene of Act IV, Mrs. Overdo attempts to play the role of proxy for her husband. Her pretensions to authority are based upon her claims upon her husband's name and her stylized vocabulary, which continually functions as a parody of the Justice's ornate language and rhetoric.[37]

36. Barish, it should be pointed out, does not find such implications in Cokes's folly, rather envisaging it as "incapable of hurting others" and therefore harmless. He concludes that "Jonson is pronouncing a kind of blessing on the idiots of the world, on the gulls and naïfs, and their state of being perpetually deceived" (*Ben Jonson*, p. 222).

37. She tells Wasp, for example, that he should "shew discretion, though he [Cokes] bee exorbitant (as Mr *Ouer-doo* saies,)" and, when rebuked by Wasp, answers: "I am content to be in *abeyance,* Sir" (I.v.12–13, 21).

Mrs. Overdo's position in society is emphasized by continual reference to the outstanding feature of her dress, her French hood. The privilege of wearing such a hood, as both the text of the play and other references make clear, is limited to those who enjoy a particular rank in city society, such as the wife of a mayor or judge;[38] so Wasp refers to Mrs. Overdo as "goody she-*Iustice,* Mistris *French-hood*" (I.v.15). Besides placing her in the social scale by means of emblematic costume, Jonson is also providing (at least until Act IV) an ever-present symbol of the ideal role such a ranking member of society should be playing towards the social disorder and anarchy of the Fair. But Mrs. Overdo is no help to Cokes against the threat of the cutpurse, but rather identifies herself with his "vanity of the eye" (III.v.48) and joins him in his denunciation of the "preaching fellow" whom she describes as "a lewd, and pernicious Enormity: (as Master *Ouerdoo* calls him.)" (ll. 193, 206–7). Rather than helping to restore social order, Mrs. Overdo's pretensions to rank and authority only serve to make her husband appear even more ridiculous while establishing her kinship with her hopelessly foolish brother. Given a society in which justice has ceased to be an effective agency, such a "she-*Iustice*" will be equally inept and the symbol of her station will become meaningless.

A third "estates" figure is Proctor John Littlewit whose

38. See *Tale of a Tub,* IV.v.95; *Alchemist,* V.ii.23; *Devil is an Ass,* I.i.98–99; *Underwoods,* xliii, 69–71. The significance of the French hood is clearly spelled out in Dekker's *Shoemakers' Holiday* (*The Dramatic Works of Thomas Dekker,* ed. Fredson Bowers, 4 vols. [Cambridge, Eng., 1953–61], I, 7–89). In Act III, scene ii, Margery Eyre, about to become Madame Sheriff, asks: "Art thou acquainted with neuer a fardingale-maker, nor a French-hoode maker, . . . how shall I looke in a hoode I wonder?" (ll. 32–34) Simon Eyre then returns with his gold chain and tells his wife: "I shal make thee a Lady, heer's a French hood for thee" (l. 132). The next scene opens with the stage direction: "*Enter* Lord Maior, Eyre, *his* wife *in a French hood.*"

particular brand of folly is established by the opening lines of the play. Upon finding the "*Bartholmew* vpon *Bartholmew*" correspondence between Cokes and St. Bartholomew's Day, he joyously announces: "A Pretty conceit, and worth the finding! I ha' such luck to spinne out these fine things still, and like a Silkeworme, out of my selfe" (I.i.1–3). In a discussion in his *Discoveries* of the workings of the mind in the pursuit of knowledge, Jonson describes the rational soul as "a perpetual Agent, prompt and subtile; but often flexible, and erring; intangling her selfe like a Silke-worme" (ll. 814–16); in her investigations "oft-times new Sents put her by; and shee takes in errors into her, by the same conduits she doth Truths" (ll. 818–20).[39] Littlewit is using the silkworm analogy to describe his ability to spin out seemingly endless series of "conceits" (e.g., ll. 13–19), but Jonson is calling attention to the "sick mind" or "silkworm mentality" behind such outpourings which can lead to entanglement and error.[40]

Littlewit, like Cokes, has a valued possession he will lose in the Fair—his wife Win. Here, outside the Fair, he demonstrates his lack of jealousy and, for that matter, his lack of concern over his wife's safety; as he tells Winwife, "I enuy

39. This connection between the silkworm and the workings of the mind is probably, as Simpson suggests, derived from Montaigne, who argues that the mind "uncessantly goeth turning, winding, building and entangling her selfe in hir owne worke; as doe our silke-wormes, and therein stifleth hir selfe." See H & S, XI, 239; and the Everyman edition of Florio's translation of the *Essays*, III, 325. See also *Staple of News*, I.ii.104–6.

40. For a general analysis of such false wit and its implications see *Discoveries*, ll. 745–59, where Jonson criticizes "such as presuming on their owne *Naturals* (which perhaps are excellent) dare deride all diligence, and seeme to mock at the termes, when they understand not the things." For a helpful discussion of Jonson's position on "wit," see Wesley Trimpi, *Ben Jonson's Poems: A Study of the Plain Style* (Stanford, Calif., 1962), chap. I and *passim*.

no man, my delicates, Sir" (I.ii.13). When Quarlous kisses Win, who cries out for help, her husband reassures her that "they'll do you no harme, *Win,* they are both our worshipfull good friends" and even urges her to "know" Quarlous, not quarrel with him (I.iii.46–48). Littlewit is assuming a certain standard of behavior from such "an honest Gentleman" (l. 42) and therefore has no fears for his wife's safety, but his unintentional sexual pun on the word "know" suggests the type of danger to which Win will later be exposed because of her husband's blindness.

Littlewit's obsession with "wit" and "conceits" is displayed in the next two scenes. Such behavior (e.g., the assertion of priority of wit in I.v.68–70) elicits ironic warnings from Winwife and Quarlous who point out that such wit "will doe you no good i' the end," "will bring you to some obscure place in time, and there 'twill leaue you," and will turn out to be "a dangerous thing, in this age" (ll. 71–79). Despite the irony and condescension in these speeches, such advice is quite relevant to the problems Littlewit must face in the world of the Fair. As with Overdo's oration or Busy's tirade, valuable admonitions are here for the listener able to hear or see.

By virtue of his wit, Littlewit succeeds in setting up a visit to the Fair. Once there, he instructs Win to "long to see, as well as to taste" (III.vi.13–14), thereby advocating the "vanity of the eye" which has led to Cokes's undoing. Busy, however, resists such a suggestion, urging instead that Win "fly the impurity of the place, swiftly, lest shee partake of the pitch thereof" (ll. 43–44). With his plans temporarily foiled by Busy (whose advice is deemed only needless restriction), Littlewit bribes Leatherhead to eliminate this man of religion. From his point of view, his wit is once again successful, for the officers soon drag away the zealous Busy, leaving the proctor to exult: "Was not this shilling well ventur'd, *Win?*

for our liberty? Now we may goe play, and see ouer the *Fayre*, where we list our selues" (ll. 114–16). Littlewit here sees the Fair as a children's paradise in which he and his equally foolish wife can "goe play" and "see" all the sights.[41] Their liberty to go "where we list our selues," gained by escaping from an authority figure who offered at least some protection and guidance, does not prove to be such a valuable acquisition. Throughout his work Jonson stressed the distinction between true "liberty" and license.[42] Here he is testing such "liberty" by letting loose in the Fair, Littlewit, with his "silkworm mentality" and his blindness to danger, and Win, with her various desires both feigned and real.

The last of the representative "estates" is Dame Purecraft. Early in the play we are told that this widow "has had her natiuity-water cast lately" and has been told that "shee shall neuer haue happy houre; vnlesse shee marry within this sen'night" to "a Gentle-man Mad-man" (I.ii.46–51). Win, on the other hand, points out that her mother-in-law "will neuer consent to such a *prophane motion*" as a visit to the Fair because she is "a most elect *Hypocrite*, and has maintain'd us all this seuen yeere with it, like Gentlefolkes" (I.v.149–50, 163–65). Here is a shrewd yet basically superstitious widow who has used her religious professions as a

41. Littlewit's vision of the Fair here is quite similar to that provided by many of the critics quoted above. Subsequent events, however, especially the fate of Win in Acts IV and V, make clear the dangers of such attitudes in the world of the Fair.

42. Catiline, for example, in his description of the "libertie" and "freedom" in store for the conspirators, promises them that the world will be "a field, to exercise your longings in" (I.410, 421, 480). The true "libertie" referred to in the closing line of "Inviting a Friend to Supper" (*Epigrams*, ci) can be contrasted to the "licence" practiced by the irresponsible nobles in "A Speech according to Horace," l. 70. The contrast between the terms is made quite explicitly in *Time Vindicated* (H & S, VII, 651–73), where Fame points out: "There's difference 'twixt liberty, and licence" (l. 216). See also ll. 79–80.

source of income with great success but is still dependent upon outside authority, whether in the form of spiritual advice or "natiuity-water" prophecy, for guidance.

In her first appearance, Dame Purecraft tries to combat Win's pregnant longing for pig with a stern lecture on the "foule temptations" of "the wicked Tempter" with his "carnall prouocations" and his appeal to "flesh and blood" (I.vi.14–19). Although the daughter's desires are feigned, Win in Act IV will be subjected to just such provocations by the tempters of the Fair, in her case Knockem and Whit. Because she fears a miscarriage, Dame Purecraft asks Busy "to make it as lawfull as you can" (ll. 60–61), in effect bullying him into acquiescence. Her "discipline" or "scruples" are from the outset subject to her will and desires, not to some absolute standard.

In the course of her journey through the Fair, Dame Purecraft (like Mrs. Overdo) attempts to play the role of an authority by proxy for her daughter and son-in-law. She reminds Littlewit of Busy's "wholesome admonition" about "the vanity of the eye" (III.ii.73–74) and decides that her daughter may look on the "fine sights" of the Fair so long as "you hate 'hem, as our Brother *Zeale* do's" (III.vi.63–65). By the end of Act III, this widow has twice been deceived by her daughter's feigned desires and has seen her chosen figure of authority dragged away to the stocks. Jonson has let loose in the Fair one more character in need of authority who can exhibit the effects of the failures of Wasp, Busy, and Overdo.

The "Quality"

A third group of outsiders who visit the Fair—Winwife, Quarlous, and Grace—have yet to be considered. Winwife, whose rank in society makes him an attractive suitor for

Dame Purecraft (I.ii.26–27), is characterized by a refined sensibility and concern for propriety; thus he can ask Quarlous to stop kissing Win "for my respect" (I.iii.56). Quarlous, another of Jonson's pragmatic gamesters (whom Littlewit describes as "an honest Gentleman"), is less concerned with such niceties. After complaining how "respectiue" (l. 57) his friend has become, he tries to persuade Winwife to "leaue thy exercise of widdow-hunting" (ll. 62–63); so he points out that even if Winwife succeeds there will be little profit because Dame Purecraft will "ha' conuey'd her state, safe enough from thee, an' she be a right widdow" (ll. 102–3). In Winwife, Jonson is portraying a man of rank and sensibility looking for a profitable marriage who may not be shrewd enough to gain what he wants on his own terms. Quarlous, on the other hand (who does eventually win the rich widow), is a gamester who, like Surly, exhibits a firm grasp of the real nature of the world around him.

Throughout the early scenes, Winwife and Quarlous act as choric commentators who for the most part stand aloof from the other characters and call attention to the different types of folly. Their place in the social hierarchy is recognized and appreciated; they are continually addressed as "gentlemen," and their judgments and opinions carry a good deal of weight. To such gentlemen, Cokes is obviously an ass, but Grace is "discreete," "sober," and "handsome." They admire the "restrain'd scorne she casts vpon all his [Cokes's] behauiour, and speeches" (I.v.55–58), castigate Cokes for his failure to understand what Grace means by "quality" and "fashion" (ll. 131–37), and decide to follow this group to the Fair as a source of "excellent creeping sport" (l. 141).

From the outset Grace Wellborne is associated with those social virtues and "manners" alien to Cokes. Her comments link her to Winwife in a common concern for "quality" or "respect" (the "wellborne" emphasis) and a common distaste for the Fair and its social anarchy. In going to the Fair, Winwife and Quarlous assume that, as men of "manners," they will retain their aloof position. When they are accosted by the various venders, Winwife asks in astonishment: "doe wee looke as if wee would buy Ginger-bread? or Hobby-horses?" (II.v.14–15). Quarlous, who is more realistic about his relationship to the Fair, points out that "our very being here makes vs fit to be demanded, as well as others" (ll. 17–18). Their inability to remain aloof is emphasized once more when they are recognized by Knockem ("who's yonder! *Ned Winwife?* and *Tom Quarlous*" ll. 20–21), who asks them to join him. To Winwife's sensibility, such an invitation represents "an inconuenience" (l. 29), so that Knockem is informed that "we knew not of so much familiarity betweene vs afore" (ll. 35–36). In this world of "Punque" and "Pigge" (l. 41), however, such attempts to uphold social propriety only lead to an argument. Similarly, the gentlemen's attempts to continue the witty commentary they had indulged in outside the Fair bring on rejoinders from Ursula who, with her "*Bartholmew*-wit," showers them with a torrent of abuse. Although Winwife and Quarlous do escape intact from the ensuing skirmish, Jonson has shown us that their pretensions to "quality" with its distance from such crudity and vulgarity are quite out of place here. The only way to remain unsoiled by contact with the Fair (to avoid, as Busy would put it, "the impurity of the place") is to adopt the policy advocated by Grace (or practiced by Lady Aubigny) and not go at all.

In their next appearance the two gentlemen once again fail to remain aloof. Quarlous observes that they have missed Cokes's "prologue o' the purse" but still have "fiue *Acts* of him ere night" (III.ii.1–3); to him the folly of the outsiders and the vulgarity of the Fair are only convenient spectacles established for their "sport." But such detachment is immediately challenged by "Captain" Whit who addresses them as "Duke *Quarlous*" or "Prinsh *Quarlous*" and "vorshipfull *Vinvife*" (ll. 4, 12, 18) and offers to "help tee to a vife vorth forty marks" (ll. 7–8). Although Quarlous berates Whit for being a rogue and a pimp, Winwife hands over twelvepence to get rid of him, an action which elicits the comment "Tou art a vorthy man, and a vorshipfull man still" (l. 16) and pointers on how to find ale or "punque" or both. Like Edgworth,[43] Whit knows his "trade" well and has successfully played upon Winwife's sensibilities in order to extort money from him. Like Knockem, Whit assumes that the "quality" of these gentlemen is merely a surface that covers "flesh and blood" desires for the satisfactions offered by the Fair (ale, pig, prostitutes). His deliberately exaggerated recognition of such "quality" (Duke, Prince, worshipful Winwife) demonstrates the lip service gladly (and irreverently) paid by the forces of the Fair in their quest for profit.

Jonson now develops an important distinction between these two men of "quality." After Busy leads his flock to their feast, Quarlous comments: "Now were a fine time for thee, *Win-wife,* to lay aboard thy widdow," because "shee that will venture her selfe into the *Fayre,* and a pig-boxe, will admit any assault" (ll. 132–36). When Winwife hesitates, Quarlous adds: "But you are a modest vndertaker, by circumstances, and degrees; come, 'tis Disease in thee, not Iudgement, I should offer at all together" (ll. 143–45). The opportunistic Quarlous, whose favorite imagery is from hunt-

43. The cutpurse had earlier classified Winwife and Quarlous as "too fine to carry money" (II.v.176–77) and had therefore not attempted to rob them.

ing or piracy, sees life as a hardheaded pursuit of profitable, realizable goals. In contrast, Winwife tells us that he has no liking for "enterprises of that suddennesse" (l. 137) but would rather observe the proprieties and act "by circumstances, and degrees." If the Fair is to be the arena and success is to be the yardstick, Winwife's approach does represent a "Disease" or failing, not a "Iudgement" or considered course of action. Quarlous' opportunism and Winwife's propriety are orchestrated here so that the audience, on the basis of the subsequent action, can evaluate the merits (and implications) of each attitude.

With the reappearance of Cokes's group, the two gentlemen decide to "goe enter our selues in *Grace*" (III.iv.75). While Cokes, Overdo, Wasp, and Mrs. Overdo (the "mess" of fools) are entranced by the ballad, the two gentlemen act as a chorus for Grace's benefit, first castigating Cokes, then observing with relish the activities of Edgworth and Nightingale. Rather than expressing dismay at Edgworth's successful crime, Winwife exclaims: "God hee is a braue fellow; pitty hee should be detected" (III.v.157). Although the two gentlemen have casually observed what Cokes and his protectors have missed, they see no particular significance in the young man's loss but rather applaud the dexterity of the cutpurse. Their discussion of the theft, which they regard as "sport" (l. 147), coincides with the final stanza of the ballad in which England is described as a "*vile nation of cutpurses all.*" This disturbing suggestion of universal villainy is thereby juxtaposed with the failure of those of rank and social obligation (significantly the only perceptive individuals on stage) to exert any moral authority over the chaotic world of the Fair, even when such control is within their power. As in the poems cited earlier, the lack of good example and true "manners" among the "quality" is an important factor in the corruption of society. Overdo's reference to "*O Tempora! O mores!*" here becomes relevant and meaningful, for, as with Catiline's conspiracy, obvious crimes go unpunished when those in positions of eminence fail to uphold moral standards.

With the departure of Cokes, Wasp, and Mrs. Overdo, the opportunistic Quarlous accosts Edgworth and commissions him to steal the black box from Wasp. When the cutpurse volunteers to bring back the license and leave the box, Winwife is delighted, for " 'twill make the more sport when 'tis mist" (l. 256). Once more theft is seen as "sport" when characters ignore the larger implications of their actions. Grace now reveals that Overdo has purchased her wardship, so that she must marry Cokes or pay Overdo the value of her land.[44] Rather than earning or developing by degrees such "wellborne" grace or "manners," Cokes and those responsible for him expect to purchase such marks of "quality."[45] But Grace, who is self-sufficient because she is "secure of mine owne manners" (ll. 298–99) is now separated from and, in effect, totally lost to Cokes and his group.

44. Commenting upon the abuses of such sales of wardships, H. E. Bell points out: "Only by paying [his guardian] a heavy fine could the ward compound for his marriage and obtain freedom of choice as to whom he would marry, failure to compound resulting in a stay of his livery and right to enter upon his lands. . . . Even at the recognized rates, fines to compound were severe, being assessed . . . for females at three years' [value] for lands in possession and two years' or one and a half, for lands in revision. Remembering the other expenses that the heir had to meet in connexion with suing out of his livery, a fine of this magnitude must have acted as a substantial discouragement from marrying otherwise than as the committee elected." *An Introduction to the History and Records of the Court of Wards and Liveries* (Cambridge, Eng., 1953), pp. 125–26.

45. In his "Epistle to Dorset" quoted above Jonson argues that it is "by degrees that men arrive at glad / Profit in ought," not only "in money, but in manners too." For an interpretation of the theological implications in the buying and selling of "Grace," see Cope, "*Bartholomew Fair,*" esp. p. 137.

Authority in the Stocks

By the end of Act III, the original groups of outsiders to the Fair have begun to disintegrate.[46] Cokes, who has left Grace behind, has also been separated from Wasp and Mrs. Overdo; the Littlewits, who are looking for a "*Iordan*" at Ursula's, have been separated from Busy and Dame Purecraft; while Quarlous and Winwife are showing signs of contention over Grace. Act IV can now dramatize the individual fates of the figures directly faced with the threat of the Fair and sum up the causes of such a situation in one central dramatic image, authority in the stocks.

To focus our attention on the consequences of the failure of authority, Jonson introduces a new character, the madman Trouble-All, with his insistent question: "I do only hope you haue warrant, for what you doe" (IV.i.14–15). Trouble-All's function in the play has been ably analyzed by Ray L. Heffner, Jr., who envisages this madman's "absurd humor" as "the ultimate extreme, the fantastic caricature of the widespread and not unnatural human craving for clearly defined authority." Trouble-All, who "is obsessed with the necessity of documentary sanction for even the slightest action," forces the various characters (and, one might add, the audience) into "a new scrutiny of what warrant they really have and what they pretend to have for their beliefs and their deeds." [47]

46. For a helpful analysis of the composition, disintegration, and interrelationships of these groups, see Richard Levin, "The Structure of *Bartholomew Fair*," *PMLA*, LXXX (1965), 172–79.

47. "Unifying Symbols in the Comedy of Ben Jonson," in *English Stage Comedy*, ed. W. K. Wimsatt, Jr., English Institute Essays, 1954 (New York, 1955), pp. 90–91. See Cope, "*Bartholomew Fair*," pp. 140 ff. for a treatment of Trouble-All as "the omnipresent destiny" of the play.

The madman, who considers Justice Overdo's warrant to be "the warrant of warrants" (IV.i.20), makes his first appearance while the officers are putting Overdo in the stocks. The Justice has assumed once more his Stoic pose. "The world," he points out, will now see "how I can beare aduersity" and how "I carry my calamity nobly," for "in the mid'st of this tumult" he plans to achieve "a *Triumph*" by sitting calmly in the stocks (ll. 29–33, 43–46). Such Stoic resignation is of dubious value for the reforming justice or "Cicero reincarnate" that Overdo has sought to be. His Stoic equanimity, moreover, soon receives a series of shocks. First he hears the truth about Trouble-All, who had formerly been an officer of his court but went mad upon being dismissed. Next he is exposed to an evaluation of himself by the Watch for whom "warrant" or authority "is contained entirely in the unpredictable personality of the judge whom they serve," for "if there is ethics behind the law, they do not comprehend it."[48] The meaninglessness of such a "warrant" is, of course, further emphasized by the presence of the source of that authority in the stocks.

The stocks, moreover, are not merely a means to expose Overdo's pretensions. Rather, as in Kent's similar discomfiture in *King Lear,* the placing of a representative figure in the stocks is an important piece of Elizabethan symbolic stage business which has its roots in the morality tradition. In his discussion of "the temporary fettering, sometimes in the stocks, of a virtue by the vices," T. W. Craik offers examples from *Youth, Hickscorner,* and Lindsay's *Ane Satyre of the Thrie Estaits.* In *Youth,* as he points out, the imprisonment of the virtue "is wholly symbolic of Charity's powerlessness in a mind where Riot holds sway."[49] In Lindsay's play, the

48. Heffner, "Unifying Symbols," p. 92.

49. *The Tudor Interlude: Stage, Costume, and Acting* (Leicester, Eng., 1958), pp. 93–94.

symbolic imprisonment is extended to both Veritie and Chastitie in order to act out the effect of the vices upon Rex Humanitas. The implications of this device can be pursued even further. In *Hickscorner,* for example, Pity, having been bound and perhaps stocked by Freewill, Imagination, and Hickscorner, offers a long lament upon the evil conditions in contemporary society. He tells us that "virtue is vanished for ever and aye" and points out how lechery is masquerading as love and murder as manhood while "God's commandments we break them all ten." The theme of his discourse, repeated four times, is "worse was it never." [50] Similarly, Charity in *Youth* laments not his own fate but rather the fate of youth in general when "vice is taken, and virtue set aside." [51] In *Ane Satyre,* Veritie spells out the significance of her fate:

> The Prophesie of the Propheit Esay
> Is practickit alace, on mee this day:
> Quha said the veritie sould be trampit doun
> Amid the streit, and put in strang presoun.[52]
>
> (ll. 1176–79)

The implications of Veritie's fate are further developed through the fortunes of Chastitie, who is rejected by all three estates and ordered to the stocks by Sensualitie. In all three instances, the fettering or placing in the stocks of figures of virtue provides a meaningful dramatic symbol for the general state of affairs in the world of the play—the failure of authority or absolute standards and the rise of moral anarchy.

In Act IV of *Bartholomew Fair* the audience is presented with the same image of authority in the stocks while vice runs

50. Dodsley, I, 174–75.
51. Dodsley, II, 28.
52. *The Works of Sir David Lindsay of the Mount,* ed. Douglas Hamer (Edinburgh and London, 1931), II, 131.

rampant. In this particular scene Overdo does not remain in the stocks very long; both he and Busy, ironically, are taken away in custody "to *Iustice Ouerdoo*" who will "doe ouer 'hem as is fitting" (ll. 98–99). With two of the men in authority in custody, Jonson begins to demonstrate the effects of their failure upon the representative "estates." First Cokes, now "without his Protector" (IV.ii.16), is met by the "sport" (l. 21) prepared for him by Edgworth and Nightingale. In the previous scene, this young man had gone off to "looke for my goods, and *Numps*" (l. 40), but, as the audience knows, Leatherhead and Trash have decided to disappear (III.vi. 135–39), thereby emphasizing the transience of the "goods" with which Cokes is concerned. Here, even though the young man has lost his way, the tune whistled by Nightingale, like the ballad of Act III, scene v, or the "vile tunes," can still drive all else from his mind. His choice of the tune over answers to his various questions (ll. 29–30) is followed by a similar decision to scramble for pears while giving up his hat, cloak and sword. Once more Cokes turns the "wares" of the costardmonger into a "muss" or children's game (as in the "handy-dandy" of Act III, scene v) only to lose his emblems of manhood and rank in society.

This stripping of Cokes by Edgworth and Nightingale is Jonson's Jacobean equivalent for the degradation of Youth, an integral part of the "morality of youth." During his allegorical journey to his betrothed, the Wit figure of the educational delinquency plays was inevitably stripped by his enemies of the clothing with which he had started, a simple yet effective way of visually conveying the disparity between his present and original state.[53] Similarly, Cokes has been

53. Thus in Redford's *Wit and Science* the hero is stripped by Idleness and thereby "cuniurd from wyt vnto a starke foole" (l. 614). In *The Marriage of Wit and Wisdom*, Wit is sung to sleep by Wan-

separated from his fiancée and guardian, has lost his way in the Fair, and now, as made clear by his visible reduction in costume, has fallen easy prey to his enemies. Edgworth's scathing remarks call attention to Cokes's symbolic degradation, especially the description of the young man's soul as if it were no more than a preservative for his body (ll. 54–58). Cokes, we are told, has gathered up pears "in exchange, for his beauer-hat, and his cloake" (l. 63), once more trading the valuable for the ephemeral. After the loss of two purses and his clothing, Cokes finally realizes that there is nothing "but thieuing, and cooz'ning, i' this whole *Fayre*" (l. 70). Separated from all the available figures of authority, the young man can turn for help only to the madman Trouble-All, an appeal which conveys Jonson's final comment on the futility of Cokes's position in the world of the Fair. Instead of providing a figure such as Instruction or Discipline as Redford might have done, Jonson offers one last dramatic image to sum up the isolation of Cokes and the absence of any authority to remedy such a situation.

Between the degradation of Cokes and the anarchy of the "vapours" scene, Jonson presents in Act IV, scene iii, the one potential source of reason and order in the Fair. The opening stage business quickly establishes the difference between conduct supervised by Grace and the general behavior encouraged by the Fair. Although Winwife and Quarlous "*enter with their swords drawne*" (IV.iii.s.d.), Grace stops them,

---

tonness, who then blackens his face and sets a fool's bauble on his head while Idleness steals away with his purse. Later moralities use a similar device. In *Like Will to Like*, Ralph Roister and Tom Tosspot, who have lost everything through gambling and drinking, make their final entrance "*in their doublet and their hose, and no cap nor hat on their head, saving a nightcap*" (Dodsley, III, 346). Similarly, Simplicity in Wilson's *Three Ladies* is stripped and beaten by the beadle while the vices prosper.

pointing out that they "do but breed one another trouble, and offence, and giue me no contentment at all" because "I am no she, that affects to be quarell'd for, or haue my name or fortune made the question of mens swords" (ll. 1–5). After providing reasonable arguments against such open conflict, Grace states that the two gentlemen "are both equall, and alike to mee, yet" (l. 33); therefore, at this point, she refuses to choose either: "For you are reasonable creatures, you haue vnderstanding, and discourse. And if fate send me an vnderstanding husband, I haue no feare at all, but mine owne manners shall make him a good one" (ll. 35–38).

In keeping with the "wellborne" grace with which she is nominally associated, this character (like Celia) is a walking symbol of desirable qualities. In contrast to Ursula, who berated Mooncalf for stopping a fight in her booth (II.v.59–64), Grace exercises a reasonable restraint over contention that can only be damaging to all concerned. In place of the hotheaded approach of the two gentlemen (and, for that matter, of most of the characters in the play), she provides a logical and accurate appraisal of the present situation and then moves towards some form of resolution. Her fundamental faith in her own "manners" (established in III.v.298–99 and amplified here) is the key to her role, for, as she points out, the influence of such "manners" upon a man capable of reason and understanding must produce a good husband or a valuable member of society. Given such a criterion, Cokes's behavior in the previous scene has certainly disqualified him from eligibility for any such "grace" or "manners." The arrival of Trouble-All to act as the arbiter of the names chosen by the gentlemen provides a further comment upon the limitations of Grace's influence, for in this chaotic world with its inevitable contamination and "impurity" even the most rationally constructed plan is brought to a conclusion by a madman.

Grace's rule of reason quickly gives way to the much-discussed "vapours" scene.[54] The exact stage business here is difficult to ascertain from the text, but clearly Nordern and Puppy drink themselves into oblivion while the others partake freely.[55] Given, in addition, Overdo's earlier tirade against ale *and* tobacco and given the constant reference to "vapours," it is also likely that Jonson intended to have the characters on stage smoking and, in fact, producing a good deal of such "vapours." Such profusion, in Overdo's terms, of "the fome of the one, and the fumes of the other" (II.vi.1–2) provides a key to both the significance of the "game" and the behavior of the outsiders to the Fair.

Overdo, it should be remembered, had pointed to the role played by tobacco and ale in the "diseases of the body" but had emphasized the "mallady it doth the minde" as manifested in swearing, swaggering, and "the quarrelling lesson." Similarly Busy, within his frame of reference, had identified ale as "a drinke of Sathan's" which was "deuised to puffe vs vp, and make vs swell in this latter age of vanity, as the smoake of tabacco, to keepe vs in mist and error" (III.vi. 30–33). Such a "mallady" and such "mist and error" are here embodied in "*their game of* vapours, *which is* non sense. *Euery man to oppose the last man that spoke: whether it concern'd him, or no*" (IV.iv.27s.d.). Such a "game" reduces human "vnderstanding, and discourse," which Grace had just

54. Most critics have discussed the "vapours" in terms of the Jonsonian theory of "humours." See, for example, Enck, *Jonson and the Comic Truth*, p. 190; Barish, *Ben Jonson*, pp. 216–19. For an argument that such "vapours" represent the controlling theme for the entire action, see James E. Robinson, "*Bartholomew Fair:* Comedy of Vapors," *SEL*, I (1961), 65–80. See also Cope, "*Bartholomew Fair*," pp. 142–46 for a treatment of vapors as "the clouds of discord which rise from the passions of the pig booth hell" (p. 146).

55. The stage direction, "*They drinke againe*" (IV.iv.75.s.d.), suggests that the entire assemblage was drinking periodic rounds, an action that would explain Nordern's iterated protestation, "I'le ne mare" (ll. 3, 13, 82).

termed the requisites for "reasonable creatures," to "non sense," thereby revealing the truth in the strictures of Overdo and Busy against ale and tobacco.

As the opening line in the scene makes clear, moreover, the "game" is staged by Knockem, Whit, and Val Cutting for the express purpose of fleecing Nordern, Puppy, and especially Wasp.[56] The statements of this erstwhile protector of youth indicate how, under the catalytic effects of ale and tobacco, his perversity has been metamorphosed into sheer meaninglessness and intellectual anarchy. So, once the Fair people start the game, Wasp objects "to any thing, whatsoeuer it is, so long as I do not like it" (ll. 31–32). When Knockem and Whit raise the issue of Wasp's "reason," he replies: "I haue no reason, nor I will heare of no reason, nor I will looke for no reason, and he is an Asse, that either knowes any, or lookes for't from me" (ll. 42–44). This "angry man" (l. 48) is here using "reason" primarily in the sense of "cause" or "motive," but, given Grace's definition of "reasonable creatures," he is also demonstrating the failure of his own rational faculty. His subsequent comments further demonstrate this failure, for the Fair people easily get him to contradict himself again and again until he states: "I am not i' the right, nor neuer was i' the right, nor neuer will be i' the right, while I am in my right minde" (ll. 72–74). The "mallady" done to the mind by the Fair's ale and tobacco is here exhibited in the drunken and perverse denial by one of the potential sources of authority of both his own "reason" and his ability to discover truth or "the right."[57]

56. Knockem instructs Whit to tell Val Cutting to "continue the vapours for a lift" or, in other words, to keep the game going as a trick or ruse to cover some other purpose.

57. The amusing yet relevant strictures against the dangers of ale and tobacco provided by Busy and Overdo are characteristic of Jonson's method of indirect statement, which provides the audience with sig-

Knockem consequently has no trouble goading this "angry man" into "a noysome vapour" which provides a pretext for Whit to start a fight. Edgworth can then easily steal the license from the black box, thereby removing what earlier had been described as "his Patent (it seemes) hee has of his place" (IV.ii.64–65) or, in other words, the symbol of Wasp's authority over Cokes. Meanwhile, Quarlous, who again has sought to be an aloof observer, is once more drawn into the world of the Fair against his will. His laughter at the mad scramble, which to him is only his "christian liberty" (l. 122), is resented by Wasp, whose objection produces a second altercation and a second opportunity for Whit and Knockem to "gather vp" (l. 147) anything that is not nailed down. Despite his shrewdness, Quarlous has not seen the

---

nificant admonitions through misguided or foolish characters. See, for example, the discussion in earlier chapters of Voltore's rhetorical question or the *homo frugi* ideal. Jonson, as a result, is not satirizing King James's position on the use of tobacco (a point which has bothered some critics, e.g., Barish, *Ben Jonson*, pp. 319–20), but rather is demonstrating the truth in such strictures. With regard to the abuses of drinking, Jonson elsewhere refers to those false friends who "live in the wild Anarchie of Drinke, / Subject to quarrell only" (*Underwoods*, xlvii, 10–11). See also *Epigrams*, cxv, 12. Our author, who himself was notorious for his drinking habits, is arguing against that state of drunkenness in which meaning and order disappear and are replaced by thoughtless discourse and a propensity to quarrel. The proper approach to drink is aptly summed up in "Inviting a Friend to Supper," in which the host promises to "sup free, but moderately" of the Canary wine (*Epigrams*, ci, 35):

Nor shall our cups make any guiltie men:
  But, at our parting, we will be, as when
We innocently met. No simple word,
  That shall be vtter'd at our mirthfull boord,
Shall make vs sad next morning: or affright
  The libertie, that wee'll enioy to night.

(ll. 37–42)

Such "libertie," not "wild Anarchie," is thus the proper end of drinking.

purpose behind the "vapours" game. Once more he has demonstrated that, separated from Grace and immersed in the Fair, he is unable to remain aloof and unsoiled but instead can be brought down to the level of Knockem, Whit, or Val Cutting.

Although Quarlous manages to escape intact from another bout with the Fair, Wasp's perversity, which is soon directed indiscriminately at the Watch, leads only to his being carried off "to the pigeon-holes" (l. 179). The only outsider left behind is Mrs. Overdo, who throughout this scene has been speaking out "in termes of Iustice, and the Stile of authority, with her hood vpright" (IV.iii.121–22). Although the "termes" and the "Stile" have been those of her husband (e.g., ll. 116–19), the "gentlemen" she has been addressing pay no attention to such verbal claims to "authority." Overdo, as the audience knows, is at this point in the custody of his own officers, a situation which further undermines his wife's ineffectual use of his "name." Mrs. Overdo's various threats on the basis of her "woman-hood" and her "Iustice-hood" (ll. 149–51) show how both visually and verbally her "hood" is becoming as meaningless as Wasp's "reason," especially when confronted with the real forces of the Fair. Left alone with Whit, moreover, she whispers, since she "cannot with modesty speake it out" (l. 200), that she, like Win, is in need of a "*Iordan.*" Her "modesty" is immediately countered by the crudeness of Ursula (ll. 211–15) and the sexuality of Knockem (ll. 222–23, 230–31). Both Knockem's vision of Mrs. Overdo as a "Filly" to be "covered" and the disclosure of a "flesh and blood" need to urinate have brought to light those basic needs and desires which, when manipulated by the forces of the Fair, can make a mockery of empty pretensions to authority or station or modesty.

Littlewit now reappears, announcing his intention to leave his wife "i' this good company" so that he can check up on his puppet play (IV.v.3). When Win asks: "Will you leaue me alone with two men, *Iohn?*" her husband replies: "I, they are honest Gentlemen, *Win*, Captaine *Iordan*, and Captaine *Whit*, they'll vse you very ciuilly, *Win*" (ll. 7–9). Just as Mrs. Overdo had envisaged the "vapourers" as "gentlemen" and "Sonnes of the sword" (IV.iv.116, 148, 228), so another outsider to the Fair foolishly identifies the two supposed "Captaines" as "honest Gentlemen" who will "vse" his wife "very ciuilly" in his absence. The unintentional sexual pun on "vse," moreover, recalls the similar use of "know" in reference to two other "gentlemen," Winwife and Quarlous. Outside the Fair the restraining influence of Winwife and the presence of the husband had offset any danger to Win, but here the mistaken evaluation of "quality" in a wholly different context shows Littlewit foolishly choosing the cherished product of his "wit," the puppet play, over the safety of his wife.

With the husband out of the way, Ursula urges the two "Captaines" on Win because the concession is short on "Bird o' the game" (IV.v.18). The subsequent seduction scene is highly reminiscent of corresponding temptation scenes in the morality tradition. First the two tempters contrast the "dull honest womans life" (equated with "de leefe of a Bondwoman") with the life of "a free-woman, and a Lady" which they can offer her (ll. 27–28, 32–34). Such "freedom" from the "bondage" of marriage underlines the real nature of that "liberty" which Littlewit had purchased by having Busy arrested. To satisfy any remaining scruples, Win is assured that she can "be honest too sometimes" yet still have her fine clothing, her coach, and her opportunity to associate with the players and gallants, even "lye by twenty on 'hem, if dou pleash" (ll. 36–42). To such a vision Win responds: "What, and be honest still, that were fine sport" (l. 44), using "sport" (as do Quarlous and Winwife) as a euphemism to cloak the abuse of a moral or civil law. The seducers strengthen their case by arguing on the basis of common practice, for "it is the vapour of spirit in the wife, to cuckold, now adaies; as it is the vapour of fashion, in the husband, not to suspect" (ll. 50–51). When Win exhibits signs of acquiescence ("Lord, what a foole haue I beene" l. 53), they hastily conclude that she should "doe euery ting like a Lady" or, in other words, "know any man" (ll. 54–57). The current "fashion" among "Ladies" has been used to justify universal sexual license, here embodied in the same verb which Littlewit himself had unwittingly used.[58]

Through this seduction scene, Jonson has demonstrated how such terms as "honesty," "fashion," and "liberty," which appear to have fixed meanings, have in reality become mere pawns that the two "Captaines" (or the Fair people in general) can manipulate for their own purposes.[59] To trap a

58. Such arguments are referred to by Jonson in other anatomies of his society. In *The Devil is an Ass*, he provides an elaborate analysis of the current "*Lady* of spirit, or a woman of fashion" (including Fitzdottrel's comment: "It is ciuility to deny vs nothing"), to which Pug, the hapless devil, offers the epigraph: "why, *Hell* is / A Grammar-schoole to this!" (IV.iv.156, 169–71) In his "Epistle to a Friend" discussed above (pp. 142–43) Jonson again anatomizes the "woman of fashion" and "Lady of spirit" whose adulteries have now "growne Commoditie upon Exchange" (ll. 82, 86). With regard to the subsequent decay of morals and "manners" he points out:

> The Husband now's call'd churlish, or a poore
> Nature, that will not let his Wife be a whore;
> Or use all arts, or haunt all Companies
> That may corrupt her, even in his eyes.
>
> (ll. 89–92)

The success of Knockem's similar argument is one indication that the "hell on earth" described in the poem is relevant to the play.

59. The general corruption of language under the influence of the Fair offers an interesting parallel to the failure of authority and absolute standards in the play. In addition to such degradation of "honesty" and "fashion," the audience is also made aware of the reduction

foolish outsider like Win, who continues to attach the same absolute meaning to such terms, the tempters need only cloak their real purpose behind an apparently acceptable standard (living "the life of a Lady"). The general lack of any absolute standard or authority in this world has resulted in a decay in "manners," morals, and language which can be used by Whit and Knockem as a justification for any kind of license or "liberty." Although Busy, from whom Win has been symbolically separated, has been shown to be a hypocrite and a glutton, even a partial fulfillment of his role of man of religion (such as his advice to "fly the impurity of the place") could counter such arguments. Similarly, Grace, the true symbol of "quality" and "manners," provides a standard by which the audience can evaluate the false notions of "fashion," "spirit," and "lady" implicitly accepted by Win and Mrs. Overdo. Both of these women, drawn into this situation by their lowest bodily needs, are acting out the ultimate effects of the failure of authority and the decay of absolute standards in the Fair.[60]

To heighten the implications of this seduction scene, Jonson announces that Alice, "your *Punque* of Turnbull," has

---

of "warrant" to the level of a verb meaning "assure" (V.i.20, 23; V.iv.6, 12) and the use of "quality" (a word used indiscriminately throughout the play) to describe Leatherhead's profession as puppeteer (V.v.33). Mrs. Overdo's "hood," moreover, becomes a suffix ("womanhood," "justice-hood") which, like her French hood, is essentially meaningless. While "vapours" becomes a ubiquitous term to signify almost anything, such apparently fixed terms as "Lady" or "conscience" lose their absolute meaning (see, for example, IV.vi.176; V.ii.123). The technique already seen in Ananias' quibbles (e.g., "coining" vs. "casting") has here been expanded to fit the scope of this play.

60. The contrast between Grace and Win is enhanced by parallel stage groupings, for both of these young women in their respective major scenes (IV.iii; IV.v.) are alone on stage with two men who contend for them. Grace, of course, controls her situation, while Win is easily controlled by Whit and Knockem.

seized Mrs. Overdo and "pull'd her hood ouer her eares, and her hayre through it" (ll. 61–63). Alice's subsequent comments reveal that "the poore common whores" of the Fair view "the priuy rich ones" (her way of summing up what Win and Mrs. Overdo are to become) as business competitors who divert their "traffique" and "take our trade from vs" (ll. 65–67, 69–71). Jonson is bluntly calling our attention to the implications of Win's and Mrs. Overdo's decision to believe the two "Captaines" and "liue the life of a Lady." Win's velvet cap and Mrs. Overdo's hood (which has now lost both its visual *and* verbal identity) are to be replaced by the green gowns and crimson petticoats of the "priuy rich" prostitutes decried by "*Punque*" Alice. Like Cokes, these two figures have been separated from the support of "men in authority" and left helpless before the forces of the Fair.

Jonson has now prepared his audience for a summary presentation of what lies behind such representative degradations. First, Knockem forges Overdo's "name" to a "warrant" so that Trouble-All can join him in a drink. As in the arguments justifying adultery to Win, the Fair people have no trouble finding authority or "warrant" for any action. Next, Quarlous discharges Edgworth, who has carried out his commission, with the warning, "beware of being spi'd, hereafter" (IV.vi.16–17). To Quarlous, the cutpurse is at fault primarily for having been detected rather than for his thefts. As Volpone told Celia, "*to be taken, to be seene, / These haue crimes accounted beene.*"

In return, Edgworth asks the "gentleman" to join him in sampling the women promised by Ursula, an invitation that evokes Quarlous' most significant speech:

> Keepe it for your companions in beastlinesse, I am none of 'hem, Sir. If I had not already forgiuen you a greater

> trespasse, or thought you yet worth my beating, I would instruct your manners, to whom you made your offers. But goe your wayes, talke not to me, the hangman is onely fit to discourse with you; the hand of Beadle is too mercifull a punishment for your Trade of life. I am sorry I employ'd this fellow; for he thinks me such: *Facinus quos inquinat, aequat*. But, it was for sport.
>
> (IV.vi.22–30)

Throughout the play the Fair people have assumed (in most cases quite correctly) that "flesh and blood" desires exist in any individual who would venture into their domain. Here as earlier, Quarlous expresses righteous indignation that Edgworth (or Knockem or Whit) should suppose such "beastlinesse" in him and considers such "offers" to be a clear breach of "manners." But Quarlous, as we have seen, is scarcely a paragon of "manners." The frequency with which he has been drawn into open conflict with the forces of the Fair, in fact, has shown the limitations of the aloofness he claims on the basis of his "quality." Quarlous, moreover, has already "forgiuen" the cutpurse "a greater trespasse" and thereby implicated himself in another form of "beastlinesse," complicity in a crime, much more significant than Edgworth's breach of "manners."

The reference to the cutpurse's "Trade of life," moreover, is an echo of Wasp's ironic statement to Cokes that, given the lapse of authority, both the "trade" of breeding cutpurses and the "trade" of cutting purses would "lye open." Edgworth's earlier success, we should remember, had been a result not only of Cokes's "foolish hauing of money" but also of the failure of "men in authority" and the complicity of men of "quality." The regarding of such obvious crimes as "sport," along with the concomitant denial of the responsibility that should accompany one's station in society (the obligation, as

Quarlous puts it, to "instruct your manners"), exposes the hollowness of the "quality" upon which this "gentleman" bases his pretensions. As shown in his quotation from Lucan, this opportunist does at least recognize the debasing effect of his complicity in the various thefts (once more emphasizing the contamination and "impurity" of the Fair). However, his final assertion that "it was for sport" sums up his refusal to accept any responsibility for others or recognize any basic flaw in his own attitude. Jonson is here raising the question: how much really separates Quarlous from Edgworth and his "companions in beastlinesse," and, for that matter, which "Trade of life" under examination offers the deeper threat to the general health of society?

The officers now place Wasp in the stocks, and Haggis announces that Justice Overdo cannot be found so "there is no Court of *Pie-poulders* yet" (ll. 71–72). The lack of either court or judge is another effective symbol for the absence of authority here in Act IV. The subsequent placing of Busy and Overdo in the stocks along with Wasp is then the primary dramatic emblem used by Jonson to sum up what is wrong with the world of the Fair. As in *Hickscorner* or *Youth* or Lindsay's *Ane Satyre*, the presence of figures of authority (religion, justice, education) in the stocks while their respective "charges" (Win, Mrs. Overdo, Cokes) are being preyed upon by rampant vice (Knockem, Whit, Edgworth) serves as an effective dramatic summary of the author's view of conditions in his society. Quarlous, moreover, whose complicity has helped to produce this situation, is once more on stage as an aloof observer who feels no responsibility for this debacle. After almost four acts of groundwork and preparation, Jonson, in one dramatic moment, epitomizes his vision of the "hell on earth" to which his contemporary society can descend.

In the absence of any clearly defined authority, Quarlous emerges as the only outsider able to achieve even a limited control over the Fair. So when Dame Purecraft tries to join Trouble-All as "a yoakefellow in your madnesse" (V.ii.38–39), the figure she accosts turns out to be Quarlous, who has taken on "*the habit of the madman*" (l. 14.s.d.). Dame Purecraft, realizing that she "must vncover my selfe vnto him, or I shall neuer enioy him" (ll. 48–49), confesses how she has used her pose of "a wilfull holy widdow" (ll. 53–54) for seven years as a profitable source of income and begs the "madman" to "enioy all my deceits" (l. 72) and the accrued profits.

The opportunistic Quarlous now "*considers with himselfe of it*" (l. 75.s.d.). Since "no expectation" remains for Grace, this offer of six thousand pounds represents "some sauer" or, in other words, an adequate compensation for his losses (ll. 75–79). After reasoning with himself ("It is money that I want, why should I not marry the money, when 'tis offer'd mee?" ll. 80–82), he concludes: "I were truly mad, an' I would not!" (ll. 84–85) To Dame Purecraft, madness is the ultimate truth in a chaotic world, but for Quarlous true madness is the failure to act in one's own best interest. In contrast to Winwife, who had been castigated for passing up such opportunities, Quarlous categorically states: "There's no playing with a man's fortune" (ll. 83–84) and thereby takes the widow and her money. This gentleman's shrewdness, like that of the Fair people (to whom he is moving closer and closer in outlook and behavior), is being used to gain a profit, not order the world around him. His decision, moreover, is conditioned by the picture he himself had drawn of the miseries of such a marriage. He had pointed out, for example, that "a right widdow" could easily convey her estate away from a new husband to prevent him from gaining any profit (I.iii.102–3) and had observed: "A sweet course for a man to waste the brand of life for, to be still raking himselfe a fortune in an old womans embers" (ll. 77–79). On the basis of his own remarks, Quarlous' success is not as clear-cut as he would have it.

By the end of Act V, scene ii, Quarlous has gained possession of the license, Dame Purecraft, and the "hand and seale" (l. 103) of Overdo who, now disguised as a porter, has revealed himself to the "madman" for whom he feels responsible. The false madman has obtained a true "warrant"; as Quarlous observes, "this mad mans shape, will proue a very fortunate one" (ll. 111–12), for from a pragmatic point of view, it has not yet failed to produce results. The success of madness after the failure of authority shows how "quality" must inevitably be degraded in such circumstances and is one more indication of the anarchy and meaninglessness which now hold sway in the world of the Fair.

The Puppet Play

At the outset of Act V, when Leatherhead arrives to present Littlewit's play "in the name of *Wit*" (V.i.2), Jonson introduces a new dramatic center. After pointing to his previous successes (associated with the anarchy of Shrove Tuesday), Leatherhead sums up his concept of good theater:

> Your home-borne proiects proue euer the best, they are so easie, and familiar, they put too much learning i' their things now o' dayes: and that I feare will be the spoile o' this. *Little-wit?* I say, *Mickle-wit!* if not too mickle!
>
> (ll. 14–18)

In contrast to such a "get-penny" as "the *Gunpowder-plot*" (l. 12), Littlewit's offering may contain "too much learning" and thereby offend popular tastes, a situation clearly unsatisfactory to this profit-minded producer. The names of the attendants (Sharkwell, Filcher) and the subsequent instructions on how to exact higher admissions from "Gentlefolks" (ll. 21–22) further underscore the ascendancy of the profit motive in this attempt to "please the people" (l. 6).

Leatherhead's views on his "art" and his audience reflect Jonson's scornful evaluation of the puppets—along with ballads, jigs, and dances—as symbols of degenerate popular taste. Lovewit, for example, includes puppets along with baboons and other devices in his list of attractions Jeremy might have used to draw crowds (V.i.14), while the speaker in *The King's Entertainment* scornfully refers to the practice of labeling emblems so that the populace will be sure to understand, "after the most miserable and desperate shift of the Puppits" (ll. 260–61).[61] The continued popularity of puppets, jigs, and ballads[62] was a thorn in the side of literary traditionalists like Jonson and was often cited by satirists of popular culture.[63] Thus, in Chapman's *The Revenge of Bussy*

61. H & S, VII, 91.

62. Jonson is quite explicit on the subject of ballads, a type of "poetry" that Overdo, for one, admires (III.v.112–13). Thus he told Drummond that "a Poet should detest a Ballet maker" (l. 475), and, in a scornful evaluation of popular taste, pointed out that the general public is "taken with false Baytes / Of worded Balladrie," thinking it to be "Poësie" (*Underwoods*, xxiii, 20–22). In *Neptune's Triumph* the Poet contrasts the true aims of literature embodied in the masque with "th'abortiue, and extemporall dinne / Of balladry" which was then in demand (ll. 163–64).

63. Nashe, for example, refers to "a puppet stage, or some such ridiculous idle childish inuention," and, in his *Lenten Stuffe*, refers to "Latinelesse dolts, saturnine heavy headed blunderers, . . . such as count al Artes puppet-playes, and pretty rattles to please children." See *Works*, ed. R. B. McKerrow (Oxford, 1958), I, 356; III, 216.

D'Ambois[64] (1610), Clermont provides a lengthy analysis of his diseased world, turning finally to the contemporary stage:

> Nay, we must now have nothing brought on stages
> But puppetry, and pied ridiculous antics:
> Men thither come to laugh, and feed fool-fat,
> Check at all goodness there, as being profan'd:
> (I.i.323–26)

In his *Discoveries*, Jonson offers similar comments on the decay of contemporary literary tastes. To Jonson: "*Nothing* in our Age, I have observ'd, is more preposterous, then the *running Iudgements* upon *Poetry*, and *Poets*" (ll. 587–88), a statement he develops at length:

> But a man cannot imagine that thing so foolish, or rude, but will find, and enjoy an Admirer; at least, a Reader, or *Spectator*. The Puppets are seene now in despight of the Players: *Heath's Epigrams*, and the *Skullers Poems* have their applause. There are never wanting, that dare preferre the worst *Preachers*, the worst *Pleaders*, the worst *Poets:*
> (ll. 608–14)

The popularity of the puppets at the expense of the legitimate stage is thereby typical of a general decline in contemporary taste and standards.

Earlier in his *Discoveries*, Jonson had pointed to the causes for such a decline. Adapting J. J. Scaliger, he observes that "it is but convenient to the times and manners wee live with, to have then the worst writings, and studies flourish, when the best begin to be despis'd. *Ill Arts* begin, where good end" (ll. 274–77). The failure of "good arts," like the failure of

64. Text used is *The Plays of George Chapman: The Tragedies*, ed. T. M. Parrott (New York, 1961), I, 75–148.

"good men," provides a key to the degeneration of "the times and manners wee live with." Scurrility and petulancy, jeering and lying are now "the food of mens natures: the diet of the times! *Gallants* cannot sleepe else. The Writer must lye" (ll. 287–88). In a paragraph entitled *"Sed seculi morbus,"* he concludes that lying is "the disease of the Age" (l. 300): "It is long since the sick world began to doate, and talke idly: Would she had but doated still; but her dotage is now broke forth into a madnesse, and become a meere phrency" (ll. 302–5). The corruption of the true function of literature and the degradation of the role of the poet are here major symptoms of the diseases of "the sick world." In this *Dunciad*-like vision, moreover, the sickness has broken forth "into a madnesse" embodied in the idle and senseless outpourings of scurrilous writers and pretenders to "wit."

At least part of Jonson's reaction against the literary standards of "the sick world" can be attributed to the failure of the popular audience to grant him the reception he thought he deserved. So, in the dedication to the 1611 Quarto of *Catiline*, Jonson refers to *"these Iig-giuen times"* in which *"so thick, and darke an ignorance, . . . now almost couers the age."* Similarly, he tells the reader of the 1612 Quarto of *The Alchemist* that *"thou wert neuer more fair in the way to be cos'ned (then in this Age) in* Poetry, *especially in Playes: wherein, now, the Concupiscence of Daunces, and Antickes so raigneth."* In the dedication to the *Epigrams* in 1616 (again roughly contemporary with *Bartholomew Fair*), Jonson characterizes *"the trade of the world"* as the preference for *"their deare* Mountebanke, *or* Iester" over *"all the studie, or studiers of* humanitie."[65] Finally, in a well-known passage in

65. The above passages can be found in H & S, V, 431; V, 291; VIII, 26. Jonson conveys the same sense of general decline in his discussion of oratory, for although Bacon represents a peak, "Now things daily fall: wits grow downe-ward, and *Eloquence* growes back-ward" (*Discoveries*, ll. 921–22).

the Induction to *Bartholomew Fair,* Jonson (carping at Shakespeare's symbolic romances) asserts he is "loth to make Nature afraid in his *Playes,* like those that beget *Tales, Tempests,* and such like *Drolleries,* . . . let the concupiscence of *Iigges* and *Dances,* raigne as strong as it will amongst you" (ll. 129–32). The Induction, in general, indicts such popular taste and judgment. Although the old Stage-Keeper (whose tastes are associated with the farcical stage business of the 1580s) suggests various "fine sights" (l. 20) he would like to see (a juggler with an ape, a "Punque" under a pump), he is driven off by the Book-Keeper who derides such "*spectacles.*" The Articles of Agreement then call upon each spectator to "exercise his owne Iudgement" (ll. 97–98) and mock the "vertuous and stay'd ignorance" (l. 110) which would use *The Spanish Tragedy* or *Titus Andronicus* as standards.

For Jonson, then, the absence of "good arts" like the absence of "good men" has caused "the sick world" to break forth "into a madnesse," producing an equivalent to the "hell on earth" described earlier. The popularity of puppets, moreover, becomes one symbol for the ascendancy in "*these Iiggiuen times*" of corrupt standards of taste over traditional views on the function of literature and the role of the poet. The puppet show of Act V, the joint product of a false wit and a producer whose aim is to "please the people," can thereby serve as Jonson's dramatic symbol for the effect of the Fair and all it represents upon literature and the theater.

The first character to come to terms with the puppets is Cokes, whose childish state is epitomized by the "*boyes o' the* Fayre" (V.iii.14.s.d.) who follow him and obviously include him in their number. This young man, who has "lost all i' the *Fayre*" (l. 29), characteristically transforms the puppets into his own toys ("*Leander* my *fiddle-sticke: . . . Damon,* my *drum*" ll. 135–36), once more showing how he inevitably turns every situation into a game (or "sport"). When Cokes asks, "Doe you play it according to the printed booke?" he is told that Marlowe's version "is too learned, and poeticall for our audience" (ll. 106–7, 110–11). Rather, Littlewit has been commissioned "to reduce it to a more familiar straine for our people" and make it "a little easie, and *moderne* for the times" (ll. 116–17, 121). As Littlewit sums it up:

> for the *Hellespont* I imagine our *Thames* here; and then *Leander*, I make a Diers sonne, about *Puddle-wharfe:* and *Hero* a wench o' the *Banke-side*, who going ouer one morning, to old fish-street; *Leander* spies her land at *Trigs-stayers*, and falls in loue with her: Now do I introduce *Cupid*, hauing *Metamorphos'd* himselfe into a Drawer, and hee strikes *Hero* in loue with a pint of *Sherry* . . .
>
> (ll. 122–28)

Such a plot is designed to "delight you, Sir, and please you of iudgement" (ll. 129–30), so long as the level of judgment is that of Cokes or the Fair.

Winwife and Grace are the next to arrive, but they stay aloof, observing the antics of Cokes as their entertainment. Although these representatives of the "quality" do maintain successfully the distance demanded by their propriety, they fail to exert any control over the anarchy evident in the "art" or "manners" around them. After Littlewit departs to seek his wife, Knockem, Whit, and Edgworth arrive with Win and Mrs. Overdo, a juxtaposition which contrasts the real threat to Littlewit's reputation (the seduction of his wife) with his misguided concern for the success of the play. While Edgworth "*courts Mistresse* Littlewit" (V.iv.39.s.d.) who is enjoying the life of a "Lady," Overdo wonders "that persons of such fashion, should resort hither" (ll. 37–38); meanwhile Win is addressed so often as "Madame" or "Lady" that she exclaims: "They doe so all-to-be-*Madame* mee, I thinke they thinke me a very Lady!" (ll. 41–42) The audience, however, is kept aware of the true meaning of such "ladyship." When Overdo asks, "Is this a *Lady*, friend?" Whit replies, "If dou hasht a minde to 'hem, giue me twelue pence from tee, and dou shalt haue eder-oder on 'hem!" (ll. 49–53); and Win is told that her husband "must not know you, nor you him" (ll. 47–48) and that hers is "a finer life" than being "clogg'd with a husband" (ll. 56–57). When she tries for the last time to identify herself as Littlewit's wife, she is told: "That was you, *Lady;* but now you are no such poore thing" (ll. 66–67). Under the aloof and unconcerned eyes of the symbols of "quality" and "manners," the institution of marriage is being undermined by an appeal to false "fashion" and a false concept of "Ladyship."

The next arrival is Wasp who finds that the news of his sojourn in the stocks has preceded him:

> Do's he know that? nay, then the date of my *Authority* is out; I must thinke no longer to raigne, my gouernment is at an end. He that will correct another, must want fault in himselfe.
>
> (ll. 97–100)

Having lost his sword, the license (he is carrying an empty black box), and any remaining influence over his charge, Wasp too is reduced to the level of a spectator. Cokes can promise, "I'le interpret to thee" (l. 110), thereby summing up the level of mentality at which the show is directed.

The subsequent play within a play is Jonson's final exhibition of the anarchic forces which reign supreme in the Fair.

Now that the audience has once more been exposed to the degradation of Cokes, Win, and Mrs. Overdo and the failure of Wasp, the puppet play itself sets forth an uninhibited display of those very "flesh and blood" forces that had proved their undoing. In an early exchange, for example, Leander tells the puppet-master: "*A pox o' your maners, kisse my hole here, and smell,*" to which Leatherhead replies: "*there's manners indeed*" (ll. 134–36). Such crudity on the lowest possible level is the natural result of the Fair's contempt for "quality" and true "manners." Similarly, the puppets' "compulsive trading of insults" and quarreling "out of sheer perversity"[66] recall the inability of Wasp and Quarlous to stay out of trouble and suggest the anarchy in store for a society that has failed to maintain adequate controls. More specifically, the emphatic association of drinking and sexuality (Cupid "*strikes* Hero *in loue*" with Leander "*with a pint of Sherry*" l. 202) recalls the fate of Mrs. Overdo, while the two "true friends," Damon and Pythias, who immediately start fighting over Hero, parody Winwife and Quarlous in their squabble over Grace. The ascendancy of "flesh and blood" desires over any restraints here produces, albeit in miniature, the "madnesse" or "hell on earth" that Jonson had envisaged.

Littlewit's debasement of this famous story, moreover, attempts to bring it down to Cokes's level of judgment where any form of "conceit" is too learned. When Leander asks Old Cole, "*What fayerest of Fayers, / Was that fare, that thou landedst but now at* Trigsstayers?" the young man can "scarce

66. Barish, *Ben Jonson*, p. 231. Barish had earlier (p. 229) pointed to "the uninhibited debauch" of the puppets and then described their play as "an absolute orgy of quarrels . . . which raises to a hysterical pitch the vulgar bickerings of the day" (p. 231).

vnderstand" (ll. 143–46). When Cole, on the other hand, exclaims, "*You Rogue, I am no Pandar,*" Cokes tells us, "He sayes he is no *Pandar*. 'Tis a fine language; I vnderstand it, now" (ll. 162–64). Cokes is the ideal audience for such a debased form of theater and, as a result, is once more contributing to the diseases of his society by his support of something corrupt or ephemeral. When Wasp (who has already failed to wean his charge away from "vile tunes," Overdo's oration, or Nightingale's ballad) joins him in appreciation of this spectacle (l. 267), any hope for improvement in this youth's taste and judgment is eliminated. As with his "foolish hauing of money," Cokes's depraved standards of taste, when unchecked, symbolically sustain and encourage another form of corruption which threatens society.

The arrival of the second "man in authority," Rabbi Busy, provides the first of two symbolic interruptions to the puppet play. This man of religion, who rails against the "prophanations" of the puppets and the stage in general, is once more espousing the right cause (the restraint of such abuses) for the wrong reason (their "contempt of the *Brethren*, and the *Cause*" V.v.11–12). In spite of his obvious failings, Busy can at least recognize the false liberty and false authority invoked here (ll. 14–17, 21), but his various charges (e.g., that the puppets lack any "lawfull *Calling*") are easily parried by Dionysius. Here the man of religion, whose interpretation of what is "lawfull" has been suspect from the outset, is confronted with the implications of his own mode of argument. Thus, Busy (who offers no arguments or "reasons" for his pronouncements) and the puppet can loudly proclaim the opposite sides of the same issue ("It is prophane." "*It is not prophane.*") in what is clearly a satire on "the vain Disputes of Divines" in which there is "no Measure to end the Controversie."[67] After all of Busy's charges have been rejected, Dionysius concludes:

> *Nay, I'le proue, against ere a* Rabbin *of 'hem all, that my standing is as lawfull as his; that I speak by inspiration, as well as he; that I haue as little to doe with learning as he; and doe scorne her helps as much as he.*
>
> (ll. 109–12)

The "confuted" Busy now permits the play to continue: "For I am changed, and will become a beholder with you!" (ll. 116–17)

That Dionysius has been able to convince Busy that his "*standing*," "*inspiration*," and "*learning*" are as valid as those of any "Rabbin" is not an indication that the puppets represent Jonson's "agent of reform" or norm of "pleasure," nor is it meant to establish the "role of spectator" to which Wasp and Busy are reduced as a "wholesome" one.[68] Rather, as the entire weight of the action has made clear, the capitulation of these two figures of authority is the final symbolic representation of the failure of Wasp's type of education or good counsel and Busy's type of religion to cope with the puppets, who function as a microcosm of the world of the Fair. Through the representative failings of the good counselor

67. Remarks by Jonson's friend, John Selden, quoted in H & S, X, 213. Selden points out: "The Puritan would be judged by the Word of God: If he would speak clearly, he means himself, but he is ashamed to say so." Referring to the Puritan's manner of disputation, Selden continues: " 'Tis just as if Two Men were at Bowls, and both judg'd by the Eye: One says 'tis his Cast, the other says 'tis my Cast; and having no Measure, the Difference is Eternal." Selden then uses this scene as his example.

68. See Barish, *Ben Jonson*, pp. 236–38. Jonson, according to this argument, is concluding that only "by acknowledging his kinship with the puppets can a man begin to transcend his own grossness, vaporousness, and automatism."

and the man of religion, Jonson is calling attention to those contemporary abuses of education and religion which prevent such authorities from adequately defending society from the moral and social anarchy embodied in the puppet play and the Fair.

With Wasp subdued and Busy confuted, Cokes cries out "on with the Play!" (l. 119) only to be disappointed by the final interruption in which Justice Overdo "*discouers himselfe*" (l. 120.s.d.). Although the audience has been kept aware of Overdo's mistakes and misconceptions, a slim possibility still exists that the justice, the last hope for the forces of authority and order, may yet be able "to take Enormity by the fore head, and brand it" (ll. 125–26). After preventing the Fair people, who are in "terror" of his "name," from stealing away, Overdo acts as stage manager, giving the various characters (including the recent arrivals—Quarlous, Dame Purecraft, and Littlewit) "places" in which to stand and promising to "reprehend" them in turn. The Justice then strikes his pose:

> Now, to my enormities: looke vpon mee, O *London!* and see mee, O *Smithfield;* the *example of Iustice,* and *Mirror of Magistrates:* the true top of formality, and scourge of enormity. Harken vnto my *labours,* and but obserue my *discoueries;* and compare *Hercules* with me, if thou dar'st, of old; or *Columbus; Magellan;* or our countrey man *Drake* of later times:
>
> (V.vi.33–39)

Overdo then reveals his "*discoueries*" by going around the circle of characters he had just established: Busy is a "*superlunaticall* hypocrite"; Leatherhead a "prophane professor of *Puppetry,* little better then *Poetry*"; Knockem a "Debaucher, and Seducer of youth"; Edgworth an "easie and honest young man"; Whit an "*Esquire* of Dames, *Madams,* and twelue-penny *Ladies";* and Win a "greene *Madame* her selfe, of the price" (ll. 40–46). The Justice's series of truths, half-truths, and misconceptions is soon halted, however, by the revelation that the other of the "twelue-penny *Ladies*" is his own wife.

Here Quarlous takes over as stage manager. Lightly dismissing Edgworth's crimes (ll. 74–81), the gamester makes an impressive public display of the profits reaped by his opportunism and "madnesse." He first thanks Overdo for the gift of his ward, pointing to the Justice's hand and seal which have been used to change Grace's guardianship. He congratulates Winwife, who is "possest o' the Gentlewoman," but adds that "she must pay me value, here's warrant for it." By virtue of Overdo's "warrant" (a true and effective one this time), Quarlous has become Grace's guardian, so that she must pay him a large sum for the privilege of marrying without his consent. The gamester has thereby covered his losses in the lottery of names and achieved a financial coup by virtue of this substantial payment and the acquisition of a rich widow. He has also outwitted "carefull *Numps*" by his success in obtaining the license. Through his ingenuity and opportunism, Quarlous has outwitted Overdo, Busy, and Wasp in his acquisition of Grace's wardship, Dame Purecraft's jointure, and Cokes's license. If results are to be the yardstick, his shrewd and amoral self-interest proves to be the only successful "warrant" to guide men's actions in the world of the Fair.

With almost everyone on stage in some way discomfitted, Quarlous offers his final instructions to Overdo:

> remember you are but *Adam,* Flesh, and blood! you haue your frailty, forget your other name of *Ouerdoo,* and inuite vs all to supper. There you and I will compare our

> *discoueries;* and drowne the memory of all enormity in your bigg'st bowle at home.
>
> (ll. 96–100)

To Quarlous, who views all the activities of the Fair as "sport," any pretension to authority or the suppression of "enormity" is in defiance of the "flesh and blood" frailty of man. The various "*discoueries*" made by Overdo (e.g., prostitution) can be transformed into light conversation to be exchanged over drinks. Quarlous' insight into the "enormity" of the Fair, however, is not as extensive as he himself fancies. Although he has uncovered the truth about the theft of Cokes's second purse, he is still unaware of the extensive organization which lies behind the other events witnessed by the audience (Cokes's other losses, the seduction of Win and Mrs. Overdo, even the "vapours" device in which he himself was involved). Just as Quarlous, in his desire to seize a profitable opportunity, has forgotten his own strictures against marrying widows, so here he is ignoring the threat to society to be found in the "sport" practiced by Edgworth, Whit, Knockem, and Ursula. This gamester's opportunistic self-interest has led to financial success, which according to his point of view ("It is money that I want") is everything, but such success (as in *The Alchemist*) has ominous implications for the future health of society.

Quarlous' success, moreover, is at the expense of the three men in authority and is juxtaposed with the symbolic failure of Overdo. This reforming justice, we should remember, had earlier announced that "a publike good designe" should never be abandoned owing to any "particular disaster" and had prided himself on his Stoic ability to withstand "aduersity" and "calamity." In the denouement, however, he is turned away from his good design by just such a disaster, the discovery that his own wife is an "enormity." Instead of rising above such a setback, this supposed figure of justice is persuaded to forget his discoveries and "drowne the memory of all enormity" in wine. Like Wasp and Busy, Overdo offers no hope for the future fulfillment of his particular role, and, in a violation of "quality," indiscriminately invites all those present home with him (ll. 111–13). No one need fear Overdo now (as had the Fair people when he revealed himself), because his concept of justice has been overruled by Quarlous' concept of "sport." The ironic misapplication of his final scraps of Latin[69] provides one last indication of the failure of this justice to use his discoveries for the good of the kingdom.

Cokes's final words can then have a telling effect. Given the successive failures of men in authority to control the abuses of the Fair and prevent the presentation of the puppet play, that microcosm of the Fair, both the play and the abuses which it

69. So Overdo's description of his "intents" as being "*Ad correctionem, non ad destructionem*" can be glossed by Jonson's discussion of the ideal prince whose concern is "the publike good, and common safety" and whose "punishments are rather to correct, then to destroy" (*Discoveries,* ll. 988–99, 994). In his general amnesty to all "enormity," Overdo is not showing princely mercy but rather is giving up any possibility for that correction or punishment of vice which is necessary for "common safety." The Horatian context of the other reference ("*Ad aedificandum, non ad diruendum*") is equally revealing. Maecenas had just been told that he would surely laugh if Horace's clothing or hair were at fault: "What, when my judgement is at strife with itself, scorns what it craved, asks again for what it lately cast aside; when it shifts like a tide, and in the whole system of life is out of joint, pulling down, building up (*diruit, aedificat*), and changing square to round? You think my madness is the usual thing, and neither laugh at me nor deem that I need a physician or a guardian assigned by the court . . ." (*Horace: Satires, Epistles and Ars Poetica,* trans. H. R. Fairclough, Loeb Classical Library [London and Cambridge, Mass., 1961], p. 259). Overdo's *volte-face* on "enormity" and justice has just demonstrated such madness or judgment "at strife with itself" to the audience.

sets forth will continue unchecked. Since Bartholomew Cokes has come to represent that debased level of taste and mentality at which the various appeals of the Fair are directed, his decision after the two abortive interruptions to "ha' the rest o' the *Play* at home" indicates how "*Bartholmew*-wit" and "*Bartholmew*-termes" are about to spread to all of society. Like Face's epilogue to *The Alchemist*, the final words of this representative figure, whose "diseases of youth," childish whims, and "foolish hauing of money" have not been controlled, project into the future the abuses found in both the play and the puppet show and offer the final comment upon the failure of justice, religion, and education in the world of the Fair.

Bartholomew Fair is undoubtedly Jonson's most ambitious attempt at a panoramic treatment of both the causes and effects of society's diseases, contamination, and impurity. Sacrificing the unity and focus of *The Alchemist*, he has painted the broadest possible canvas in a manner reminiscent of *Every Man Out*. Comparison to Jonson's earlier attempt to dissect the deformity of the times is revealing. In both plays the audience is offered a host of characters and a wealth of incidents; in both a series of plots and counterplots exhibits the folly and culpability of representative figures. But *Bartholomew Fair* has a total structure, movement, and rationale not to be found in the earlier comical satire, even granting its satyr-satirist figure. The careful preparation of Acts I and II sets up the major scenes of Act III (the cutting of Cokes's second purse, Busy's arrest) which then lead into the holocaust of Act IV wherein we are shown the symbolic failure of men in authority, the degradation of the "estates," and the limitations of the "quality." Act V, like the denouements of *Volpone* and *The Alchemist*, can then resolve the intricate plot in the traditional comic manner without diminishing the many disturbing implications of the play. Thanks to a combination of morality structure and comic expertise, the tendency towards panorama and scope evident throughout Jonson's career has here achieved its fullest expression.

Such added scope accounts for many of the differences between *Bartholomew Fair* and the other two great comedies. The small group of Vice-like intriguers who had served as prime movers in *Volpone* and *The Alchemist* has given way to a wider range of salesmen, bawds, and thieves, who can display more fully the antisocial forces threatening the visitors to the Fair. As Jackson Cope has pointed out, Jonson has even associated Ursula with *Discordia* to give greater depth and significance to the vapors and influences emanating from her booth.[70] The techniques and appeals of the Fair people are often quite similar to those used by Subtle, Face, and Dol (witness the analogous temptations of Dame Pliant and Win), but the conspiracy against society is found not in one well-defined group but rather in the Fair itself and all it comes to represent. The play's richness and variety (certainly its strongest point) and its plethora of characters and incidents (which at times strains the understanding of the viewer) both arise from Jonson's grand conception.

Significantly, there is no figure analogous to Cicero in *Bartholomew Fair*. In *The Alchemist*, Surly had sought some ordering and justice during Act IV, only to be laughed off the stage and superceded by Lovewit in Act V. Similarly, in *Bartholomew Fair* those characters seeking some ordering of the Fair are continually defeated and degraded owing to their folly and inadequacy, while the one outsider shrewd enough to get an effective "warrant" and deal with the Fair people on their own terms is (like Lovewit) only interested in his own profit. Cicero's ideals and abilities are thus split between two

70. "*Bartholomew Fair*," pp. 143–46.

characters, Overdo and Quarlous, neither of whom can or will play the role that can bring sanity and order back to society. The absence of any "good men" to "make good the times" and the projection of the puppet play into the future thereby link *Bartholomew Fair* in theme and effect to *The Alchemist* and *Sejanus.* For the third and last time, Jonson has succeeded in fusing together morality structure and technique with comic tone and surface in order to provide an image of his times. Here is the last of Jonson's great moral comedies.

CHAPTER 6

The Decline of Moral Comedy: *The Devil is an Ass* and *The Staple of News*

In *Bartholomew Fair,* Jonson set forth a panoramic treatment of contemporary society by adapting a dramatic pattern from the late morality. In substituting the sprawling canvas of Smithfield for the tightly knit structure of *The Alchemist,* he achieved a more complex and diversified statement at the expense of dramatic unity and clarity. Taken together, these two plays show Jonson developing the "estates" pattern to its full potential for literal comedy. His next two plays, on the other hand, although concerned with similar issues, exhibit new and not always successful experiments in dramatic form. Investigation of *The Devil is an Ass* and *The Staple of News,* with their various virtues and failings, is a necessary final step in evaluating the achievement of Jonsonian moral comedy.

The Devil is an Ass

Jonson's next play has been a source of concern to some of his critics. L. C. Knights, to be sure, has argued that the play successfully "formulates an attitude towards acquisition" by penetrating "beneath the superficial follies, the accidental forms" to "the root of the disease," greed,[1] but others have sensed an inconsistency between this blatant "devil play" and Jonson's derisive comments which classify fools and devils as "*antique reliques of barbarisme.*"[2] Herford, for one, is forced to postulate a "growing willingness to relax the severity of his canons, to accommodate himself to popular tastes and make use of popular traditions."[3] The presence of Pug, Iniquity, and Satan becomes evidence for the author's concession to a public demanding entertainment upon its own terms.

But such relaxation of standards is not in keeping with the belligerent attitude towards his audience that Jonson manifested in many public pronouncements throughout a long career. The Induction to *Bartholomew Fair*, the intermeans of *The Staple of News*, and the choric commentary of Damplay and the Boy in *The Magnetic Lady* all attest to his continuing desire to bring the "understanders" up to his level. In the case of *The Devil is an Ass*, Jonson was apparently not ashamed of his devil plot and, in fact, specifi-

1. *Drama and Society in the Age of Jonson* (London, 1937), pp. 188, 218. More recently, Larry S. Champion (*Ben Jonson's "Dotages": A Reconsideration of the Late Plays* [Lexington, Ky., 1967]) has pointed out how Jonson has employed various elements from the morality tradition here ("the inverse pattern of two evil forces contending for power over a third person, the devil-figure Pug throughout the work, and the framing scenes in Hell") and has concluded that "an awareness of the structure of the play and the manipulations of morality elements to sharpen the satiric exposure of the earth's vices indicates that Jonson has neither allowed his comedy to deteriorate under a heavy didacticism, nor suffered any serious decline in inventiveness and ingenuity" (p. 44). Champion, however, devotes only one note (pp. 145–46, n. 16) to the devil plays central to this discussion.
2. H & S, V, 19.
3. H & S, II, 153.

cally called attention to that feature of the play. The description recorded by Drummond is prefaced by a statement that "according to Comedia Vetus, in England the divell was brought in either wt one Vice or other, the Play done the divel caried away the Vice." But Jonson's play as he describes it "brings in ye divel so overcome wt ye wickednes of this age that [he] thought himself ane ass" (ll. 409–13). Jonson has thereby sketched in for Drummond a dramatic convention of the "Comedia Vetus" or morality and then summed up what he felt to be the basic irony of the play, that "the wickednes of this age" was too much for the poor devil. He *is* admittedly using "popular traditions" as Herford argues but in a typically self-conscious manner as in his deliberate inversion of the traditional relationship between devil and Vice. Rather than catering to the expectations of his audience, Jonson is once more violating those expectations to make a sardonic comment about contemporary society.

Jonson's attitude towards the use of devils in Jacobean plays is therefore rather complex. In the Prologue to *The Devil is an Ass*, he asks that his play be granted only "*the same face*" that the audience would give their "*deare delight, the* Diuell *of* Edmunton" (ll. 21–22). His scorn for this immensely popular play is explained during the first intermean of *The Staple of News*. After Mirth has described one type of play in which the Devil was a fine gentleman who "*would carry away the* Vice *on his backe, quicke to* Hell, *in euery Play where he came*" (ll. 64–66), the discussion turns to "*the* Diuell *of* Edmonton" who was "*no such man*," having been "*coosen'd*" by the conjurer (Peter Fabell). The gossips' main recollection of *The Merry Devil of Edmonton* (in an account that appears to have been deliberately garbled by Jonson) is of the antics and buffoonery which they associate with Smug the Smith. Echoing the tastes and prejudices of the popular audience, these foolish gossips demand the titillation provided by clowns and devils rather than the moral enlightenment of a more ambitious play. As with Littlewit's puppet play, Jonson is objecting not necessarily to the subject matter per se (Hero and Leander, the devil play) but rather to the reduction of such raw materials "to a more familiar straine" in order to "please the people."

The horseplay associated with *The Merry Devil of Edmonton,* however, does not represent the sole type of action offered by all the devil plays. Jonson's various comments linking devils and the Vice, for example, recall a series of plays—sometimes comic, sometimes serious, sometimes both—in which Satan or his emissaries come to earth to win more denizens for Hell. In Fulwell's *Like Will to Like* (1568), the Vice is enjoined by Lucifer to use his "new-fangled fashions" to "procure men to set their minds aside" from virtue.[4] After the Vice successfully leads three different pairs of figures to their destruction, he is carried away upon the Devil's back. Similarly, in Garter's *Virtuous and Godly Susanna* (1569) the Devil commissions Ill Report to destroy Susanna, who represents an admitted exception to his diabolic power and influence, and later bears off the Vice after his failure.[5] In *Enough is as Good as a Feast,* Satan makes his appearance after Covetouse and Ignorance have destroyed Worldly Man. The Devil rejoices at the population explosion

4. Dodsley, III, 312.

5. This play, unlike the other moralities cited as evidence throughout this study, was probably produced under what Bevington terms "cloistered and amateur auspices." See David Bevington, *From "Mankind" to Marlowe: Growth of Structure in the Popular Drama of Tudor England* (Cambridge, Mass., 1962), pp. 32, 67. Still, the presence of the Devil-Vice relationship in a play somewhat removed from the popular canon offers further evidence for the influence of this feature of the late morality.

in his kingdom, praises the Vice for a job well done, describes what lies in store for all such Worldly Men, and finally carries off the latest victim on his back. The Devil also makes an appearance in *A Knack to Know a Knave* where he bears off the Bailiff of Hexham, the father of the four knaves who act out the evils in the kingdom. In all these instances, the relatively brief appearances of the Devil have established the ultimate source of evil and temptation by connecting the Vice or vicious figures with Hell.

The Devil need not always use a Vice to achieve his ends. In better known plays like *Doctor Faustus* and Barnes's *The Devil's Charter* the protagonist makes a pact with a devil which leads to tragedy. Most interesting for Jonson's play is the popular vehicle referred to in the last line of his Prologue, Dekker's *If this be not a good play, the Devil is in it* (1611–12), in which Pluto sends forth three devils to pose as courtier, friar, and merchant. The emissaries successfully exploit weaknesses in each of these "estates" so that, with a few exceptions, the court and the friars are corrupted while the merchant Barterville, the chief human villain, teaches one devil some new tricks. Dekker has combined his diabolic emissaries with a limited "estates" structure to demonstrate how representative vices lead to an increase in Hell's population.

Not all of the English devil plays take such a serious view of the emissary's role. Haughton's *Grim the Collier of Croydon* or *The Devil and His Dame,* based in part upon Machiavelli's *The Devil Takes a Wife* or *The Tale of Belfagor,* uses the misfortunes of the diabolic agent to stress the tribulations of marriage. After Malbecco (borrowed from Book III of *The Faerie Queene*) has attributed his sad demise to marriage and women, the somewhat dubious infernal tribunal sends the mild-mannered Belphegor and his servant Akercock to survey the situation on earth. The play that results is more complex and considerably less unified than Machiavelli's tale, but the moral of the main plot is the same. Having been duped into marrying the wrong woman (Marian instead of Honorea), then tormented and brazenly outfaced by his shrewish wife, and finally poisoned, threatened by an assassin, *and* accused of murder, Belphegor gladly retreats to Hell, exclaiming: "O vile earth, / Worse for us devils than hell itself for men!"[6] Helpless before the ingenuity and depravity of the contemporary world, this particular devil becomes a convincing and well-informed spokesman against the institution of marriage and the wiles of women.

Jonson, who was assuredly aware of many of these plays (and perhaps others not extant), would have found in them both interesting possibilities and distinct limitations. His own devil play, needless to say, would not rely upon the horseplay and antics which the gossips associate with *The Merry Devil of Edmonton*. Dekker's play, which has a scope and structure that might have appealed to the author of *Bartholomew Fair*, had been put forward only a few years previously by a dramatist Jonson considered a rogue (*Conversations with Drummond*, l. 51). Temptation of representative figures by diabolic emissaries, moreover, would have represented a departure from the general practice of Jonson's major comedies which display corruption from within society by forces created and condoned by the general public. The "devil outwitted" play would solve this particular problem by allowing a con-

6. V.i., p. 177. Text used is *Five Anonymous Plays*, ed. John S. Farmer, 4th ser. (London, 1908), pp. 101–80. See also Dodsley, VIII, 468. For a treatment of *The Devil is an Ass* in terms of Machiavelli's tale (without using *Grim*), see Daniel C. Boughner, *The Devil's Disciple: Ben Jonson's Debt to Machiavelli* (New York, 1968), pp. 214–26.

trast between an inept or inefficient devil and a superior earthly antagonist, but the only extant play of this type, *Grim the Collier of Croydon,* is primarily concerned with marriage and the role of women and lacks the broader import sought by Jonson.

In a sense, *The Devil is an Ass* draws upon the most viable features of its popular antecedents by developing the inept devil depicted in *Grim* and expanding the number of earthly figures who are more than a match for him (Wittipol, Meercraft, Everill, Engine, Gilthead), thereby achieving the scope of Dekker's play. The opening scene establishes the assumptions of this particular devil play. For the benefit of both Pug and the audience, Satan paints a picture of a Hell hard pressed to keep pace with the wickedness of man; the inexperienced Pug's request for a "braue" Vice like Iniquity as his aide-de-camp is derided by the more worldly senior devil who observes that such a figure might have been able to "aduance the cause of *Hell*" in 1560 "when euery great man had his *Vice* stand by him, / In his long coat, shaking his wooden dagger" but would be obsolescent and ridiculous in 1616 when human vices are "stranger, and newer: and chang'd euery houre" (ll. 79, 84–85, 102). The reputation of Hell itself is currently at stake, for the infernal powers foresee an inability "to keepe vs vp in credit" among mankind unless they can provide "extraordinary subtill" vices "of quality, or fashion" (ll. 111–12, 116–17). The world, as Satan describes it, is obviously too subtle for an unsophisticated devil; men "haue their *Vices,* there, most like to *Vertues;* / You cannot know 'hem, apart, by any difference" (ll. 121–22). Still, Pug is conceded his day among men with the stipulation that he is to be "subiect / To all impression of the flesh, you take, / So farre as humane frailty" (ll. 137–39). Like the Belphegor of both Machiavelli and Haughton, Jonson's devil must face mankind upon equal terms. At the outset, moreover, Jonson has made explicit what had been implicit in his major comedies, that "modern" forms of evil have adapted themselves to the fashions and predilections of contemporary society.

The results of Pug's sojourn in Jacobean London, as any reader of the play is aware, are highly amusing. Despite his inordinate desire to sin, especially to indulge in "a little venery, / While I am in this body" (III.vi.7–8), he is unable to satisfy any of his desires, either diabolic or human. Even more than Belphegor, Jonson's inept devil finds himself outwitted at every turn by his more adept human opponents and ends up disgraced and in prison. While on earth Pug is even unable to convince his master, Fitzdottrel, that he *is* a devil and at one point is forced to change his name to De Vile in order not to offend the ears of the ladies. The essential point of the devil plot is summed up in the scene to which Jonson called Drummond's attention. Having thoroughly disgraced "the name of *Deuill*" (V.vi.3), Pug is first taunted by Iniquity and then by Satan himself, who "*enters, and vpbraids him with all his dayes worke*" (l. 36.s.d.). Pug is accused of being "a scarre vpon our Name" because he has revealed to mankind their ability "to out-doe a *diuel* / Put in a body" (ll. 58–60). Satan asks:

> whom hast thou dealt with,
> Woman or man, this day, but haue out-gone thee
> Some way, and most haue prou'd the better fiendes?
> (ll. 60–62)

Finally, in contrast to the traditional morality pattern, the inept Devil is carried away on the back of the Vice, who calls our attention to the inversion, "The *Diuell* was wont to carry away the euill; / But, now, the Euill out-carries the *Diuell*" (ll. 76–77). Outdated forms of iniquity and deviltry are clearly ineffectual in wickedly sophisticated 1616.

Much of the action of the play is devoted to a demonstration of this theme, for again and again "*men and women o' the time*" prove themselves "better fiendes" than the diabolic emissary. Pug's attempted seduction of Mrs. Fitzdottrel provides a good example. First, we are shown how Wittipol, with Engine's help, successfully uses Fitzdottrel's greed and gullibility through the offer of the cloak to gain access to his wife (albeit in the husband's presence). After observing Wittipol's success, Pug decides that he too should sue for her favors, but already, without realizing it, the inept devil has become an unsuspecting messenger between the gallant and his mistress, having carried back and forth bits of information he is incapable of understanding (II.ii.52–54, 81–84). When Pug makes his own declaration of love to Mrs. Fitzdottrel, she not only rejects such advances but assumes that such impertinence must have been instigated by her husband who, she suspects, must therefore be spying upon her at that moment. While Meercraft, another successful plotter, waits within, Pug is soundly beaten by his master for his presumption, an action which indicates the disparity between such outdated deviltry and the "modern" wiles of Wittipol, Mrs. Fitzdottrel, and the projector. By the time Pug finally realizes that he has been "made an instrument! and could not sent it!" (II.vi.26), he can only show his "malignity" and avoid "discredite" for Hell (ll. 29, 31) by informing Fitzdottrel who interrupts the tryst set up by the wit of the lovers. From the diabolic point of view, however, such intervention has "profited the cause of Hell / But little, in the breaking-off their loues" (II.vii.25–26). Ironically, Pug has not only failed at this first attempt at active deviltry but has, in fact, succeeded in furthering the cause of the angels.

The folly of Pug's master, Fitzdottrel, also demonstrates the sophistication of "modern" evil. His lecture to Pug (II.i.160–76) listing the various devices that might be used by Wittipol to gain access to his wife consists of a very amusing compilation of bits of knavery and "bawdy intelligence" borrowed from the plots of romantic comedies. Wittipol, on the other hand, needs no such puddings or empty tubs or lace women to arrange his assignation but makes expert use of the unwitting Pug as go-between. Similarly, the obsession of Fitzdottrel, "the Diuell-giuen *Elfine* Squire" (I.vi.95), with magic and deviltry to the exclusion of common sense can be contrasted to the statements of Wittipol, who assures Mrs. Fitzdottrel that she does not need "the extraordinary aydes, / Of spells, or spirits" to recognize her own misery nor does he require "false arts, medicines, or charmes / To be said forward and backward" in order to communicate with her (I.vi.106–10).

In contrast to such pragmatism and good sense, Fitzdottrel's folly shows itself in his naïve association between magic and the acquisition of riches. When he hears Engine's description of a projector (one "that proiects / Wayes to enrich men, or to make 'hem great"), his immediate reaction is: "Can hee not coniure at all?" (I.vii.10–11, 14) At first, diabolic assistance seems to be the only possible source of the "hidden treasure, / Hee hopes to finde," because Fitzdottrel's imagination, like Pug's, is shackled to the outmoded situations of 1560. But the foolish squire, who "cares not what he parts with, of the present" so long as he is given the promise of future treasure (I.v.17–21), soon falls under the spell of Meercraft, who "coniures" by means of projects and promises carefully tailored to the world of 1616. Jonson specifically calls our attention to the contrast between the outmoded diabolic magic and "modern" wit. When Mrs.

Fitzdottrel suggests that Meercraft and his cohorts, despite their fine promises, may be "false spirits," her husand replies:

> Spirits? O, no such thing! wife! wit, mere wit!
> This man defies the *Diuell*, and all his works!
> He dos't by *Ingine*, and deuises, hee!
> He has his winged ploughes, that goe with sailes,
> Will plough you forty acres, at once! and mills,
> Will spout you water, ten miles off!
>
> (II.iii.44–49)

Armed with "*Ingine*, and deuises" rather than a Vice and infernal magic, the projector of 1616, according to this foolish squire, can successfully defy the Devil and still promise extravagant rewards to the initiate.

Meercraft, like Volpone and Mosca, the "venter *tripartite*," and the Fair people, is another of Jonson's Vice-like figures of control in "modern" dress. His various projects (e.g., the recovery of drowned land, the dressing of dogs' skins, the promulgation of oral hygiene through centrally controlled toothpicks) are both disturbing in their relevance to contemporary chimeras and highly amusing in their hyperboles and overwhelming effect on the gullible victims. In the opening scene Satan had warned Pug to "stay i' your place, know your owne strengths, and put not / Beyond the spheare of your actiuity" (ll. 24–25), but Meercraft's power arises from his ability to recognize the hidden dreams of his victims and encourage them to ignore any such sense of limitations. The vision which the projector plants in Fitzdottrel's foolish mind, for example, breaks all bounds:

> All *Crowland*
> Is ours, wife; and the fens, from vs, in *Norfolke*,
> To the vtmost bound of *Lincoln-shire!* we haue view'd it,

And measur'd it within all; by the scale!
The richest tract of land, Loue, i' the kingdome!
There will be made seuenteene, or eighteene *millions;*
Or more, as 't may be handled! wherefore, thinke,
Sweet heart, if th' hast a fancy to one place,
More then another, to be *Dutchesse* of;
Now, name it: I will ha't, what ere it cost,
(If 't will be had for money) either here,
Or'in *France,* or *Italy.*

(II.iii.49–60)

Also vulnerable to such visions are Gilthead, the city merchant who wants his son to become a gentleman, and Lady Tailbush, whose "ambition, / Sir, to grow great, and court it with the secret" (III.iv.55–56) leads her into the fucus project.[7] Unlike Subtle's analogous handling of figures such as Mammon and Dapper, Meercraft's explanation of this process is couched in agricultural rather than alchemical terms. Describing Lady Tailbush to the Spanish Lady (Wittipol), he confesses

that wee poore Gentlemen, that want acres,
Must for our needs, turne fooles vp, and plough *Ladies*
Sometimes, to try what glebe they are: and this
Is no vnfruitefull piece.

(III.iv.45–48)

Given the highly sophisticated and subtle devices used by such "modern" husbandry to "turne fooles vp," the audience

7. Interestingly, Meercraft's own fall (like the equivalent fall of Volpone in Act V) is attributed to such overreaching. Thus Everill tells him that "you are so couetous, still, to embrace / More then you can, that you loose all" (V.v.61–62).

can appreciate why a Vice like Iniquity or an inept devil like Pug can only be comically obsolescent in 1616.

The inadequacy of traditional deviltry is most evident in the denouement. Throughout *Volpone,* as shown earlier, the behavior of the birds of prey had suggested how man's obsessions, especially with gold, had made superfluous the old-fashioned notions about diabolic temptation. During the second trial Voltore's highly ironic dispossession had acted out the theme. Here in *The Devil is an Ass,* with its more extensive diabolic apparatus, the same ideas and ironies are made more explicit, even to a fault. Thus, after Pug has been disclaimed by Fitzdottrel, even though he has promised to teach his master some "fine *diuels* tricks," Meercraft quite accurately observes: "Why, if he were the *Diuel*, we sha' not need him, / If you'll be rul'd" (V.v.35, 38–39). Meercraft's subsequent plot is an elaboration upon the impromptu device hurriedly set up by Volpone during the second trial, for Fitzdottrel, like Voltore, feigns diabolic possession to convince a judicial audience (Sir Paul Eitherside, the Avocatori) that previous statements or commitments (the enfeoffment bestowed upon Manly, the advocate's papers and confession) should be disregarded. As in *Volpone*, the real "possession" of Fitzdottrel and his fellow victims, so adroitly encouraged and harvested by Meercraft, has been evident throughout the play, so that the shamming of Act V calls to our attention not the power of the Devil but rather the extremes to which man is driven by his greed and gullibility. Because of this plot, moreover, Wittipol, Manly, and Mrs. Fitzdottrel (like Celia and Bonario) are threatened both with the loss of the ascendancy they have arduously achieved over the foolish squire and with punishment. With the gullible Sir Paul (like the Avocatori) convinced of Fitzdottrel's possession, all that saves the sympathetic characters is the news brought to the squire in the midst of his supposed fit that Pug actually had been a devil, a revelation which prompts him for once to "tell truth, / And shame the *Feind*" (V.viii.142–43). For a second time Pug's contribution to the events of this corrupt world has been an ironic assist to virtue and the side of the angels.

A good deal of the action of *The Devil is an Ass,* then, has been used to demonstrate that "*men and women o' the time*" have proved themselves "better fiendes" than the traditional figures borrowed from 1560. Such a system of contrasts between "old" and "modern" forms of temptation has served as a variation upon or a development from the related pattern of vices and "estates" found earlier. The best moments in the play arise from the ironic situations engendered by the devil plot, while the slack moments mostly result from Jonson's attempt to provide further demonstration of his thesis. In contrast to his earlier comic achievements with "estates" figures (Corvino, Mammon, Cokes), at least some of the equivalent personae in this play (Gilthead, Plutarchus, Lady Tailbush, Sir Paul)[8] appear pale, underdeveloped, and even at times peripheral. Similarly, Meercraft lacks the central position and control of the previous pseudo-Vices (partly owing to the primacy of the devil plot),[9] while the Wittipol-Manly-Mrs. Fitzdottrel segment lacks the integral connec-

8. The exposure of Sir Paul's foolish credulity with regard to diabolic possession is certainly an outgrowth of events involving King James, Sir Humphrey Winch, and John Smith in 1616. See G. L. Kittredge, "King James I and *The Devil is an Ass*," *MP*, IX (1912), 195–209. Jonson's compliment to his king, however, is at the expense of dramatic credibility.

9. Because of the dependence upon contrasts between devils and "modern" tempters, Meercraft is not allotted the central position of the equivalent figures in the major plays. The half-hearted attempt to use Everill, a parasite upon the projector, to enlarge the antisocial forces of this play into a warring group analogous to that found in *The Alchemist* also emphasizes the disparity between the conspirators of that play and their pale cousins here.

tion to the total structure found in the actions involving either Celia and Bonario or Winwife, Quarlous, and Grace. Jonson's devil play thus exhibits a proliferation of individuals and a weakening of satiric control reminiscent of his early plays.

Still one cannot help admiring Jonson's ingenuity and skill in adapting the devil play of the popular tradition to his own ends. Steering a course between the horseplay of *The Merry Devil of Edmonton* and the serious diabolic action of *If this be not a good play* or *Doctor Faustus*, Jonson has used the inept devil as depicted in *Grim the Collier of Croydon* while also recalling the relationship between Satan and the Vice found in late moralities such as *Like Will to Like*. Such a devil play does differ somewhat in structure from the three major comedies but, with its demonstration of how "Euill out-carries the *Diuell*" or its postulation that "*Hell* is / A Grammar-schoole" in comparison to the society of 1616 (IV.iv. 170–71), still carries on the analysis of contemporary mores and manners through comedy which we have come to expect from the author of *Volpone*, *The Alchemist*, and *Bartholomew Fair*. Once more the audience has been shown the power and appeal of the Vice in "modern" dress and the willingness of his victims to participate enthusiastically in their own destruction. The same forces, condoned and even encouraged by the general public, which almost destroyed Celia and Bonario, made ridiculous Surly's honesty, and degraded the various visitors to the Fair, have here displayed their power by showing in comparison how a devil is an ass.

The Staple of News

Jonson's next attempt, after a lapse of ten years, to deal again with money and power and greed and gullibility through a comedy on the popular stage does not, unfortunately, live up to the promise sustained by his devil play. The continuity in issues and concerns between *The Staple of News* and the preceding plays, in fact, only calls attention to the disparity in execution. Partridge has pointed out that "what had been left to implication in his major plays is in *The Staple of Newes* brought out and explicitly insisted upon." For example:

> in *The Staple of Newes* Pecunia is a character constantly before our eyes, and as a symbol of money she keeps our imagination in close check so that we think of her more in terms of a lady than of money. This potential humanity of Pecunia makes any worship of her less profane than Volpone's worship of gold. The shock is less, and the satire is blunted.[10]

Other limitations of this play can be cited. Too often missing is that acting out of folly, venality, and amorality by the literal denizens of the comic worlds provided by the major comedies. Similarly, the contrast between the titular center of this play and more effective dramatic centers (Lovewit's house, the Fair) suggests the limitation of Jonson's critique of nascent journalism as a container for his satiric thrusts.

In spite of the various faults of *The Staple of News,* of which critics since Dryden have been aware, the play can still provide revealing insights for the reader seeking better understanding of the major comedies. Ideas and techniques implicit in such earlier plays, such as the power of money or

10. *The Broken Compass* (London, 1958), pp. 185–86. For other critiques of the play, see H & S, II, 186; Freda L. Townsend, *Apologie for Bartholmew Fayre* (New York, 1947), pp. 85–86; C. G. Thayer, *Ben Jonson: Studies in the Plays* (Norman, Okla., 1963), pp. 194–98; and Robert E. Knoll, *Ben Jonson's Plays: An Introduction* (Lincoln, Nebr., 1964), p. 179. For a defense of the play as an allegory of the golden mean see Champion, *Ben Jonson's "Dotages,"* pp. 45–75.

the modernization of the Vice, here become explicit, even blatant, thereby helping us to understand what has gone before. To take one example, the ironic contrast between the ideal role that should be played by men in authority and the symbolic failures of figures such as Mammon, the Brethren, Overdo, Busy, and Wasp is here made explicit in Penniboy Canter's denunciation of the various jeerers. The father observes to his son:

> If thou had'st sought out good, and vertuous persons
> Of these professions: I'had lou'd thee, and them.
> For these shall neuer haue that plea 'gainst me,
> Or colour of aduantage, that I hate
> Their callings, but their manners, and their vices.
> (IV.iv.135–39)

Then follows a lengthy speech (paralyzing the dramatic movement in a manner not seen in the comedies since *Cynthia's Revels*) which distinguishes in great detail between the ideal and the reality in each of the "estates."

> A worthy *Courtier*, is the ornament
> Of a *Kings Palace*, his great *Masters* honour.
> This is a moth, a rascall, a Court-rat,
> That gnawes the common-wealth with broking suits,
> And eating grieuances! So, a *true Souldier*,
> He is his *Countryes strength*, his *Soueraignes safety*,
> And to secure his peace, he makes himselfe
> The *heyre* of danger, nay the *subiect* of it,
> And runnes those vertuous hazards, that this Scarre-crow
> Cannot endure to heare of.
> (ll. 140–49)

After dealing in turn with the herald, the doctor, and the poet, Penniboy Canter concludes:

Away, I am impatient of these vlcers,
(That I not call you worse) There is no sore,
Or Plague but you to infect the times.

(ll. 169–71)

Once more the disease which infects "the times" is associated with the absence of "good men" in positions of responsibility and trust. The reader familiar with *The Alchemist*, *Bartholomew Fair*, *Discoveries*, and much of the nondramatic poetry can recognize Jonson's repeated indictment.

Perhaps the main reason for the presence of such helpful yet static passages in *The Staple of News* is the unfortunate transformation of that delightful and meaningful comic enactment of Jonson's various themes found in the major plays into the description (often allegorical) and pure talk of this play. The jeerers, for example, who could have been the dramatic equivalent to Corvino, Corbaccio, and Voltore, *do* practically nothing; their intermittent appearances are almost wholly devoted to exercising their persistent brand of vilification. To demonstrate the power of gold in Volpone's Venice, Jonson had presented Corvino's prostitution of his wife and had shown in specific terms how purchased evidence could undermine justice. Here in *The Staple of News*, although the theme is basically the same, the audience is offered little of such enactment (with the exception of Penniboy Junior's misuse of Lady Pecunia during Act IV) but instead, for the first time since *Cynthia's Revels*, is given an abundance of overt allegorical description and analysis.[11] At the outset of

11. A revealing parallel is provided by a comparison of the behavior of the prodigals of both plays in their respective fourth acts. In *Cynthia's Revels*, Asotus, who has already won Argurion (an earlier version of Lady Pecunia), decides to follow Moria (Folly) and therefore freely gives away the gifts of his original mistress to the other ladies. Like Penniboy Junior, Asotus provides a summary presentation of his prodigality by scattering the favors of a female figure who stands for

Act II, for example, we are introduced to both Penniboy Senior and Lady Pecunia by a series of interchanges that allegorizes their relationship. So the miser describes his "adoration, and iust worship" of Pecunia, shows his pride in turning himself into "your *Graces Martyr*" and "the slaue of money," and ends up rejoicing in his suffering for her sake (II.i.8, 11, 13). When Pecunia objects that such "selfe-tormentings" are unnecessary, Penniboy Senior defends his sacred rites by treating her as a goddess whose mysteries are understood only by the initiate.

> All this *Nether-world*
> Is yours, you command it, and doe sway it,
> The honour of it, and the honesty,
> The reputation, I, and the religion,
> (I was about to say, and had not err'd)
> Is Queene *Pecunia's*.
>
> (ll. 38–43)

Perhaps the disparity between this speech, directed at a figure named Pecunia standing before the audience, and Volpone's morning hymn to a real and impressive pile of gold and treasure[12] best sums up what has happened to the literal surface of Jonsonian comedy. In place of a Volpone or a Corbaccio to act out the idea of avarice or miserliness, Jonson here directly presents the idea itself, thereby foregoing that comic demonstration which had distinguished the major plays and parts of *The Devil is an Ass*.

---

money. For a revealing literal contrast, see Cokes's foolish use of *his* resources in Acts II and III of *Bartholomew Fair*.

12. The echo of the opening scene of *Volpone*, especially ll. 21–27, is unmistakable here. See also the similarity between Penniboy Canter's lecture on the effect of "base money" upon "all iust, true reputation" (III.ii. 241–48) and Celia's lament (III.vii.133–38), and the analysis of Picklock's discomfiture below. *Volpone*, the great success of twenty years ago, was apparently much in Jonson's mind during the writing of *The Staple of News*.

Equally revealing is the contrast in denouements between *Volpone* and *The Staple of News.* The second trial of the former, which brought together into a highly compelling finale most of the strands of the plot, here gives way to a rather diffuse fifth act which disposes in turn of Picklock the lawyer, the jeerers, and Penniboy Senior. In particular, the presentation of the "justifiable" cheating of Picklock by Penniboy Junior illustrates the disparity between the comic worlds of the two plays. In *Volpone,* the near destruction of Celia and Bonario, who could offer as witnesses or evidence only their consciences and "heauen, that neuer failes the innocent," acted out the vulnerability of justice to money as an effective climax to a searching play. In *The Staple of News,* Jonson deals with quite similar issues by introducing Picklock's attempt to enrich himself by playing off father against son, thereby violating his oath of "trust" to Penniboy Canter. When Penniboy Junior seeks to aid his father "with *truth,*" the lawyer, who lives "by *Law,*" demands witnesses who can attest to such truth (V.ii.56–61). The former prodigal, like Bonario, can only make a plea to Picklock's conscience, thereby eliciting the legal point of view:

> No *Court*
> Grants out a *Writ* of *Summons,* for the Conscience,
> That I know, nor *Sub-poena,* nor *Attachment.*
> I must haue witnesse, and of your producing,
> Ere this can come to hearing, and it must
> Be heard on oath, and witnesse.
>
> (ll. 62–67)

But, in contrast to Celia and Bonario, Penniboy Junior *does* have such a witness, Thomas the Barber, who has overheard and can attest to Picklock's admission of his "trust." The reformed prodigal, in addition, has cleverly regained the deed which had been in the lawyer's possession. Since the audience has been aware throughout this scene that Penniboy Junior had arranged for this eavesdropper, the impact of the events on stage is considerably less than that of the trial scenes in *Volpone*. In place of the searching appraisal of Venetian justice, we are given this rather perfunctory discomfiture of one lawyer in an action introduced, developed, and resolved within 150 lines. The acting out of an ominous threat to innocent figures helpless in a situation beyond their control has been replaced by a recently reformed prodigal's clever manipulation of a wicked antagonist who receives his just deserts.

The presence of Picklock's discomfiture in Act V shows us that Jonson's moral concerns in comedy have not changed. What *is* missing is the organizational ability that constructed the complex denouements of the major comedies, the intellectual questioning that squarely faced various issues without resorting to pat answers or conclusions, and the inventive facility that provided literal display of a thesis without violating the comic world of the play. Although the second intermean provides the statement about modernization of allegorical figures which helps to pinpoint Jonson's technique, this particular play fails largely because many of its figures are not satisfactorily transformed into "*men and women o' the time.*" Ironically, yet perhaps inevitably, the Jonsonian play which on the surface is most like the morality turns out to be the least successsful of his attempts at moral comedy.

Jonson himself certainly recognized his own lapses, for his subsequent plays strike out in new directions and no longer attempt to parallel his earlier successes. *The New Inn,* for example, leaves behind the questions of money and power in favor of an ironic treatment of love, valor, and appearances. As the apologetic Epilogue makes clear, this new concoction was offered with some trepidation. There is admittedly some return to a critique of society in *The Magnetic Lady* with its exposé of figures such as Sir Moth Interest, but the emphasis here, as Jonson keeps telling us, is upon reconciliation of humours and the shutting up of his circle. The "magnetic" allegory, in particular, in which Lady Loadstone is at last attached to Captain Ironsides, shows how far the play has come from the literal surface of Jacobean comedy. *A Tale of a Tub* and fragments such as *The Sad Shepherd* also point to Jonson's various experiments at the end of his career. Although to dismiss these plays as "dotages" would be unfair or unwise, to view them as a continuation of the themes and purpose of Jonson's moral comedies is equally unfruitful.

Partridge has described *The Staple of News* and the subsequent plays as "only more rigid, more obvious, and less unified versions of *The Alchemist* and *Volpone*."[13] Certainly, if the major plays are to be the yardstick, such depreciation is just. The subtle control over conventions and expectations by which Jonson engaged and manipulated his audience in the major comedies and even in *The Devil is an Ass* seems to have slackened during his ten-year absence from the stage. So too the springs of comic inventiveness which had provided a seemingly endless series of gulls and knaves to populate Jonson's comic world seem to have dried up. *The Staple of News* in particular, with its many echoes of *Volpone*, leaves the reader with the impression of an author of declining powers nostalgically seeking to rival or perhaps recreate past successes by venturing onto new and somewhat shaky ground. Still, *The Devil is an Ass* and *The Staple of News*, both in their strengths and their weaknesses, provide the revealing final stage in the rise and fall of Jonson's moral comedy.

13. *Broken Compass*, p. 212.

CHAPTER 7

Jonson's Moral Comedy

THROUGHOUT a long career, Jonson's goals are markedly consistent. In *Discoveries*, for example, he argues that the good poet (like Quintilian's good orator) requires not only "mere *Elocution;* or an excellent faculty in verse; but the exact knowledge of all vertues, and their Contraries; with ability to render the one lov'd, the other hated, by his proper embattaling them" (ll. 1038–41). There is ample evidence, moreover, that his contemporaries recognized and appreciated the moral emphasis of his comedies; the elegies in *Jonsonus Virbius* (1638), in fact, consistently call attention to the educational value of the plays. Lord Falkland cites

> th' *Ethicke Lectures* of his *Comedies*,
> Where the Spectators act, and the sham'd age
> Blusheth to meet her follies on the stage;
> Where each man finds some *Light* he never sought,
> And leaves behind some vanitie he brought.[1]

1. H & S, XI, 432–33, ll. 116–20.

According to Sir John Beaumont, in his plays Jonson

> painted Vertues, that each one might know,
> And point the man, that did such Treasure owe . . .
> But vice he onely shew'd us in a glasse,
> Which by reflection of those rayes that passe,
> Retaines the figure lively, set before,
> And that withdrawne, reflects at us no more.[2]

Edmund Waller says of the comedies:

> Who ever in those Glasses lookes, may finde
> The spots return'd, or graces, of his minde.[3]

He also finds "*Vertue* too, as well as *Vice*, is clad, / In flesh and blood" in the plays (ll. 21–22). To Richard West: "Thy *Scoenes* are *precepts*, every *verse* doth give / Councell, and teach us not to *laugh*, but *live*";[4] to Jasper Mayne: "Men were laugh'd into *vertue*, and none more / Hated *Face* acted then were such before." [5] And Sir Thomas Hawkins states:

> *Folly*, and braine-sicke *Humours* of the time,
> Distempered *Passion*, audacious *Crime*,
> Thy Pen so on the stage doth personate,
> That ere men scarce begin to know, they hate
> The *Vice* presented, and there lessons learne,
> *Virtue*, from vicious Habits to discerne.[6]

Even granted their elegiac bias, such comments indicate that some of Jonson's contemporaries recognized the moral-ethical dimension of his comedies.[7]

2. *Ibid.*, p. 438, ll. 17–24.
3. *Ibid.*, p. 448, ll. 13–14.
4. *Ibid.*, p. 468, ll. 31–32.
5. *Ibid.*, p. 453, ll. 103–4.
6. *Ibid.*, p. 439, ll. 17–22.
7. For a discussion of Jonson's views on the moral function of his art, see Helena Watts Baum, *The Satiric and Didactic in Ben Jonson's*

With the advantages of hindsight, moreover, the modern reader can appreciate the many problems Jonson had to face in his attempts to establish his scenes as precepts or deliver "th' *Ethicke Lectures* of his *Comedies*"—problems of tone, structure, characterization, emphasis. Jonson's strength as a dramatist was clearly in comedy, particularly in the portrayal of comic eccentricities and aberrations. But to achieve the larger goals announced in *Every Man Out* he had to find some way to make such individual comic creations into a larger whole that could provide an image of the times. In the early plays, whether through Asper-Macilente or the Fountain of Self-Love, we can see interesting experiments in tone, structure, and technique, but still unsolved is the basic problem: how to go beyond exposés of individual folly to some larger statement whereby the thoughtful laughter of the audience is directed at the world around them and also at themselves.

Each of the three great comedies has a distinctive solution to this problem and draws upon a wide variety of sources and raw materials for its dramatic flesh and blood. But if the proper allowances are made for the many *aliena castra* explored by this learned dramatist, Jonson's major comedies can be seen as a logical final step that results from trends found in the morality tradition, especially those plays concerned with the health of Respublica. The early Elizabethan moralities often displayed a public Vice, who acted out those attitudes responsible for society's evils, and a series of "estates" figures, who showed the effects of his power. Because of their limited facilities, such early "estates" plays had to rely a good deal

---

Comedy (Chapel Hill, N.C., 1947), pp. 22–58; for a provocative revaluation of this material, see Gabrielle Bernhard Jackson, *Vision and Judgment in Ben Jonson's Drama* (New Haven, Conn., and London, 1968), pp. 5–52 and *passim*.

upon allegorical summary, but by the 1580s a play like *The Three Ladies* could use both allegory and literal action on a much broader scale to demonstrate both the causes and effects of contemporary evils. By the 1590s this trend towards greater specificity of action led to a greater emphasis upon the literal surface. Such plays as *A Knack to Know a Knave* or *A Looking Glass for London and England* achieve the same ends as had the plays of the previous two decades but with little recourse to overt allegory. *A Knack,* in effect, is only one small step away from a play like Middleton's *The Phoenix* in which a prince rather than an allegorical principle uncovers representative abuses in Ferrara-England. The goals and techniques of Wager, Lupton, Wapull, and Wilson are not rejected or ignored during the 1590s and early 1600s but rather are conditioned by the prevailing tastes and assumptions of the age.

In this sense, Jonson's moral comedies can be seen as the final stage in the process of dramatic evolution that began with *Respublica, Wealth and Health,* and *The Tide Tarrieth No Man.* In the hands of a skillful comic dramatist, many of the essential features of the late morality could be transformed into equivalents that could set forth the "proper embattaling" of virtues and vices on the Jacobean stage. Thus the late morality Vice could find new life in the seventeenth century as the highly entertaining yet profoundly disturbing Jonsonian rascal who lures his victims to their destruction by appealing to their baser nature and clouding their judgment. The various "estates" figures scattered throughout the Elizabethan morality reappear as Jonsonian merchants, misers, youths, lawyers, knights, gamesters, clerks, and men of religion whose behavior comically yet meaningfully acts out what the commonwealth has become. Even the virtuous figures make an occasional appearance, helpless in a world they cannot control or understand.

Such a listing of affinities, however, is but a starting point for any fair evaluation of Jonson's moral comedies, because the analogy or connection can take us only so far. Consider *The Tide Tarrieth No Man* and *Bartholomew Fair*. In both plays, an antisocial force (Courage, the Fair people) corrupts and degrades a series of representative figures who, taken together, stand for society as a whole. In both, such forces are granted power only as a result of the acquiescence of the victims, who willingly participate in their own destruction, and the absence of any spiritual authority to counter the Vice or pseudo-Vice. Both provide a summary definition of the problem: either Christianity is forced to bear the "titles" of Riches and Policy or Overdo, Busy, and Wasp are placed simultaneously in the stocks.

But the differences between the two plays are as revealing as their similarities, for *Bartholomew Fair* achieves its goals without recourse to overt allegory and without any signs of the didacticism associated with the morality tradition. Instead of the ultimate triumph of Faithful Few whose perseverance is finally rewarded, Jonson presents the success of Quarlous who, like Lovewit, may be superior in many ways but does not rank very high on any moral scale. The movement from morality play to moral comedy could have led to black-and-white formulations, albeit in literal terms, along the lines of Fulwell's *Like Will to Like*, which, according to its title page, is designed to show "*not onely what punishment followeth those that wil rather followe licentious liuing, then to esteeme & followe good councel: and what great benefits and commodities they receive that apply them vnto vertuous liuing and good exercises.*"[8] Or the modern reader might

8. Dodsley, III, 304.

expect the kind of poetic justice envisaged by Albany in the final scene of *King Lear* in which "all friends shall taste / The wages of their virtue, and all foes / The cup of their deservings." Some Elizabethan-Jacobean comedies do, in fact, end with such neat moral formulations. *A Knack to Know a Knave* ends with Honesty's elaborate critique of the four knaves before the king, along with a warning for similar knaves in the audience. At the close of *A Knack to Know an Honest Man* (1594), Sempronio devotes over fifteen lines to a general summary of the lessons conveyed by the play, particularly how "to scan out knaues from perfect honest men." [9] During the final moments of *How a Man May Choose a Good Wife from a Bad* (1602), young Arthur places himself between the good wife (Mistress Arthur) and the bad (Mary the courtesan) and draws an elaborate moralization of over twenty lines (e.g., "A good wife will be carefull of her fame . . . And such art thou. A bad wife will respect / Her pride, her lust, and her good name neglect, / And such are thou" [10]). Similarly, in the execution scene of *The Fair Maid of Bristow,* Florence, the repentant courtesan, types various figures on stage: "Heere is a glasse for such as liues by lust, / See what tis to be honest, what tis to be iust." [11] Both plots of *The Royal King and Loyal Subject* end with such clear distinctions among the characters. So Captain Bonville provides an elaborate critique of each of the false friends who denied him in his apparent poverty (Match, Touchbox, Lord Clinton, Lord Bonville, Lord Audley, the Host), praising only Mary Audley who is "of another element, / A mirrour of thy sex"; similarly, at the climax of the

9. Ed. H. De Vocht for the Malone Society (Oxford, 1910), ll. 1783–98.

10. Ed. John S. Farmer for the Tudor Facsimile Texts (1912), L2ʳ.

11. Tudor Facsimile Text (1912), Flᵛ.

play the King addresses the Lord Martial and the false lords: "I observe in thee / The substance of all perfect Loyalty; / In you save flattery, envy, hate, and pride / Nothing, or ought to goodnesse that's ally'd." [12] Here are plentiful examples of moralized comedy in which a climactic scene, without recourse to allegory or a Vice, provides black-and-white distinctions that edify an audience in the tradition of the morality play.

Occasionally Jonson's comedies do end with a clear distinction between a Horace and a Crispinus or between a Crites and an Anaides or with a satisfying arraignment that punishes the licentious and rewards the virtuous. But in his major plays Jonson creates a moral comedy that is neither pat nor didactic in the traditional sense. Instead, the audience is presented with a Bonario, a Surly, or an Overdo whose fate conveys far less confidence in the triumph of virtue. Similarly, Angelo's attempted rape of Rachel or Picklock's threat to the Penniboys (with Paulo and Thomas the Barber readily at hand) can be contrasted to Celia's analogous plight, whether in Volpone's chambers or during the two trials, with its far more unsettling effect upon the audience. To render virtues loved and vices hated on stage, Jonson does not, in his best plays, resort to moral extremes in the manner of many morality plays but offers his audience complex situations that challenge and perplex. *The Tide Tarrieth No Man* shows us a preacher bringing hell-fire and damnation to his dramatic congregation; *Bartholomew Fair* (or *Volpone* or *The Alchemist*) shows us the satiric manipulator forcing his audience into untenable positions and making them find their own way out. The laughter evoked by moral comedy is carefully controlled

12. *The Royal King and Loyal Subject*, ed. Kate Watkins Tibbals, *Publications of University of Pennsylvania*, Series in Philology and Literature (Philadelphia, Pa., 1906), IV.287–88; V. 398–401.

so that eventually it turns back upon the laugher. The man who told Drummond "of all stiles he loved most to be named honest" (l. 631) could not in his best plays fabricate a dramatic world built upon a wished-for reality or a moral formulation that did not exist in the world as he knew it. To improve that world (to close the circle, in the terms of his imprese) Jonson forced his audience to recognize the truth about themselves *and* the implications of that truth, whether through the rhetorical question of a Voltore or the epilogue of a Face or Cokes or the failure of a Surly or Overdo. Only by forcing the viewer to see himself in the glass of satire can moral comedy succeed.

Along with *Doctor Faustus* and *Othello*, Jonson's three great comedies represent the culmination of the English morality tradition. In the hands of an original and skillful dramatist willing to explore all available *aliena castra*, the vices, virtues, and "estates" of the Elizabethan morality can truly become "*men and women o' the time*." In contrast to the puppet play of Littlewit and Leatherhead, where a famous story was debased to please the people, Jonson's great plays alchemize the base metal of the allegorical-didactic dramatic tradition into a unique form that can stand in opposition to the disorder and anarchy of his contemporary society. "His own style, his own instrument" is moral comedy.

Index

Albion Knight, 14
Alchemist, The, 5–6, 38–39, 41, 108–41, 143–44; and *Catiline*, 138–41; and *Bartholomew Fair*, 152, 160, 162, 166, 216, 218–21; and *The Devil is an Ass*, 231, 234–35; and *The Staple of News*, 237–38, 242, and moral comedy, 108, 136–37, 249–50
All for Money (Lupton), 12, 22, 25; and *Volpone*, 76–80, 91–95, 103
Apius and Virginia, 18–19

Barish, Jonas, 51, 56–57, 105; on *Bartholomew Fair*, 148, 150–51, 156–57, 160–61, 176 n, 211, 213
Bartholomew Fair, 39, 41, 148–222; and *The Devil is an Ass*, 224, 231, 234–35; and *The Staple of News*, 237–38; and *The Tide Tarrieth No Man*, 247; and moral comedy, 218–20, 249–50
Baskervill, C. R., 37, 55–56
Beaumont, Sir John, 244
Bevington, David, 8, 10 n, 15, 20–21, 25

Cambises (Preston), 20, 23
Case is Altered, The, 43–44; and *Volpone*, 44, 102, 249; and moral comedy, 249
Castle of Perseverance, The, 10
Catiline His Conspiracy, 138–41, 143; and *Bartholomew Fair*, 160–62, 219–20
Chapman, George, 205–6
Cobbler's Prophecy, The (Wilson), 13, 27–28, 35–36; and *Every Man Out*, 48–49; and *Cynthia's Revels*, 55–56; and *Volpone*, 81

Comedy: conventional, and *Volpone*, 6–7, 103–4; Jonson's complex view of, 6–7, 53–54, 249–50; marriage in, 169; moralization in, 248–49; Roman, and *The Case is Altered*; Roman, and *Every Man In*, 44–45, 76; Roman, and *Volpone*, 76; traditional notions of, in Jonson's early plays, 53–54, 67. *See also* Moral comedy; Satire
Comical satires, the, 48–69; and *Sejanus*, 73–74; and *Volpone*, 75, 101–2; and *The Alchemist*, 135; and the morality play, 68–69; as structural satire, 67. *See also Every Man Out of His Humour; Cynthia's Revels; Poetaster*
Cynthia's Revels, 5, 42, 55–60, 143, 145; and *Poetaster*, 61, 64, 66–67; and *Sejanus*, 70–74; and *Volpone*, 82; and *Epicoene*, 106–7; and *The Alchemist*, 135; and *Bartholomew Fair*, 160; and *The Staple of News*, 237–38; and moral comedy, 245, 249; and the morality play, 37, 55–57, 60, 68–69

Dekker, Thomas, 66; *If this be not a good play, the Devil is in it*, 225–26, 235; *Satiromastix*, 61, 63; *The Shoemakers' Holiday*, 177 n
Devil is an Ass, The, 5, 198 n, 221–35, 242; and the morality play, 37, 38, 223
Devil plays, 5, 223–27; and *The Devil is an Ass*, 227–28, 235
Devil's Charter, The (Barnes), 225
Doran, Madeleine, 23, 37–38, 67

Eliot, T. S., 6, 103, 250
Enough is as Good as a Feast (Wager), 12, 41, 224–25; and *Volpone*, 76–79, 81, 86
Epicoene, 106–8; and *The Alchemist*, 135–36
"Estates" technique, the: in *Volpone*, 81, 100–101, 107; in *The Alchemist*, 109, 113–22; in *Bartholomew Fair*, 166–81, 190–91, 196–200, 202, 218, 221; in *The Devil is an Ass*, 234–35; in *The Staple of News*, 238; in the devil play, 225–26; and Jonsonian comedy, 246–47, 250; in Jonson's early plays, 48, 55–57, 67–69; in the morality play, 20–36, 76–77, 245–46
Every Man In His Humour, 43–48; and *Every Man Out*, 53–54; and *Sejanus*, 74; and *Volpone*, 75–76; and *Epicoene*, 106–8; and *The Alchemist*, 121; as incidental satire, 67; and the morality play, 37–47
Every Man Out of His Humour, 3, 5, 48–54, 67, 69; and *Cynthia's Revels*, 56–57, 59–60; and *Poetaster*, 61; and *Sejanus*, 70–71, 74; and *Volpone*, 75, 102; and *Epicoene*, 107; and *The Alchemist*, 118; and *Bartholomew*

Fair, 218; and moral comedy, 245

Fair Maid of Bristow, The, 248
Falkland, Lord, 243
Farnham, Willard, 8–9, 12, 20

Grim the Collier of Croydon (Haughton), 225–28, 235

Harington, Sir John, 26
Hawkins, Sir Thomas, 244
Herford, C. H., 2, 138; on Jonson's early plays, 43, 51, 56; on Jonson's mature comedies, 88 n, 106, 123, 148–49, 222
Hickscorner, 188–89, 202
Horestes (Pickeryng), 16–18, 20
How a Man May Choose a Good Wife from a Bad, 248
Humanum Genus figure: and Cokes, 168; departures from, in the late morality, 15–16, 20–21, 23, 25; "fission" of, 14; Jonson's use of, 38–39, 168; traditional use of, 13–14, 34

Impatient Poverty, 20, 78–79

Jonson, Ben: on ballads, 205; on classical authority, 2–3; on comedy, 6–7; on the decline in the arts, 206–8; on the Devil and the Vice, 223–24; on diseased society, 141–43, 198 n, 207; on drinking, 195 n; as *explorator*, 4, 50; on the Fair as symbol, 149–50, 158, 173; on false fashion, 143, 198 n; on false wit, 178; on the good counselor, 151; on good men, 143–47, 185–86, 208, 220, 238; on the good poet, 243; on "hell on earth," 142–43, 198 n, 202, 208, 211; on honesty, 250; on *imitatio*, 3, 45; on justice, 160; on liberty vs. license, 180; on "manners," 143, 145–47, 185; and the morality play, 5–6, 37–42, 245–50; on puppets, 205–6, 208
Jonsonus Virbius, 243

Kernan, Alvin, 49–51, 89 n, 97, 133
King Darius, 11, 15–16, 135
Knack to Know an Honest Man, A, 28, 248
Knack to Know a Knave, A, 225, 246, 248; and *Volpone*, 81, 89; and *Bartholomew Fair*, 160, 164; as an "estates" play, 28–31, 35–36; role of Honesty in, 29–31, 33, 35, 160, 164

Liberality and Prodigality, 11
Like Will to Like (Fulwell), 78, 168–69, 191 n, 247; the Devil in, 224, 235
Lindsay, Sir David, *Ane Satyre of the Thrie Estaits*, 188–89, 202
Longer Thou Livest, The (Wager), 20, 23, 168, 171

Looking Glass for London and England, A (Lodge and Greene), 27–28, 33, 35, 246; and *The Alchemist*, 122
Lusty Juventus, 21, 76, 166–68, 171–72

Machiavelli, *The Tale of Belfagor*, 225–27
Magnetic Lady, The, 37, 222, 242
Mankind, 10, 76
Marlowe, Christopher: *Doctor Faustus*, 9, 13, 129, 225, 235, 250; "Hero and Leander," 209
Marprelate, Martin, 11
Marriage of Wit and Wisdom, The, 20, 153, 190–91 n
Marston, John, 66; *The Fawn*, 67; *Histriomastix*, 31–32, 35; *The Malcontent*, 67
Masque, the: and *The Alchemist*, 135–36
Mayne, Jasper, 244
Merry Devil of Edmonton, The, 223–24, 226, 235
Moral comedy, 221, 243–50; in *Volpone*, 101–6, 108; in *The Alchemist*, 108, 136–37; in *Bartholomew Fair*, 218–20; in Jonson's late plays, 241–42; and the morality tradition, 245–47, 249–50; and moralized comedy, 248–49
Morality play, the: and *Volpone*, 79–81, 88, 90, 103–4; allegorical superstructure in, 25–26, 28, 31–32; concern with justice in, 22, 91–92; dramatic legacy of, 8–36; historical overplot in, 28, 30, 33, 35; and Jonson, 5–6, 37–42, 223, 245–50; and Jonson's comical satires, 68–69; new dramatic formula in, 25–26, 34–36; suppleness of Elizabethan, as form, 10–12; unification in, 12–13. *See also* "Estates" technique, the; Humanum Genus figure; "Morality of youth"; *Psychomachia* conflict; Thesis-and-demonstration structure; Vice, the; Virtue figures
"Morality of youth," 166–71; 173; 175 n; 190–91
New Custom, 11, 23
New Inn, The, 241
Nice Wanton, 167–68
Nobody and Somebody, 32–33, 35

Partridge, Edward, 133, 236, 242; on *Volpone*, 6, 80, 87
Patient Grissill (Phillips), 23
Phoenix, The (Middleton), 160, 164, 246
Plautus, 5, 43, 54, 76; *Mostellaria*, 108, 132
Play of the Cards, The, 26–27
Play of Plays and Pastimes, The, 11–12
Poetaster, 60–70, 143; and *Sejanus*, 70–74; and *Epicoene*, 106–7; and *The Alchemist*, 135; and *Bartholomew Fair*, 160; and moral comedy, 249
Pope, Alexander, "Epistle to Dr. Arbuthnot," 60
Psychomachia conflict, 19–21; and *The Alchemist*, 129

Respublica, 14–15, 22–23, 76, 246
Royal King and Loyal Subject, The, 248–49

Sad Shepherd, The, 242
Satire: as a glass, 135, 250; incidental vs. structural, 67; and Jonson's early plays, 67–69; nondramatic, and *Every Man Out*, 49–51; Roman, and *Volpone*, 75
Sejanus His Fall, 5, 70–74; and *Volpone*, 71, 75, 92 n, 102–3; and *Epicoene*, 107; and *The Alchemist*, 112–13, 126, 134; and *Catiline*, 138–41; and *Bartholomew Fair*, 160, 220
Selden, John, 212–13
Seneca, 4–5
Shakespeare, William: *Henry IV*, 9; *King Lear*, 89, 130, 188, 248; *Macbeth*, 13; *Measure for Measure*, 160, 164; *Othello*, 9, 13, 89, 100, 250; *Titus Andronicus*, 208
Sir Thomas More, 172
Spivack, Bernard, 8–10, 13–14, 21, 27
Staple of News, The, 221–24, 235–42; and *Cynthia's Revels*, 60–61, 238; and moral comedy, 249; and the morality play, 37, 39–42
Stocks, the: in *Bartholomew Fair*, 188–90, 202, 247; in the morality play, 188–89
Swift, Jonathan, 135

Tale of a Tub, A, 43 n, 242
Terence, 5, 76
Thesis-and-demonstration structure: in *Volpone*, 80, 83 n, 101–3; in *Bartholomew Fair*, 169; in the late morality play, 21–22, 25–26, 31–32, 34, 76–79
Three Ladies of London, The (Wilson), 12, 23–26, 28, 33–35, 246; and *Volpone*, 76–79, 81, 83, 89, 97 n; and *The Alchemist*, 122; and *Bartholomew Fair*, 169; as "estates" play, 13, 24–26, 35, 41
Tide Tarrieth No Man, The (Wapull), 12, 20–21, 25, 246; and *Every Man Out*, 48–49; and *Volpone*, 89; and *Bartholomew Fair*, 169, 247, 249; and moral comedy, 249–50; virtues in, 78–79, 81
Trial of Treasure, 78; and *Volpone*, 81

Vice, the: and *Volpone*, 75–76, 81, 91, 95, 100–104, 107; and *The Alchemist*, 109, 111, 113, 122, 129–30, 133, 135; and *Bartholomew Fair*, 219; and *The Devil is an Ass*, 227–29, 231, 233–35; change in the role of, 10, 15–16, 20; and the Devil, 40, 223–25, 228–29; and Jonson's early plays, 47, 55–57, 68–69, 74; and justice, 91; in the late morality, 20–23, 27; as men and women of the time, 40–42, 60, 81, 103, 109,

228–29, 235, 237, 241; public emergence of, 14–20, 34, 36, 245, 249; traditional role of, 10, 14
Virtue figures: in *Volpone*, 81, 85–86, 89, 93, 95, 123; in *The Alchemist*, 123–25, 130, 136; in *Bartholomew Fair*, 155, 170–71, 219–20; and Jonsonian comedy, 246–47, 250; in the morality play, 21, 30, 78–79
Virtuous and Godly Susanna (Garter), 224
Volpone, 39, 41–42, 67, 74–106, 143–44, 149; and *Epicoene*, 107–8; and *The Alchemist*, 108–9, 112–13, 123, 126–29, 134, 136–37; and *Catiline*, 138–39; and *Bartholomew Fair*, 160, 162–63, 200, 218–19; and *The Devil is an Ass*, 231, 233–35; and *The Staple of News*, 238–42, 249; and moral comedy, 101–6, 108, 249–50; and the morality play, 5–6, 37, 69, 79–81, 103

Waller, Edmund, 244
Wealth and Health, 14–15, 246
West, Richard, 244
Wit and Science (Redford), 170, 175 n, 190–91

Youth, 167–68, 188–89, 202